David T. Hill

THE PRESS IN NEW ORDER INDONESIA

EQUINOX
PUBLISHING
JAKARTA   KUALA LUMPUR

PT Equinox Publishing Indonesia
PO Box 6179 JKSGN
Jakarta 12062 • Indonesia

www.EquinoxPublishing.com

The Press in New Order Indonesia
by David T. Hill

ISBN 979-3780-46-0

First Equinox Edition 2007

Copyright © 1994 by David T. Hill
This is a reprint edition authorized by the original publisher, University of Western Australia Press

Printed in the United States.

1 3 5 7 9 10 8 6 4 2

All rights reserved. No part of this publication may be reproduced, stored in a retrieval system, or transmitted in any form or by any means, electronic, mechanical, photocopying, recording or otherwise without the prior permission of Equinox Publishing.

THE PRESS IN NEW ORDER INDONESIA

Contents

Acknowledgements 7
A note on spelling 9
A note on currency conversion 9
Introduction 11

Chapter 1: Before the New Order 25
Chapter 2: Surveying the New Order 34
Chapter 3: Government Agencies and Industry Bodies 61
Chapter 4: The Rise of Press Empires 81
Chapter 5: Marginal Presses 111
Chapter 6: Facing the Future 139

Tables 164
A Note on Further Reading 173
Biographical Note 176
Index 177

Acknowledgements

This study owes its existence to the encouragement, advice and support of numerous friends and colleagues in Australia and Indonesia. I would like particularly to thank Atmakusumah Astraatmaja who, together with his wife Sri and their family, not only provided help, hospitality and friendship, but also made available the wealth of his personal research files and his encyclopaedic knowledge of the press industry. I am deeply indebted also to Harry Bhaskara who has been more than a friend and informant; he has been a caring confidant and gentle guide in my exploration of Indonesian society for two decades now.

In a wide range of ways Richard Robison, David Bourchier, Paul Tickell, Ricardi S. Adnan, John McGregor, Umniyati Kowi, Adam Schwarz, and Hans Beutenmuller have all helped me at crucial times with my research and writing, for which I thank them greatly. Needless to say, all are absolved of any complicity in the arguments made in the study which follows!

The influence of a diverse range of current or former Indonesian editors, notably Mochtar Lubis, Hasyim Rachman, Yusuf Isak, Gunawan Mohamad and Aristides Katoppo, has been enormously valuable towards this and previous germane projects since 1981. Dozens of others have contributed by their willingness to discuss this project. I mention particularly Amir Daud, Amir Effendi Siregar, Bambang Harymurti, Fikri Jufri, Ariel Heryanto, Benny Harman, Dahlan Iskan, Daniel Dhakidae, Mohd Elman, Hardoyo, Hersri Setiawan, Slamet Jabarudi, Andrew Rosser, R.E. Stannard, Cuk Suwarsono, Vedi Hadiz and the late Zulharmans. Many others preferred not to have their opinions attributed, but to all those who have assisted me I extend my thanks.

Most particularly I appreciated the warm hospitality of Nasir, Nur and Niar Tamara and their families, together with our neighbours and friends, during our three month stay at the Indonesian Journalists Association housing complex, Kompleks PWI, in Cipinang Muara in 1991. It was a friendly and conducive environment in which to conduct this research, where the very neighbourhood itself, home to perhaps the largest single concentration of journalists in the country, proved an inspiration.

Research was based mainly on written Indonesian-language materials collected between 1990-1994, and augmented by numerous interviews with practitioners in the press conducted primarily during two visits to Indonesia, for three months at the end of 1991 and four weeks in January-February 1993, with some follow-up interviews in July 1994. The research trips were made possible by the financial support of the Asia Research Centre on Social, Political and Economic Change at Murdoch University and by the university's Outside Studies Program. I would like to thank my colleagues in the Asian Studies Program at Murdoch for enabling me to take such leave, which inevitably increased their own workloads. The assistance of Helen Gibson and others in the Murdoch library was greatly appreciated, as was the hospitality of several Indonesian institutions, including the Dr Sutomo Press Institute in Jakarta, then under director D.H. Assegaff.

Parts of this study have appeared previously in earlier forms in a Murdoch University Asia Research Centre Working Paper, *The Press in 'New Order' Indonesia: Entering the 1990s* (1991), in "The Press in a Squeeze: Operating Hazards in the Indonesian Print Media", *Southeast Asian Journal of Social Science* (National University of Singapore), Vol. 20 No. 2 (1992), pp.1-28, and in several shorter articles in *Inside Indonesia* magazine. I would like to thank these bodies for permission to include such material in this longer study.

It would be foolish to proceed on such a study as this without noting an obvious caveat. There are enormous pitfalls in writing about a subject like the Indonesian press: the industry is typically in a state of constant flux and change, most dramatically in the areas of press restrictions and bans, ownership patterns, advertising and circulation statistics (always of dubious reliability). As an example of risks in predicting trends in an industry so prone to extraordinarily rapid change, within weeks of the publisher accepting what I had regarded as the final manuscript of this monograph two key incidents took place which necessitated revisions to several chapters. On 2 June 1994, a joint ministerial announcement opened up the possibility of foreign investment in the Indonesian mass media, and on 21 June three major weekly publications were banned in the first mass closures since 1978. Both incidents caught the industry and outside observers by surprise, causing animated public debate, and shaking confidence in the economic future of the industry.

Information in this study is generally based on the situation in 1992-4. While effort has been made to ensure the accuracy of details provided, I offer my apologies to those organisations or individuals who feel they have been disadvantaged by any inaccuracy or oversight. I am keen to rectify any such errors brought to my attention.

Most of all, I thank Krishna Sen for sharing all this (and so much more) with me, invariably to the detriment of her own research and personal goals. It would, truly, have been impossible to imagine this project without her. Finally, this volume is dedicated to Su-mita Sen Hill, born 6 July 1991, who has grown alongside these pages from her first foray into the 'field' as a three-month old. Her contribution has been more than just patient resignation towards her father's 'work on the computer'; she has offered up the incomparable preciousness of babyhood.

A NOTE ON SPELLING

For the sake of simplicity, consistency and ease of pronunciation all Indonesian words, including personal names, mentioned in the main body of this text are spelt according to the current post-1972 spelling system (Ejaan Yang Disempurnakan). The exception to this is that authors' names appearing in the Endnotes and Bibliography retain the original spelling.

In essence, this means that the pre-1972 'oe' becomes 'u' (e.g. Sukarno, not Soekarno), 'j' changes to 'y' (e.g. *priyayi*, not *prijaji*), 'dj' is reduced to 'j' (e.g. Bersenjata, not Bersendjata) and 'tj' changes to 'c' (*mercu*, not *mertju*).

To those individuals who object to this liberty being taken, particularly with their preferred spelling of personal names, I apologise and present as justification only the belief that to do otherwise would be to make the pronunciation of all Indonesian words in this text considerably more problematical for those unfamiliar with the language.

A NOTE ON CURRENCY CONVERSION

In the early years of the 1990s, to which most of the following discussion refers, the exchange rate was approximately $US 1.00 = Rp. 1,900 or $AUD 1.00 = Rp. 1,400.

Introduction

'Freedom of association and assembly, of expressing thoughts and of issuing writing and the like, shall be prescribed by statute.'

> The 1945 Constitution
> of the Republic of Indonesia,
> Article 28[1]

After coming to power in the wake of the 1 October 1965 putsch, Major-General Suharto and his self-proclaimed 'New Order' cut a swathe through the country's newspapers. In a crackdown unlike anything the country has ever seen nearly one-third of all newspapers were shut down. As the New Order approaches its thirtieth anniversary, it is facing its greatest challenge since initially imposing its tight press policy: While surviving diminishing oil revenues, can it successfully develop an open national economy, yet still suppress growing demands for an unfettered media?

The forces constraining the Indonesian press are changing, as the market, more than the military, shapes its fate. While the President wields ultimate authority and is capable of banning a newspaper at whim, around him swirls a tide of competing interests including a new generation of economic rationalist technocrats and entrepreneurs striving to integrate into the global economy. Unlike the first decade of New Order rule, in the early 1990s it is not so much the military commander as the media capitalist who calls the shots in the industry. When soldiers' gunfire on peaceful demonstrators outside Dili's Santa Cruz cemetery echoed around the world on 12 November 1991, it was the major newspaper proprietors and their editors rather than the Armed Forces Information Centre that determined what the Indonesian papers said and how. The die was cast and the stakes were raised as the media gambled on a new spirit of political 'openness'.

The New Order has put in place an intricate, if chaotic, web of security restrictions and draconian legislation controlling the press. Indisputably such constraints moderate the messages of the media, even if one accepts that readers have honed abilities to read between the lines. As the banning of three major weekly publications in June 1994 dramatically demonstrated, stepping out of line may still result in an uncontestable ban and financial disaster. Today's astute press entrepreneur still needs to keep one eye warily on 'all the President's men', while fixing the other squarely ahead at the market.

But, over the past decade, the operation of power within the Indonesian State has become more complex with the rise of capital and the slow decline in the grosser displays of unlimited military power. Military officers are gradually being called to account, brought before the courts, charged with exceeding their legitimate authority. While such moves are tentative, the press' call for a National Investigative Commission to look into the Dili massacre, the media's detailed reporting of these events and more general coverage of breaches of human rights, contributed significantly towards the push for more accountability of the government and its Armed Forces.

Power, so long centralised in the hands of the President and exercised through the Armed Forces, is gradually fragmenting as market pressures override the old military obsession with a nebulous and ill-defined 'national security'. Now into his fifth five-year term, President Suharto himself is leaning more upon his civilian ministers, to the chagrin of miffed military chiefs. When the Department of Information brought down the triple bans in June 1994, it was almost certainly on the explicit instruction of the President, although Information Minister Harmoko had much to gain by such a show of force. Yet, unlike similar actions in the 1970s, this time it served the military's interests to dissociate itself from the banning, publicly querying the need for such closures.

The bans were arguably a sign of political ineptitude, a rear-guard action by a President, poorly advised, engaged in a futile attempt to slow the march for democratisation. Indonesian social commentators cite it as evidence that the aging President is loosing touch with the rapidly changing community, having difficulty balancing competing ministers within the Cabinet and competing interests within the society. Indonesia is enthusiastically pursuing integration into the world economy and is being inevitably incorporated into the international information order. In his attempts at stemming global information flows and withstanding the tide of social change, Suharto will be as successful as Canute, such critics argue.

As ally of the open press, the emerging middle-class demands access to information and knowledge from a mass media, both print and electronic, that is free to provide comprehensive coverage of matters of public interest. They now insist their domestic print media equal what is freely beamed into their homes by international satellite television. While the capacity to ban newspapers still lies in the hands of the Information Minister, the vociferousness of the public response to such bans demonstrates that such authority will no longer be tolerated in silence. A recent legal suit lodged by prominent editor Gunawan Mohamad against the Information Minister seeks to expose to public and judicial scrutiny whether the Minister had the constitutional authority to ban *Tempo* magazine in June 1994. The pressures for ministerial accountability and the right to a legal defence for erring newspapers are becoming irreversible.

Even more likely to alter the Indonesian media-scape is the predicted loosening of the historic cordon against foreign investment in the industry. In early June 1994 key economic ministers announced that the mass media was to be one of several previously off-limits industries to be opened to overseas investment as part of the general rationalisation of the economy. Demonstrably offended at not being consulted in this, the Minister of Information countered with emphatic denials declaring that President Suharto would never support such an encroachment in the sensitive area of media.

Despite a flurry of ministerial rebuttals, analysts read much into a brief visit to Jakarta by media magnate Rupert Murdoch only months before. The industry's quest for capital to fuel expansion was becoming evident as electronic and print media companies lobbied privately for government permission to 'go public' and list on the stock exchange. For the most entrepreneurial media conglomerates, it mattered little whether the funds were domestic or foreign. Inevitably Indonesia's media market place will go international. Both those for and against such internationalisation see it further diminishing the Indonesian Government's media control.

* * * *

With an estimated 193 million people in 1994, Indonesia is potentially the greatest newspaper-reading (and richest advertising) market in the Southeast Asian region. Its press companies include some whose advanced technologies and staff professionalism are the equal of any in the world. By contrast, numerous others strung across this archipelago are antiquated family concerns slowly winding down into oblivion.

Indonesia is home to the second largest daily newspapers in

Southeast Asia.[2] In 1992 week day sales of the prestigious daily *Kompas* exceeded 525,000, with more than 575,000 for the Sunday edition. Since most copies pass through several readers' hands, often being re-cycled through second-hand newspaper stalls in markets, the actual readership of Kompas is currently estimated to be in excess of 3 million people.[3] And *Kompas* is but one of 160 daily and weekly newspapers published across the country whose total sales exceed 10.5 million copies.

Kompas' sales are more than double comparable quality broadsheet dailies in Australia such as the *Sydney Morning Herald* (267,000) or Melbourne's *The Age* (236,000). Sales of the Indonesian market leader even exceed the Sydney Sunday middle-brow tabloid the *Sun Herald* (550,000) and closely rival Australia's largest selling paper, Melbourne's down-market Sunday tabloid the *Herald-Sun News Pictorial* (590,000).[4]

Such statistical comparisons, however, can blur the enormous differences between the two countries' press industries. Indonesia's press is closely monitored by an interventionist government. It is frequently subject to bans, without any recourse to open trial. Yet in contrast to the oligopolic control of the Australian press, in Indonesia there are dozens, if not hundreds of independent proprietors producing their own papers, surviving in an atmosphere of often boisterous competition and providing the community with broad choices in the types of reading material available. It has been a press with a firm nationalist commitment, forged under Dutch colonialism, shaped during the Japanese interregnum in World War Two, and finally tempered by the legendary 'struggle for independence' to expel the returning Dutch forces from 1945 to 1949.

During the initial decade of Independence the press was dubbed by founding president Sukarno a 'tool of the Revolution', responsible for energising and mobilising public opinion. The 1950s and early sixties were characterised by a vibrant, often caustically partisan press, organised along party lines, technologically and financially impoverished but richly committed to stimulating public debate and mobilising public opinion, even if this brought it into direct conflict with government policies.

With the transition of government after the putsch of 1 October 1965 and the transfer of power to Major-General Suharto on 11 March 1966, the New Order Government dropped the 'revolutioary' rhetoric in favour of a more moderate call to the industry to safeguard national security against internal and external threats, to act with a conscience as the 'guardian of the Pancasila', the five ideological principles of the nation. The Pancasila, initially coined by Sukarno in an extempore speech on 1 June 1945, was substantially re-interpreted by the New Order to become: belief in the one and only God; a just and civilized humanity; the unity of Indonesia; democracy guided by the inner wisdom of deliberations of representatives; and social justice for all the Indonesian people.[5] In promoting this adherence to a common Pancasila ideology, the Suharto Government sought to eliminate party organs or critical papers, domesticate the vociferous press, and ensure that press workers and management were answerable ultimately to the government. By 1969, savage bans by the in-coming regime cut the number of newspapers and magazines, and their total circulation, to less than half the 1964 level.[6]

From this low point in the early 1970s, over the past two decades the press industry in Indonesia has been transformed dramatically. Publications look smarter and more attractive, as full advantage has been taken of improving technologies. Two waves of mass bannings in the 1970s in the wake of sympathetic press reports of social and political opposition to the government, followed by the entry into the industry of heavy-weight investors during the late 1980s changed the patterns of press ownership and broadened the range of publications produced. This investment improved significantly the salaries and general working conditions of journalists as 'head-hunting' entered the industry, perceptibly altering the ethos of the profession, and the stakes required to play in the industry's big league. Both sales figures and the capital required to establish and run a sustainable publication rose rapidly. For the first time in Indonesian history newspaper companies graduated from cottage industry to the ranks of big business.

At the end of the 1980s the Indonesian press industry was riding the crest of a wave of media expansion. In the electronic media, in 1988 the first private-owned television station, RCTI (*Rajawali Citra Televisi Indonesia*) began test broadcasting in Jakarta. Two years later SCTV (*Surya Citra Televisi*) followed suit in Surabaya. In 1991 the nominally 'educational' television channel TPI (*Televisi Pendidikan Indonesia*) commenced broadcasting nation-wide, eight hours daily. In both the print and electronic media the new decade promised continued growth, flux and change.

The prognosis for the print media, however, became somewhat more gloomy as the big borrowers and investors of the late 1980s were caught in the squeeze of the government's tight monetary policy after over-extending themselves in the boom years. Even companies in strong financial shape had to face increasingly vigorous competition, both from within the print industry and from the expanding electronic media. A leaner economy, languishing advertising budgets draining away to a booming private television sector, sharpened competition from new stables of publications using bolder marketing methods have all combined to create greater risks and financial uncertainties in the 1990s. Yet while the optimistic investment surge of the 1980s may have slowed, the trajectory of the print media industry overall is firmly upward.

While pursuing commercial success and fulfilling its guardianship of the Pancasila for the past 30 years, the Indonesian press was declared, in New Order parlance, 'free but responsible', in contrast to the presumed irresponsibility of liberal (Western) newspapers. It is a policy with numerous staunch supporters, not only amongst safari-suited bureaucrats in the regulatory Department of Information, but more surprisingly even amongst hard-nosed working journalists.

Many informed observers in Indonesia regard it as either pompous arrogance or evidence of a laughable naivety when Australians point an accusing finger at Indonesia for not permitting 'freedom of the press'. Many would argue that 'the Indonesian press in several aspects is freer and more democratic than that of Australia'.[7] Indonesian editors talk with a wry smile of the fact that it is the Australian, not the Indonesian, press which is monotonous and dominated by a small clique of media magnates such as American national Rupert Murdoch, Canadian Conrad Black and Australia's home-grown Kerry Packer.[8]

That foreigners should play the determining role in a country's press, that a government should prove unequal to the task of protecting a country's media industry against foreign takeovers, is anathema to many Indonesians, who have so far endorsed their government's explicit prohibition against foreign investment or involvement in the country's print media. Generally, Indonesian editors take pride in what they see as their profession's role in the nationalist struggle of the past. Whatever the realities of current business pragmatics, many would still give lip-service at least to a commitment by the press to serve the perceived good of the nation as a whole rather than narrow commercial interests.

Yet in developing and maintaining the Indonesian print media industry without outside investment, the State and its press entrepreneurs face some of the world's most complex newspaper distribution and marketing problems: one thousand inhabited islands strung out across 7.9 million square kilometres of ocean, embracing the world's fourth largest population growing at about 2% per annum, with nearly 70 per cent living in rural areas. Establishing and supplying a viable readership is a major achievement, given a functional illiteracy rate of 15% even in the school-age population of five to twenty-nine year olds.[9] A 1992 survey covering the six major cities which represent the largest potential newspaper market, noted that in the over-15 age group 7.5% had no schooling at all and a further 10% had not completed primary school.[10] Even basic infrastructure is often lacking. For example, in Jakarta eight per cent of households are without electricity for lighting; in far flung East Timor only eight per cent have electric light.

In 1991 when the population was nudging 190 million, national sales for press publications - both newspapers and magazines - in Indonesia amounted to only a little over 13 million per issue. Any cursory comparison of circulation and population statistics starkly highlights the fact that purchasing a newspaper or magazine is, and has always been, a minority urban activity in Indonesia. In the six major cities, where newspaper reading is concentrated, advertising research suggests that in 1992 a healthy 48% of the population over-15 years of age had read a daily newspaper the previous day.[11] Yet, by contrast, figures for the heavily rural remainder of the population would be only a small fraction of this urban percentage. While one newspaper copy may be read by several people – estimates usually suggest about half a dozen at least – the practice of reading newspapers and magazines was not widespread, this despite an enormous boost in circulation over the past decade.[12]

The marketing problems faced by the Indonesian press, of course, parallel those faced by many other industries. Some observers see the fate of the press as a barometer of broader economic trends. Christianto Wibisono, head of the influential Indonesian Business Data Centre (PDBI) and an astute media analyst, has stressed that 'the ups and downs in the life of the press in Indonesia are attuned to the changes and developments we experience in businesses' economic, political and social systems'.[13] Immediately after Independence in 1945, when the economy was dominated by giant foreign (mainly Dutch) companies and banks, so too was the press. As successful indigenous entrepreneurs grew more common so too did indigenous journalists, editors and newspaper owners, gradually absorbing the energetic ethnic Chinese who had long figured prominently in journalism.

Yet, Wibisono also argued that newspapers have been more enterprising and adaptive than industries which faced tight competition from foreign investment for, unlike many other sectors of the local economy, in time the press has succeeded in 'becoming master of its own house' (to use the frequent Indonesian expression); that is, avoiding foreign ownership, joint ventures, control by ethnic Chinese cukong (financiers) and perhaps by implication, control by financial interests close to the palace – all this while constantly facing the Damocles sword of arbitrary bannings and consequent financial ruin. While many analysts would voice grave misgivings over any argument that a 'national' media in Indonesia can insulate itself against 'foreign' influence, as state borders become increasingly porous and the flows of information lightning-fast, there are many impressive financial success stories in the indigenous press industry in Indonesia despite a disturbing history of State suppression.

As the New Order economy comes of age and enjoys the prospect of sustained expansion, successful press entrepreneurs in Indonesia are rising to the challenges of global deregulation and anti-protectionism, preparing for the possibility of foreign media incursions into the Indonesian marketplace with ambitious proposals for their own expansion off shore. The major English-language daily is seeking to become a kind of regional International Herald Tribune, aiming for distribution throughout Southeast Asia. Another thriving press conglomerate, which has already cast its distribution net widely throughout the vast, largely untapped region of Eastern Indonesia, is now seriously exploring the possibility of a substantial multi-pronged investment in the Australian regional press.

As the Australian press industry contends with complex cross-media ownership limitations, the break-up of former giants like the Fairfax group, shifting permissible levels of foreign ownership, public scrutiny of bitter foreign takeover battles, and embarrasing allegations of prime ministerial back-room deals with foreign interests aired by a 1994 Senate investigation, investors across the Timor Sea are enjoying a period of increasing economic and political deregulation. It is ever more likely that, along with current Indonesian investments in Australian real estate and tourism, Indonesian press enterprises may soon be injecting a new spirit of press competition into the Australian press industry.

Fundamental, widespread and mutual misunderstandings about the operations of the respective media in both Australia and Indonesia have been at the root of numerous bilateral diplomatic and political tensions. Yet the print media industry also offers a unique window through which to observe developments in a country's political life. For such reasons then, a detailed study of the Indonesian press, its relationship with the government, and its future role in the nation, is of very direct relevance for Australians as well as Indonesia's other regional neighbours.

While there are a variety of specialised academic studies of aspects of the Indonesian press,[14] this monograph is intended primarily as a brief, factual, ready-reference; a statement of record, for those who seek a succinct general introduction to the Indonesian print media today. It illustrates that the New Order press has been under constant pressure to conform to the government's political demands. It details the fatal consequences for those press companies which ignore or underestimate government controls. But, despite the surprising triple bans of June 1944, there is an overall trend for such pressures to diminish, and evidence that commercial imperatives are rapidly filling the vacuum, becoming a primary regulating force upon the industry.

The aim of this study is to describe for the outsider the anatomy of the Indonesian press during the New Order period, detailing the history, structure, organisations, individuals, government regulations and practices which dominate the industry. The focus is generally on Indonesian-language national daily newspapers, although reference is made to major news weeklies, periodicals and magazines, together with certain significant regional (and vernacular) publications. It concentrates primarily on the rapid changes during the past decade, locating these developments within the context of relations between the press and the State after the ascension of Major-General Suharto and the self-proclaimed New Order Government in 1966-8.

Chapter One provides a brief background history of the press in Indonesia from the birth of the first newspaper in the then Dutch East Indies in 1745, to the social and political turbulence that marked the years of the early 1960s. Chapter Two highlights developments during the New Order, noting particularly the periods of government anti-press actions and more recent economic liberalisation and expansion. It will be argued that while the early years of President Suharto's New Order were marked by sweeping bans, the industry's response has been largely to 'self-regulate', letting capital accumulation and market pressures primarily determine its mode of dealing with the State. It suggests that recent multiple bans are an aberration, a flash-back to the past, which is unlikely to stem the general trend towards liberalisation since the mid-1980s.

Chapter Three examines the artifice of legislation and corporatist control structured to contain the print media. It describes the relevant policing sections of the Department of Information, and the professional organisations governing and channelling the activities of all workers in, and all aspects of, the industry. Various regulatory government structures will be discussed, as will organisational press bodies, such as the Press Council, the Journalists Association and the Newspaper Publishers Association, themselves significant regulatory structures operating to constrain the media.

Chapter Four focuses on the recent expansion in circulations and markets, together with changing patterns of ownership and financial control, particularly the emergence of press empires and the impact on these of recent bans. Four major metropolitan press conglomerates will be discussed in some depth: those centred on *Kompas*, *Suara Pembaruan*, *Tempo* and the relative newcomer *Media Indonesia*. Along with the emergence of these press empires, the recent interests of people close to, and in, the presidential family will be examined as emblematic of a new phase in the relationship between the press and the State.

The particular problems and contributions of the regional, religious, student and foreign-language presses – frequently ignored in studies of the national Indonesian-language press – are examined in Chapter Five.

Finally, Chapter Six considers more generally the impact of changes in the industry for the society at large, particularly in terms of contradictions within the ruling elite, and posits some prognoses for future trends in the industry. It discusses the increasingly sophisticated market segmentation and expansion strategies employed by the successful operators in the press as they adapt to the demographic, social and geographic divides, in an industry facing an increasingly competitive future. Significantly, it seems likely that the previous emphasis on 'national' flagship newspapers will decline, as market niches are increasingly filled by innovative, well-managed sub-national or regional papers on the one hand, and even 'transnational' publishing ventures (made possible by the globalisation of information technology) on the other.

For those readers interested in delving deeper into research on the print media a note on further reading is appended.

* * * *

While giving details of the clashes between government and the press, between the national leviathan conglomerates and the lilliputian regional papers, between corporatist professional organisations and press workers, the study attempts, too, to raise some general questions about social and political change in Indonesia. Although intended primarily as a descriptive guide to the Indonesian press, throughout its chapters run several analytical themes evident the evolution of the industry in New Order Indonesia.

Firstly, the analysis highlights the sharpening contradiction between the interests of business in maximising the profit-making potential of the print media industry and the desire of the State to control the flows of information in order to maintain the 'security' of the State. The up-market broadsheets dislike having to couch their own political and economic analyses in cautious terms, to avoid the authorities' crack-down. In the early 1990s' atmosphere of greater political 'openness' such cautious publications risk losing readers to newer, bolder rival papers unless the traditionally prudent papers follow suit. Even the tabloid press, with its penchant for gore, gossip and intrigue, resents the stifling control of the State, which excludes from the list of acceptable topics unflattering tales of the politically well-connected and powerful - the grist of Western tabloids. As the June 1994 bans show, however, survival still requires of the editor and the entrepreneur the skills of a political tightrope walker. The risks for those press companies pushing back the limits of 'openness' are closure and ruin.

When a media company is associated with a member of the presidential family (as an increasing number of print and electronic media companies are) then this contradiction between State control of information and the entrepreneurs' interest in expanding markets and profits comes into sharp relief. For example, the transmission of CNN's (uncensored) international news broadcasts via Indonesia's Palapa satellite may irritate the Indonesian Government from time to time, but it benefits Bambang Trihatmojo, one of the President's sons, whose company is engaged in the CNN-Palapa deal. While the Minister for Information may be adamant about excluding foreign investment in the media lest the State's control over information flows be diminished, such funds would prove a financial shot in the arm for Bambang Trihatmojo's RCTI television company, reportedly keen for permission to accept overseas partners. As one analyst observed, if the Indonesian Government does proceed with the predicted opening up of the media market to foreign investment, its capacity to ban an outspoken paper by withdrawing its publication permit may be curtailed by the need to adhere to more stringent legal procedures or face condemnation from the World Bank's International Centre for the Settlement of Investment Disputes.[15]

Secondly, also challenging State constraints is the burgeoning middle-class with its growing desire for open access to information and greater plurality of voices in the press. Now having access to the powerful international television networks beamed in via uncensored satellite, this constituency is demanding greater coverage and probing analysis from their own domestic media services, both print and electronic. Competition for markets is increasing across national borders and between domestic media companies, to capture a public demanding more substantial, interesting and entertaining media services. Such pressure encouraged the publication and popularity of a periodical like *Forum Keadilan [Justice Forum]*, with its explicit Human Rights brief, in 1991. Similar pressure may lie behind the government's decision to permit private television companies to broadcast their own news programs from August 1993, ending the news monopoly of State-run television's TVRI.

Thirdly, however, as the study points out, many analysts of the print media industry recognise that there are significant risks if State control is simply relinquished into the hands of powerful media oligopolies, particularly where such companies are linked with the politically powerful. There is a concern that the current level of diversity of ideas and interests permitted in the Indonesian press may actually decline with the rise of media conglomerates at the expense and consequent marginalisation of older non-syndicated or family-run papers.

The print media together with its electronic competitors, has developed into one of the most dynamic sectors of the Indonesian domestic economy. The characteristics of the media generally are unlike any other commercial sector, with an often heady mix of massive capital investment, political influence, critical expression and public appeal, as the following study aims to illustrate. Unpredictable though the ultimate outcome may be, the recent tensions described in the following pages herald a new phase in the tussle between State and private enterprise in the press world of Indonesia.

ENDNOTES

1. Quoted from the translation of the Constitution in Abdul Razak (1985), *Press Laws and Systems in Asean States*, Confederation of Asean Journalists Publication, Jakarta, p.258.

2. The largest daily paper in Southeast Asia is believed to be Bangkok's *Thai Rath*, with a circulation of about 900,000, from seven editions. It claimed a boom to 1.8 million during the failed September 1985 coup attempt (see *Ensiklopedi Nasional Indonesia*, PT Cipta Adi Pustaka, Jakarta, 1991, Vol. 16, p.286). Sales in 1992 for other leading dailies in the region include Malaysia's *Berita Harian* with about 336,000, Singapore's *Straits Times* with 338,000, and the Philippines' *Manila Bulletin* with 250,000 (according to figures from *Willings Press Guide* Vol. 2, Reed Information Services, West Sussex, 1993, various pages).

3. See advertisement in the *Australian*, 15 July 1994, p.14.

4. Australian circulation figures taken from the Australian Press Council *Annual Report No. 16*, 30 June 1992, pp.154-6.

5. Paraphrased slightly from the Department of Information (1992), *Indonesia 1992: An Official Handbook*, Indonesian Department of Information, Jakarta, p.38. For a partial translation of Sukarno's initial formulation, 'The Birth of the Panca Sila', see Herbert Feith & Lance Castles (ed.) (1970), *Indonesian Political Thinking 1945-1965* Cornell University Press, Ithaca, pp.40-9. For a discussion of the 'New Order' reinterpretation, see Michael Morfit (1981), 'Pancasila: The Indonesian State Ideology according to the New Order Government', *Asian Survey*, Vol XXI, No. 8, August, pp.838-51.

6. Daniel Dhakidae (1991), 'The State, The Rise of Capital, and the Fall of Political Journalism: Political Economy of Indonesian News Industry', Cornell University Doctoral Dissertation, (available in University Microfilms International, Ann Arbor, Michigan, 1992) p.551, table 1, gives the 1964 figures as: Number of papers (including dailies, weeklies and magazines) 609 with a total circulation (per edition) of 5,561,000 compared to the comparable 1969 data of 259 and 2,528,050.

7. Subagio Sastrowardoyo (1984), 'Pengkajian Indonesia: Yang AntiIndonesia', *Kompas* 11 September, reprinted in Kitley, P., Chauvel, R., & Reeve, D., (1989), *Australia di Mata Indonesia*, Gramedia, Jakarta, pp.446-52; quotation from p.450.

8. One example of this position was put by academic and author Subagio Sastrowardoyo (1984) in Kitley, Chauvel & Reeve (1989:450-1) in which, after listing the then four major press companies, he states 'Thus the voice of the Australian press is determined and directed by that small group of businesses. This means that public opinion in Australia is generally formed by the frames of reference, and political and commercial interests of these four companies.' A similar point has been made more recently in Yosef Tor Tulis (1992),

'Sistem Pemilikan Oligopolistik Membuat Kebebasan Pers Pincang', *Suara Pembaruan*, 2/4/92.

9. Badan Pusat Statistik, 1991, *Statistik Indonesia / Statistical Year Book of Indonesia 1990*, BPS, Jakarta pp.83-8.

10. Data given in Table 4.2, 'Demography: Population by Education and Occupation (Jakarta, Bandung, Semarang, Surabaya, Medan, Ujung Pandang)' in Baty Subakti & Ernst Katoppo (ed.) (1993) *Media Scene 1992-1993 Indonesia: The Official Guide to Advertising Media in Indonesia*, PPPI, Jakarta, p.32.

11. Data given in Table 6.1, 'Media Habits (Jakarta, Bandung, Semarang, Surabaya, Medan, Ujung Pandang)' in Subakti & Katoppo 1993:41.

12. Paul Tickell makes the point that, although 'most newspapers are consumed in urban areas', not all readers are wealthy, since publications are often posted 'on public reading boards outside of newspaper offices or government offices. Old newspapers and magazines, in particular, are sold more cheaply [in markets, bus stations or by mobile vendors] and therefore open up a new audience.' ('The Indonesian Press: Past Historic, Present Political and Future Economic', unpublished, p.4.)

13. 'Piramida Pers Indonesia', *Tempo*, 15 February 1992, pp.104-5.

14. A selection of relevant titles will be provided in 'A Note on Further Reading' at the end of this volume.

15. Christianto Wibisono (1994) 'Media Massa dari Politik ke Bisnis', *Tempo*, 11 June 1994, p.102.

CHAPTER 1

Before the New Order

Revolution needs leadership. Without it there is panic and fear. It is because we are still in an economic revolution that I shall not allow destructive criticism of my leadership nor do I permit freedom of the press. We are too young a country to encourage more confusion than we already have.

President Sukarno[1]

Since the turn of this century, the press in Indonesia has been a forum for the expression of nationalist aspirations and political agitation. The *Bataviasche Nouvelles en Politique Raisonnementes*, the first of what can be regarded as the modern newspaper in Indonesia (then the Dutch East Indies) was published in 1745; about 136 years after the world's oldest regularly published weekly newspaper *Avisa Relation oder Zeitung* appeared in Strassbourg in 1609.[2] Apart from the government gazette, the earliest publications in Indonesia were largely advertising broadsheets, providing details of commercial auctions and the like. They were initially in Dutch, with a Javanese- and later Indonesian-language press (though still frequently Dutch-financed) emerging from the mid-1850s. The first of these non-Dutch-language newspapers was the Javanese *Bromartani*, published in Solo from 1855, which was printed in the Javanese (*hanacaraka*) script.[3]

By the turn of the century nationalists,[4] such as Abdul Rivai and Tirtoadisuryo (upon whom Pramudya Ananta Tur based his four-volume epic *This Earth of Mankind*[5]), recognised the power of the periodical and began publishing Indonesian-language 'news' papers providing a nationalist interpretation of the political situation. Tirtoadisuryo's *Sunda Berita [West Java News]*, published on 17 August 1903 was the first attempt to publish a newspaper with indigenous capital, but it folded quickly. More successful was Tirtoadisuryo's next venture, *Medan Priyayi [Aristocrats' Domain]*, set up in 1907, which is regarded as the first successful newspaper to be established solely with indigenous capital.[6] This growing sense of 'Indonesian' identity – embodied in the term 'pergerakan' [the movement] — was strengthened by a 1928 milestone Youth Conference and Pledge to struggle for 'One Homeland, One Nation, One Language', that of 'Indonesia'. In that year, of the country's 33 newspapers, only eight were Indonesian-language (or 'Malay' as it had been known), with the remainder being in Dutch (13) or 'Chinese Malay' (12).[7] The Indonesian Chinese community was strongly represented among the journalists and financiers of early Indonesian/Malay newspapers, making an enduring contribution to the development of the profession and the industry.

Under the Dutch colonial regime Indonesian language periodicals, both those explicitly nationalist in editorial orientation as well as those with more commercial motivations, struggled against enormous financial odds. But more intimidating were a series of colonial laws and regulations governing printed matter. Most restricting were the despised *Haatzaai Artikelen* ['Sowing of Hatred Articles'] and a 1931 Press Act *[Persbreidel Ordonnantie]*, which could be invoked against anyone disturbing 'public order' or spreading 'hatred' or dissent against the government. Under this mandate, the Dutch Governor-General had the power to ban publications deemed offensive or destabilising, a prerogative used with some alacrity. Between 1931 and 1936 at least 27 daily newspaper were subject to government action, including the detention of journalists.[8]

The role played by journalists during this period is viewed with enormous pride by the profession, which commenced a recent English-language booklet on the Indonesian Journalists' Association (PWI):

> The history of the Indonesian independence movement provides ample evidence of the Indonesian journalists as patriots and participants in the struggle against Dutch colonialism... As freedom fighters, the Indonesian journalists fulfilled two tasks simultaneously. As working journalists, they were responsible for reporting and providing information with the aim of forging the national consciousness of the people. And, as political activists, they were directly involved in the resistance movement which fought against colonial rule. These two tasks had a single objective: to establish the independence of the Indonesian nation and State.[9]

While the Japanese Occupation of the Dutch East Indies (1942–45) brought its own pre-publication censorship constraints it did offer press industry workers a greater opportunity for skilling and training.[10] In addition to fostering the establishment of many Indonesian language papers, of which *Asia Raya [Glorious Asia]*[11] was the first, the Japanese provided training programs for journalists. Senior staff positions were 'Indonesianised' to replace the ousted Dutch and since the Japanese language was difficult to master quickly and remained unpopular, Indonesian supplanted the banned Dutch language in dealings with the bureaucracy and in the press.

The Proclamation of Independence by Sukarno and Mohammad Hatta on 17 August 1945 and the subsequent establishment of the Republic of Indonesia was enthusiastically disseminated and supported by a nationalist press. The news agency Antara, originally founded in 1937 and absorbed by the Japanese DOMEI agency during the Occupation, re-emerged in September 1945. So too, appeared a growing clutch of 'nationalist' papers, primary amongst them the Jakarta-based *Merdeka [Independence]*. Founded on 1 October 1945 only 44 days after the Proclamation, *Merdeka* is today Indonesia's oldest-running, most irrepressible national daily. The young activist-journalists who established the paper (BM Diah as editor-in-chief was only in his mid-20s) took over the Japanese-sponsored Indonesian-language daily *Asia Raya*, together with its printery, De Unie, formerly owned by the Dutch, with six months supply of newsprint.[12] *Merdeka* proved to be an enormously important training ground for a generation of journalist/editors (such as Mochtar Lubis, Rosihan Anwar and Asa Bafagih).

The struggle for international recognition of the Declaration of Independence and Dutch Transfer of Sovereignty was largely a diplomatic one, in which the forces of the Fourth Estate were as much vital foot-soldiers as were the guerrillas bearing arms against the Dutch military. It was largely a paper propaganda war, in which the skills of Indonesian journalists were unrivalled. The profession attracted a number who went on to become significant political figures in the independent nation, including most notably Adam Malik, who served as both Foreign Minister and Vice-President during the New Order.

'Nationalist' papers were permitted relatively free rein under the gaze initially of a transitional Allied administration in Indonesia, and later a United Nations commission which oversaw the negotiations between the Republic of Indonesia and the Dutch. This was the *'pers perjuangan'*, the press of political struggle: partisan, and proud of it. It was this principle which largely dominated press life in Indonesia until (it can be argued) the 1980s.

In the early years of Independence, newspapers sprung up 'like mushrooms in the rainy season' throughout the 1950s, as political parties sought media promotion for their views. In 1949, the year the Dutch recognised Independence, there were 75 press publications, with a total circulation of 413,000 per issue. By 1955, the time of Indonesia's first General Elections, the number of publications had increased six-fold to 457, with an eight-fold increase in total circulation to 3,457,910 (see Table 1). The Indonesian population was by then about 85.5 million.[13]

It was a time of political turbulence. Discontent over the rationalisation of the hotch-potch of irregular troops and military forces after the Transfer of Sovereignty, the vying for political power by a throng of emerging political parties, the swift rise and fall of Cabinets, the horse-trading for government economic concessions, the disaffection of the outer regions with central government policies, all contributed to the bubbling cauldron of 'parliamentary democracy' in the 1950s. The profusion of small papers that emerged struggled to stay afloat in a sea of financial insecurity. A nucleus broke even, or survived through regular government or military procurements that enabled copies to be distributed free in government offices and to the troops. Most lost money, remaining in business only by virtue of the editors' ability to call upon sympathetic monied supporters for donations to tide them over.[14] Press workers' wages were invariably inadequate and irregular. Advertising revenue was meagre at a time when Dutch firms, which still carried considerable weight, were hesitant to put money into 'nationalist' papers, and Indonesian businesses were still struggling to survive in the new political and commercial environment.

By the late 1950s the campaign to wrest West Papua (or Irian Jaya, as it is now known in Indonesia) from the Netherlands had threatened the viability of many Dutch enterprises, not least, in the press. In 1949, the year the Dutch finally recognised Independence, there had been 13 Dutch-language daily newspapers in Indonesia with a total circulation of 102,300. As anti-Dutch sentiment mounted, these businesses gradually closed until by 1956 only seven survived, maintaining a circulation of about 56,850. None survived 1957 when symbolically perhaps the Dutch language paper, *Nieuwsgier*, was banned as part of the Irian campaign.[15] With the decline of the Dutch-language press, came a rise in English-language papers. The first, *The Times of Indonesia*, appeared in 1952 under the initial direction of the energetic editor of the controversial Indonesian-language daily *Indonesia Raya*, Mochtar Lubis, and after 1953 led by Sri Lankan managing editor Charles Tambu. The small English-language press in Indonesia has continued uninterrupted, from origins in pamphlets produced during the struggle for

Independence (1945–49) to sway the English-speaking diplomatic community and military forces, such as the Indian, English and Australian nationals, in favour of the Republican cause.[16] It has remained a small but influential sector of the industry, not least because it is read by foreign investors, researchers and diplomats, who might be regarded potentially at least as significant opinion-builders.

As part of the government's efforts to mobilise the mass media in forging a strong and unified nation, a presidential decree in 1962 brought the news agency Antara directly under the authority of the President, as the 'semi-governmental' National News Agency (LKBN Antara). While maintaining an operational autonomy, in practice, government control increased.[17] In the 1960s Antara was committed to the ongoing social revolution promoted by President Sukarno and supported by the burgeoning Indonesian Communist Party. It pursued an explicitly partisan line in news reporting, for which it was roundly criticised by more conservative sections of the media.

Of the major exemplars of the 'perjuangan' [struggle] style of politically engaged, committed journalism, which weathered the military storms despite sporadic banning orders, and succeeded in attaining some of the highest circulation figures of the time, was the Indonesian Communist Party (PKI) daily, *Harian Rakyat [People's Daily]*. From a low 1951 base circulation of 2,000 copies, by 1956 (when the country had a total population of about 87 million) it had become the largest daily with 58,000. But *Harian Rakyat* was not alone in its 'perjuangan' style. Most papers were becoming party-affiliated, explicitly or by editorial alignment, an arrangement formalised by a Decision of the Information Minister (No.29/SK/M/65) on 26 March 1965 concerning 'the Basic Norms for Press Enterprises within the Context of the Promotion of the Indonesian Press' which ruled that all newspapers and periodicals had to be affiliated formally with a political party, 'functional group' or mass organisation. Editorial and managerial staff had to be nominated by the party, which was regarded by the Minister having consequent responsibility for the contents of the paper.[18] Thus the circulations claimed by party papers should be treated with some scepticism since they were often cited as evidence of the mass base and potential public influence of the party concerned.

Not surprisingly then, papers with strong party affiliates tended to circulate well, as did those which appealed to a literate, financial comfortable urban constituency. After *Harian Rakyat* came *Pedoman [Guide]* (associated with the small but articulate Indonesian Socialist

Party, PSI, and banned in 1961) with 48,000, the PNI (Nationalist Party) *Suluh Indonesia [Indonesian Torch]* with 40,000 and the Masyumi (Modernist Islamic) *Abadi [Eternal]* with 34,000. Most other papers were lucky to sell 10,000 copies, surviving by dint of government newsprint subsidies.[19] Such unaudited figures are always open to question, but clearly the fate of party papers was closely linked to the destiny of the party.

The year 1957, when martial law (termed the State of War and Seige) was declared in March, proved to be a watershed for the press industry. In that year there were more actions taken by the government against the press - interrogation, detention and jailing of journalists, bans on publications, and the like - than any year from May 1952 until October 1965. In this year of heightened political tensions the newspaper circulation figure of 888,950 was similarly the highest of any year during the decade till 1962.[20] Sukarno was determined to rein in renegade papers and was adamant that, whatever the international odium associated with press suppression, he would 'not allow destructive criticism of my leadership'. The military, similarly, were swift to exercise the wide-reaching authority they now enjoyed (and were largely to retain to the present). Throughout the period of martial law papers were closed down for a range of 'political' reasons, such as lending editorial support for regional movements against the central government or offending the President or senior political or military figures.[21] For example, in a crackdown on the Masyumi and the PSI, *Abadi* closed down under pressure in late 1960 and *Pedoman* was banned in early 1961. By contrast, circulation of *Harian Rakyat* rose steadily to 70,000 in 1964, and finally to 85,000 copies in 1965 prior to its prohibition – along with most other 'left of centre' publications – in the aftermath of the military coup of 1 October that year.[22]

Yet, despite judgements by many observers that government constraints on the media were severe during the years prior to 1966, if one considers the multiplicity of publications and the breadth of circulation, 1964 was, on the contrary, a high-point for an amazingly resilient press industry which could then boast 609 daily, weekly or magazine-style press publications with a total circulation per edition of 5,561,000. So high was this achievement that it was only realised in one other year, 1973, prior to a boom period in the 1980s, by which time the population of 145 million was 40% larger than 1964's 103.3 million.[23]

ENDNOTES

1. Sukarno (1965), *Sukarno: An Autobiography, as told to Cindy Adams*, Bobbs-Merrill, Indianapolis, p.279.

2. On the world's first newspapers, see Kenneth E. Olson (1966), *The History Makers: The Press of Europe from its Beginnings through 1965*, Louisiana State University Press, Louisiana, p.103. Details on the early Indonesian newspapers are from Dhakidae 1991:35 (fn. 15), the most incisive recent study focusing on the New Order press. The most accessible English-language work on the history of the Indonesian press to 1966 is Oey Hong Lee (1971), *Indonesian Government and Press During Guided Democracy*, Centre for Southeast Asian Studies, University of Hull / Inter Documentation Co AG Zug, (see esp. pp.2-65). Both cite G.H. von Faber, [1930?] *Short History of Journalism in the Dutch East Indies*, G. Kolff & Co, Surabaya, (esp. p.14) for details of the colonial period. Soebagijo notes that, on the initiative of the first Dutch GovernorGeneral in the East Indies, Jan Pieterszoon Coen in 1615, handwritten 'papers', called *Memorie* der *Nouvelles*, began to be distributed throughout the colony providing government 'news', a practice which continued until around 1644 (see Soebagijo I.N., *Sejarah Pers Indonesia*, Dewan Pers, Jakarta, 1977, p.7).

3. For a discussion of the early Javanese- and Indonesian-language press, see Paul Tickell (1987a), 'Taman Pewarta: Malay Medium - Indonesian Message' (pp.7-14) in Paul Tickell (ed.) (1987b), *The Indonesian Press: Its past, its people, its problems*, CSEAS Monash University, Clayton.

4. These pioneers are regarded by some observers as 'proto-nationalists' rather than 'nationalist' in the post-1945 sense, for their vision of a future was often more ethnic or regional. The organisations they founded, for example, bore names like 'Young Sumatrans' rather than 'Young Indonesians' but their sentiments identified with their people and their land rather than the Dutch colonial presence.

5. Pramudya's tetralogy based on the life of Tirtoadisuryo has been translated into English by Max Lane as Awakenings (incorporating the first two volumes, *This Earth of Mankind* and *Child of All Nations*), *Footsteps*, and *House of Glass* (published by Penguin, Ringwood, respectively in 1991, 1990 and 1992).

6. Dhakidae *1991:10*.

7. The term 'Chinese Malay' ['Melayu Tionghoa'] is used to describe a form of Malay language that was identified linguistically with locally-born ethnic Chinese, and also to describe those papers published by and primarily for that population. See Leo Suryadinata 'Pers Melayu Tionghoa' (pp.35-64) in Abdurrachman Surjomihardjo (ed.) (1980), *Beberapa Segi Perkembangan Sejarah Pers di Indonesia*, Departemen Penerangan RI & LEKNAS-LIPI, Jakarta, esp. p.35. For statistics on the 1928 newspapers, see Abdurrachman Surjomihardjo & Leo Suryadinata 'Pers Indonesia' (pp.65-86, esp. p.80) also in Abdurrachman Surjomihardjo (ed.) (1980).

8. Tribuana Said (1988), *Sejarah Pers Nasional dan Pembangunan* Pers *Pancasila*, Penerbit Haji Masagung, Jakarta, pp.42-3, cites an unnamed 1938 article by Sujarwo Condronegoro as his source for these details. A detailed Indonesian translation of the 1931 provisions is included in H. Mohammad Said (1976), *Sejarah Pers di Sumatera Utara*, Waspada, Medan, pp.167-9.

9. Tribuana Said (ed.) (1986), *Indonesian Journalists' Association Persatuan Wartawan Indonesia (P.W. I.)*, Indonesian Journalists' Association (PWI), Jakarta, p.7.

10. See Oey Hong Lee 1971:15-29 for details of the press during the Japanese Occupation. For a more detailed study, see A. Latief (1980) *Pers di Indonesia di Zaman Pendudukan Jepang*, Karya Anda, Surabaya.

11. I have translated the names of Indonesian newspapers and magazines. Where no translation is given, the title refers to an untranslatable name (e.g. *Bobo*) or the title is in English or is readily recognisable (e.g. *Gala*).

12. J.R. Chaniago, Kasijanto, Erwiza Erman & M. Hisyam (1987), *Ditugaskan Sejarah: Perjuangan 'Merdeka' 1945-1985*, Pustaka Merdeka, Jakarta, p.xii & 12. Diah headed the paper until his retirement in January 1989. (See 'Wartawan yang Berlabuh di Tambak Udang', *Tempo*, 14 January 1989, p.91.)

13. Figures drawn from Dhakidae 1991, Table i, p.551. Numbers refer to all kinds of press publications: dailies, weeklies and magazines.

14. This was certainly the case with the daily newspaper *Indonesia Raya*, edited by Mochtar Lubis. While fervently maintaining its 'independent' status, it was receiving irregular but significant financial injections through the intervention of key military intelligence officers. See David T. Hill (1988), 'Mochtar Lubis: Editor, Author, Political Actor', unpublished doctoral thesis, Australian National University, Canberra, pp.58-66.

15. Edward C. Smith (c.1969), *A History of Newspaper Suppression in Indonesia 1949-1965*, PhD thesis, University of Iowa, gives the statistics of Dutch, English, Chinese and Indonesian daily newspapers (1949-65) in Table 16 (published in Indonesian translation as *Pembreidelan Pers di Indonesia*, Grafitipers, Jakarta, 1983, with Table 16 on p.242). See also Burhan D. Magenda (1979), 'The Press in Jakarta as a Catalyst of Cultural Change', pp.89-107, in Gloria Davis (ed.) (1979), *What is Modern Indonesian Culture?*, Ohio University Center for International Studies, SEA *Series*, No. 52, details from p.93.

16. English publications were not only produced in Jakarta during this period. In Medan, Abdul Majid headed production of the weekly *Free Indonesia*, directed at the occupying English and Indian troops (Soebagijo 1977:65).

17. See Atmakusumah's entry on 'Antara' in *Ensiklopedi Nasional Indonesia*, Vol. 2, P.T. Cipta Adi Pustaka, Jakarta, 1988, pp.132-7.

18. Oey 1971:128-9, which also notes that, as an alternative to political parties

and mass organisations, papers could be supported by a government body called the *Panca Tunggal (Unit of Five)* which 'consisted of the Heads of Local Government, Police, Attorney General's Department, Military Territorial Command and local leaders of the National Front'(Oey 1971:340, fn. 14).

19. See Atmakusumah (1980), 'Kasus *Indonesia Raya*' (pp. 181-246) in Abdurrachman Surjomihardjo (ed.) (1980), *Beberapa Segi Perkembangan Sejarah Pers di Indonesia*, Departemen Penerangan RI & LEKNAS-LIPI, Jakarta, for figures given on p.188.

20. Figures are drawn from data provided in Smith (1983) Table 6, p.169 and Table 16, p.242. In 1957 there were 125 anti-press actions of various kinds; in 1958 there were 95; compared to 14 in 1953 and 10 in 1964 and the pre-October period of 1965.

21. For a discussion of how one crusading newspaper handled the political tensions of the time, see my 'Press Challenges, Government Responses: Two Campaigns in Indonesia Raya', in Paul Tickell (ed.), (1987b), The *Indonesian Press: Its Past, its People, its Problems*, Annual Indonesian Lecture Series, No. 12, Centre for Southeast Asian Studies, Monash University, pp.21-38.

22. Kerry Groves (1983), 'Harian *Rakjat*, Daily Newspaper of the Communist Party of Indonesia - its History and Role', unpublished MA thesis, ANU, Canberra, p.110-1. Groves is using *Harian Rakyat* sources, but discounts as an exaggeration the paper's claim that the 1957 figure was 110,000.

23. Figures drawn from Dhakidae 1991 Table i, p.551.

CHAPTER 2:
Surveying the New Order

The National Press shall have the task and duty:
a. to preserve and popularize Pancasila as contained in the Preamble to the 1945 Constitution together with the Guidelines for the Substantiation and Implementation of Pancasila;...
c. to fight for truth and justice on the basis of a responsible freedom of the press.

1982 Press Act[1]

'Freedom of the press is the crown of the New Order.'
Lt.Gen. Ali Murtopo
Minister of Information (1978-83)
Head of Opsus (Special Intelligence Operations)[2]

Despite the assurances of one of President Suharto's most insidious intelligence chiefs and information ministers, press freedom has been a tarnished crown at best for the New Order. This chapter seeks to survey key incidents which illustrate the government's firm hand in controlling and penalising the press during the New Order. It will be followed by more detailed chapters examining the structures of various press industry bodies and major publishing conglomerates which emerged during this period.

The year 1965 was the worst in the history of the press in independent Indonesia. In February and March, 29 papers were closed for their support of an anti-Communist (and opponents argued, anti-Sukarno) bloc, called somewhat ironically the Body for the Support of Sukarnoism (BPS). In the backlash that followed the political chaos of 1 October 1965 46 of Indonesia's 163 remaining newspapers were banned indefinitely because of their presumed association with, or sympathy for, the Indonesian Communist Party (PKI) and its allies.[3] Many hundreds of staff were arrested. Leftists were expelled from the Indonesian Journalists Association *(Persatuan Wartawan Indonesia,* PWI) and the national Antara news agency. Antara, for example, was decimated after the events of 1 October

1965, when it was placed under the Jakarta regional military command and 30% of its editorial staff were sacked. The arrests and killing of Communist and sympathising journalists in 1965-66, carried out against a background of large-scale massacres in the countryside, cast a very long shadow over the press for subsequent decades.[4]

As Ariel Heryanto has noted: 'The mass media, including the press and particularly the electronic media, have been the most important area of maintenance and reproduction of the New Order's legitimation... Understandably, the Indonesian press has been an institution of cultural practice that went through the most severe and most frequent blows of the [New Order] State'.[5] In one of the first pieces of legislation to reflect the shift in political power after 1 October 1965, the landmark 1966 Press Act highlighted that, whatever the sweeping statements of principle adopted by the incoming regime, the qualifications and provisos would ensure that the media could be strictly controlled when necessary.

Early legislative controls

The letter of Indonesia's 1966 Act (No. 11) on the Basic Principles of the Press declares that 'No censorship or bridling shall be applied to the National Press' (Chapter 2, Article 4), that 'Freedom of the Press is guaranteed in accordance with the fundamental rights of citizens' (Article 5.1) and that 'no publication permit is needed' (Chapter 4, Article 8.2).[6] The reality made a mockery of these principles for during an unspecified 'transitional period' [*masa peralihan*] (Chapter 9, Article 20.1.a) two related permits had to be obtained by newspaper publishers: the Permit To Publish (SIT) from the ostensibly civilian Department of Information, and the Permit To Print (SIC) from the military security authority, KOPKAMTIB. It was not possible to produce a periodical legally without both of these permits and the withdrawal of either one by their issuing authority effectively banned the publication.

In 1966, the government granted a large number of these obligatory dual permits to papers such as *Harian KAMI* [*KAMI Daily*][7] and *Mahasiswa Indonesia* [*Indonesian Student*], both associated with the militant student movement whose anti-PKI and anti-Sukarno posture supported the army leaders gaining power. Some pro-Sukarno papers survived, either because of military allies or by accommodating themselves to the changing circumstances. *El Bahar* [*The Sea*], for example, was protected by influential officers from the

Indonesian Navy and Marines. But generally, in the words of one editor, the press wanted to be regarded by the government as 'a good partner in accelerating development'.[8] In the parlance of the New Order, the Indonesian press was 'free but responsible'.[9] Journalists and critics, labouring under the constant threat of bans, rejoined with 'free to do what, and responsible to whom?'. As former Jakarta correspondent for the *Sydney Morning Herald* Peter Rodgers has observed, 'There is a striking disparity between the legal basis for domestic press operations and what happens in practice'.[10]

By the early 1970s the range of major newspapers could be classified into six (partially overlapping) types. There was the New Order radical press, typified by student papers which had spilled out of the campuses and into the streets, such as *Harian KAMI* and *Mahasiswa Indonesia*, to which could be added *Nusantara [Archipelago]*, and the revived papers *Pedoman* and *Indonesia Raya [Glorious Indonesia]*, both oriented to the Indonesian Socialist Party (PSI). Secondly, there were politically cautious, high circulation prestige journals, notably the Protestant *Sinar Harapan [Ray of Hope]* (established 1961) and Catholic *Kompas [Compass]* (established 1965). There were the organs of the Armed Forces of Indonesia: *Berita Yudha [Military News]* and *Angkatan Bersenjata [Armed Forces]* (both established in 1965) which might be grouped together with *Suara Karya [Work Voice]* established in March 1971 as an organ of the government political organisation Golkar. Radical nationalist papers constituted a fourth group, including *El Bahar, Merdeka [Freedom]* (est. 1945), and *Suluh Marhaen [Marhaen Torch]* the reincarnation of the banned *Suluh Indonesia [Indonesian Torch]*, flagship of the Indonesian Nationalist Party (PNI). Muslim interests were represented by newspapers like *Abadi, Jihad [Holy War]* and the Nahdatul Ulama party's *Duta Masyarakat [Society's Emissary]*. Finally, there were popular-style, 'a-political', 'entertainment' papers, epitomised by *Pos Kota [City Post]*, with its concentration on gory Jakarta crime stories.

In 1970, most Indonesian newspapers sold less than 20,000 copies. Only four enjoyed circulation exceeding 40,000: the radical national *Merdeka* (82,000), two prestigious Christian papers *Kompas* (75,000) and *Sinar Harapan* (65,000), and the Army's *Berita Yudha* (75,000).[11] The fate of these four publications illustrates the dynamic of change which swept the press industry under the New Order: *Kompas* and *Sinar Harapan's* successor *Suara Pembaruan [Voice of Renewal]* became the flagships of empires, while *Merdeka* and *Berita Yudha* faded to relative insignificance. Both *Kompas* and *Suara Pembaruan* have been commercially pragmatic, politically cautious, emphasising their appeal to the expanding secular middle classes. Merdeka has stagnated, unable to adapt to the new commercial demands, bereft of much-needed capital, while Berita Yudha failed to cross the civilian-military market chasm and became just another paper that few people wanted to pay to read.[12]

Multiple bans in the 1970s

Key incidents which symbolise the ongoing latent tensions in the government's relations with the press in the decade of the 1970s were the crackdowns in 1974 and 1978, which were marked by sweeping multiple bans. During these periods the press, still stirred by the tradition of 'pers perjuangan', adopted a campaigning style to support public criticism of government policies. The government ultimately responded with an iron fist against the demonstrators and those papers which had given them sympathetic coverage.

In January 1974 widespread public demonstrations erupted over several days in Jakarta, triggered off by the visit of Japanese Prime Minister Tanaka, but rooted in growing hostility towards government social and economic policy and festering distrust for leading presidential confidantes and associates. In the aftermath about 470 people were arrested, including *Indonesia Raya's* Enggak Bahau'ddin (detained for nearly eleven months) and Mochtar Lubis (for two and a half months).[13] In the weeks after demonstrations (which became known by the abbreviation 'Malari', or the 'Fifteenth of January Disaster') twelve publications had their printing and publishing permits (SIC and SIT) withdrawn: *Nusantara, Harian KAMI, Indonesia Raya, Abadi, The Jakarta Times, Mingguan Wenang, Pemuda Indonesia, Ekspres weekly newsmagazine, Pedoman* (all Jakarta), *Suluh Berita* (Surabaya), *Mahasiswa Indonesia* (Bandung), and *Indonesia Pos* (Ujungpandang). Only two publications were permitted to reappear, albeit with altered names and pruned of certain staff: *Pelita* (replacing the Islamic *Abadi*) and *The Indonesian Times* (replacing the English-language *The Jakarta Times*).

Prior to the Malari demonstrations those newspapers which had supported the emergence of the New Order had enjoyed opportunities for often robust debate and rhetoric, both amongst themselves and against the new government. They were able to take advantage of the relatively cordial government-press relations over the early New Order period to highlight dissatisfaction with a government which they had basically blessed since its inception. One of the most outspoken was Mochtar Lubis's *Indonesia Raya* which criticised numerous of the President's personal assistants together with chiefs of government authorities, including the National Logistics Board. The most notable example, beginning in late 1969, was the paper's well-researched, if vitriolic, attacks on General Ibnu Sutowo, head of the State Oil Corporation, Pertamina, accusing him of gross mismanagement and corruption. While the student press and moderate dailies like *Kompas* supported *Indonesia Raya*, the paper was counter-attacked by publications like the Army's *Angkatan Bersenjata*, which accused editor Mochtar Lubis of a business conflict of interest, and the nationalist *Merdeka*, which claimed (without substantiation) that Lubis had tried earlier to extort Rp. 100 million from Pertamina.[14] It proved to be a long and bitter campaign, silenced only by the intervention of the President in August 1970 who asserted that unless papers like *Indonesia Raya* desisted, they would be dealt with firmly.[15]

Nonetheless, it was a period of press vigorousness and government tolerance without comparison for another two decades. That is not to imply that isolated bans did not occur. In July 1971 both *Harian Kami* and *Duta Masyarakat* had been banned briefly for contravening a government prohibition against election coverage or comment during the 'Week of Calm' (*Minggu Tenang*) preceding the general elections. In January 1973 Sinar Harapan had its Printing Permit (SIC) withdrawn by KOPKAMTIB for eight days for leaking details of the 1973-74 National Budget Proposal (RAPBN) prior to its formal release in a Presidential address to the Legislative Assembly (DPR).[16] But such incidents were minor in contrast to the 'slash and burn' style of press control during martial law in the late 1950s and the New Order crackdowns of 1974 and 1978.

The sweeping 1974 bans dramatically dissolved the government's fragile 'partnership' with the press, as did the demonstrations its opportunistic 'partnership' with the students. Offending journalists were 'blacklisted' by the authorities and found that employment opportunities in the industry diminished. After eight former journalists with *Pedoman* and *Indonesia Raya* attempted to join the daily *Cahaya Kita*, on 24 March the Director-General of Press and Graphics announced that all journalists who had been working with banned papers were required to obtain permission, in the form of clearance letters, from the Directorate-General before being re-employed on other publications.[17] In any event, the most radical of the newspapers had been eliminated; only the moderates were permitted to re-appear.

Four years later, further anti-government student protests, which were sweeping through the main campuses, were again reported extensively even in the moderate press, which was becoming assertive once more. Government development policies, specifically the questionable involvement of foreign investors, Chinese financiers and government officials, were targets of student censure. The President's family was specifically criticised and there were calls for him to stand down. In January 1978, KOPKAMTIB responded by disbanding all university student councils, banning seven Jakarta dailies and a further seven student newspapers, prior to the military occupation of several key campuses and the arrest of some 223 students.[18] The incident was enough to trigger a comprehensive government re-evaluation of its educational policies in universities. The Ministry of Education developed a new 'Normalisation of Campus Life' policy to de-politicise campuses and ensure student and staff activities were directed more narrowly to academic rather than activist pursuits. As we shall see in Chapter 5, this involved nobbling the student press and drawing all campus publications strictly under the control of the university administration and the local military and security authorities.[19]

Unlike 1974 when several of the papers were killed off, in 1978 the banned papers were back on the streets within weeks. But the squeeze largely wrung out their 'spirit of struggle' for, although there have been many subsequent bans, never again has the broad press community challenged the government in such a concerted frontal manner and been suppressed in such numbers.

'Surgical' bans in the 1980s

Numerous individual publications have since been killed off however. For example, *Jurnal Ekuin [Economy, Finance and Industry Journal]*, established in April 1981 by Norman Diah (son of BM Diah, hotelier, entrepreneur and founder of *Merdeka* daily), through his PT Sistem Multi Media company, was banned in April 1983 after it revealed an impending reduction in the government's floor price for export oil. In January 1983 the fortnightly news magazine Expo had its Publication Permit (SIT) withdrawn over a series of articles on 'Indonesia's 100 Millionaires', a list which included an embarrassing number of New Order confederates. In a remarkable re-run in May 1984, *Fokus* magazine lost its Publication Permit for publishing a similar list of '200 Wealthy Indonesians' in its 10 May edition.[20] (It was symptomatic of the changing attitudes to capitalism that such listings had became common by the 1990s, when it was no longer politically embarrassing to be ostentatiously wealthy.) Even the battle-scarred *Sinar Harapan*, whose editors were renowned political jousters usually capable of treading the fine line between boldness and banning, was formally shut down on 9 October 1986 over commentaries on economic policies. Eventually, after considerable negotiating and editorial restructuring the prime movers behind *Sinar Harapan* were permitted to bring out a new paper, *Suara Pembaruan*, on 3 February 1987. The new General Chairperson of this phoenix was a Member of Parliament (DPR) for the New Order Government's Golkar political organisation.

Prioritas [Priority], a burgeoning new economic daily, fell soon after, on 29 June 1987. According to the Ministerial Decision withdrawing the newspaper licence, despite prior warnings '*Prioritas* daily newspaper still continued as a general and political paper, contravening the conditions of its permit as a daily [which specified that it would] allocate 75% of its space to economic news/reports and 25% to general news/reports'. Its reporting was 'in conflict with the values of the Pancasila Press System' and various press laws and regulations. Furthermore, it 'often contained news which was incorrect, not based on facts, and which was cynical, insinuative, tendentious and clearly violating the essence of responsible press freedom'.[21] Many observers regarded these as spurious justifictions, suggesting that the ban was due rather to the accuracy of *Prioritas*' predictions of government economic policy. Despite numerous subsequent protests by owner Surya Paloh at this arbitrary exercise of ministerial power, the once flamboyant *Prioritas* remains a memory.

Lest it be assumed that only the government had the capacity to take a newspaper off the streets, the case of the enormously popular entertainment weekly *Monitor* demonstrates the potential influence of vocal sectional interests within the community.[22] *Monitor* was the most successful publication in the country's largest publishing empire, Kompas-Gramedia, until its publishing permit was curtailed in 1990. *Monitor*'s high-flying editor Arswendo Atmowiloto offended vocal Muslim groups with what he thought was an innocuous readers' 'popularity poll' in the 15 October edition. In what was interpreted by some Muslims as an unforgivable sleight against the Prophet and the Faith, the poll listed the Prophet Muhammad at 11th place (somewhat under President Suharto in first place and Arswendo himself in tenth)! A flurry of militant Islamic groups demanded the closure of the magazine and the arrest of the editor in one of the most controversial religious imbroglios in the New Order. Faced with the threat of a widespread Islamic backlash against all its publications, the nominally Catholic publisher Kompas-Gramedia willingly surrender *Monitor*'s publication permit. Arswendo was charged with offending religious sentiments and was sentenced to five years' jail.

Anachronistic bans in the 1990s

Despite the *Monitor* affair, journalists generally the early 1990s savoured a period of increasing political lattitude and liberalism. As previously taboo topics began to be broached with greater boldness, there developed a sense that the very magnitude of the publishing industry and the growing diffuseness and fragmentation of power in the New Order State would no longer enable the government to undertake the kind of mass bans that typified the 1970s.[23] At the very least, such bans could not be imposed with impunity.

Yet, in the most dramatic crack-down on the press since 1978, on 21 June 1994 the Minister of Information, Harmoko, withdrew the publication permits of the country's three major news weekly publications: the longest-running and highly prestigious *Tempo* magazine (with estimated pre-closure sales of 187,000, discussed in more detail in Chapter 4); the most critical, fastest selling political tabloid of the 1990s, *DeTIK* (with claimed sales of 400,000 but objectively estimated at something over half that); and the weekly magazine *Editor*, modelled on *Tempo* (with sales of about 80,000). Taking full advantage of a period of increasingly open politics and press coverage since 1991, these publications together with most others had pubished detailed (often critical) analyses of presidential family businesses, human rights abuses, misuse of authority, maladministration of government funds, and factional splits within the government and the military. While the issues were cumulative, in the preeceeding months these three publications had tested fate with several on-going reports. Among other stories, *Tempo* had detailed conflicts within the Cabinet between Finance Minister Mar'ie Muhammad, and Suharto protege Minister for Research and Technology, B.J. Habibie, over the purchase and refurbishment of 39 ships from the moth-balled navy of the former East Germany. *DeTIK* had highlighted military criticisms of key civilians within the government in startlingly forthright interviews with disgruntled senior officers, and had speculated openly about who would succeed Suharto. In April 1994 *Editor* ran a cover story questioning when the President's son, Hutomo Mandala Putra (known as Tomy), would be called to account in the trial of office-bearers of the collapsed government development bank, Bapindo.

The probing proved too much for the President, who in an extempore public speech at Teluk Ratai port in South Sumatra on 9 June, railed publicly against the media's licence, asserting that some publications were jeopardising national stability by provoking political controversy over issues like the the purchase of the German warships. Despite this forewarning, the triple ban caught most observers by surprise and was widely regarded as a politically counter-productive over-reaction.[24] The strategy of mass bans, used twice in the 1970s, when applied so clumsily in the liberal 1990s betrayed a leader increasingly out of touch with his country's changing society. A less dramatic 'surgical' ban on a single publication, as used against *Sinar Harapan* and *Prioritas* in the mid-1980s, would have been more politically astute and equally effective in cautioning the press, some political analysts observed privately.

Observers tried to identify who might have been behind the bans. Suharto's uncharacteristically forthright speech led many to see the order coming right from the top. As a decisive display of strength and evidence of presidential backing, the triple bans may have had advantages for Harmoko. His performance as Golkar Chairperson was under a cloud and he had been publicly embarrassed earlier in June when powerful economic ministers ignored him and changed crucial foreign investment policies affecting the media (in a document known as Government Regulation No. 20). Habibie, though offended by unflattering press coverage had reportedly engaged legal counsel to initiate a suit for $1 million damages against *Tempo*, which suggests he was quite prepared to operate openly through the courts.

Having rashly closed down the nation's major news weeklies, with a total circulation in excess of half a million copies widely read by opinion-makers, urban professionals, and the middle classes, the government had to choose between a tough crackdown on dissent across the board or a tactical back-down. For the first time since the 1974 bans, the government's attack on the media triggered widespread social protest, which broadened in focus from these specific bans to the larger principle of the right to freedom of expression. In an extraordinary display of the breadth of opposition to the bans, the Information Minister was called to account during an all-night sitting of a Parliamentary Commission on the press, facing questions from Members of Parliament from all parties, sympathetic to the hundreds of journalists and members of the public in attendance.

The opposition to the bans united left and right across the political spectrum. Even senior military officers made it clear that they did not approve of this use of ministerial authority, with spokesperson Brigadier General Syarwan Hamid stating that the bans were 'unwanted, regrettable and ... should not have happened'.[25] Lieutenant-General Harsudiono Hartas, chief of the Armed Force's social and political branch (KASOSPOL) until 1993, declared 'in this era of global openness one cannot just ban people from getting information based on truth. The ban is an unpopular action on the part of the government'. Echoing a common theme in public discussion, General Hartas added that, if the government believed certain articles had breached press guidelines, it should rather have taken legal action against the particular journalists or editors responsible for any contravention.[26]

According to some interpretations, key factions within the military had been fostering the press' willingness to criticise influential civilian Cabinet members. The military was concerned that the President was distancing himself from the Armed Forces, for the counsel of ministers like Habibie and Harmoko. Growing pressure for democratisation was evident too amongst sections of the military. Analysts, like *DeTIK* editor Eros Jarot, predicted a joint civilian-military democratic alliance, involving young generation officers joining the broad push for non-violent reform, in readiness for the anticipated departure of President Suharto in 1998. Spokespeople for the military faction in the Parliament urged the closed publications to challenge the legitimacy of the bans in the State Administrative Court (*Pengadilan Tinggi Urusan Negara*) and, pending its verdict, to request the court's permission to continue publishing to minimise their financial losses.

Government officials quickly sought to paper over the fracas, holding out the carrot of new publication permits in return for quiescence. They paid lip-service at least to continuing political openness, while covert discussions took place between the government, the publications' senior management and entrepreneurs close to the government, aimed at replacing or re-opening the magazines under more pliable editorial leadership. The crackdown, however, strengthened opposition forces by eroding further the fragile public confidence in the government's rhetoric on political openness and public accountability. Such declarations had been necessary accompaniments to the more crucial economic deregulation in the search for foreign investment to ease the strain of declining oil revenue since the mid-1980s.

After the June bans a myriad of ad hoc opposition groups sprung up, many collecting under the banner of 'SIUPP' (*Solidaritas Indonesia untuk Pembebasan Pers, Indonesian Solidarity for Press Freedom*). These groups asserted the right to free speech and a free press, in a campaign of low-level agitation for the restoration of the publication licences and a return to the process of democratisation. The support given to sacked journalists by students, workers in the fledgling independent labour unions, lawyers and white-collar professionals generally was given good coverage in the remaining newspapers.[27] Although the national press became cautious in its political reporting, it was not yet cowering. For example, in the weeks that followed, at least two magazines, *Forum Keadilan* and *Sinar* (the latter owned by a relative of President Suharto) received formal warnings from the Department of Information, and several others had editors called in for questioning, over their coverage of the bans and demonstrations.[28]

Despite some high-level military support for a more open press, in the streets Armed Forces troops harassed and viciously beat peaceful demonstrators, including the poet W.S. Rendra and artist Semsar Siahaan.[29] In the courts, however, many of the protesters arrested during the following weeks received extraordinarily light fines of a token Rp. 2,000 [=$AUD 1.30], described by defence lawyers as 'the biggest joke of the year'.[30] Rendra reportedly claimed that, at the trial, popular support for the demonstrators was evident even from the judge. Some analysts interpreted this beneficence as an indication that the usually heavy-handed judiciary is becoming more responsive to changing attitudes, aligning more with the civil society and less with the executive and the security-minded hardliners in the military.[31]

(At the time this book goes to press, negotiations between the government and the management of these three banned publications continue, with no clear outcome in view.)

Warnings and taboos

While most closures during the New Order have been permanent, in some instances publications suffered only temporary bans. For example, in April 1982, during the build-up to the general elections, Tempo was banned for two months for its incisive reporting of the campaign, which included forthright coverage of opposition party electioneering. *Topik [Topic]* (published by the Merdeka group of companies since January 1971) had its permit withdrawn for two months in 1984.[32]

More unusual was the strategy adopted to coerce *Pelita [Lamp]*, established to replace the banned Modernist Islamic *Abadi [Eternal]*, which was closed during the mass prohibitions of January 1974. Seen as a voice of Islamic opposition to the New Order, *Pelita* was closed briefly in 1978, then again between May and September 1982, before reopening under new, more pro-government leadership. In 1985 ten Golkar leaders bought 60% of *Pelita's* shares and in May 1988 the then Vice-President Sudharmono became an official 'adviser' to the editorial board. Rather than shut the paper down, those with clear government interests had simply taken over the paper as a valuable voice through which to speak to a Muslim constituency.

Though generally papers are cautioned or banned for criticism of government policies, even government-sponsored publications are not always immune from the occasional editorial error of judgement. In June 1989, the Golkar newspaper, *Suara Karya* of which the then Vice-President Sudharmono was also the 'adviser', was given a rap over the knuckles by the Department of Information because of an article on the Sultan of Brunei Darussalam, deemed likely to hurt the feelings of a neighbouring Head of State.[33] *Editor* news weekly magazine was also given a warning over a similar article 'The Sultan of Brunei: between myth and fact' (27 May 1989).

In practice, restrictions on what can be published in the Indonesian press are largely determined, not by official legislation, but by a 'telephone culture' (budaya telepon). A phone call to editors from the authorities, usually in the form of an 'appeal' *(imbauan)* from a senior official, is frequently enough to quash any sensitive revelations. Only if a paper is recalcitrant enough to breach such instructions is it sent written warnings. The last resort is the revocation of the company's licence, representing a total ban and often financial collapse.

A range of topics are widely recognised as off limits, and have been dubbed with the mnemonic 'MISS SARA' which refers to anything deemed seditious, insinuating, sensational, speculative, or likely to antagonise ethnic, religious, racial or 'group' (class) tensions.[34] Under such guidelines, for example, religious clashes, insurgencies or resistance to central government authority by separatist groups (in East Timor, Aceh or West Papua) are reported only under the strictest guidelines. In addition to MISS SARA, certain topics are widely known to be unprintable, unless a paper is prepared to risk a ban. The First Family is beyond explicit criticism. So too, generally, are senior government officials, senior military officers, and their families, unless some internal rivalry within the power elite permits some press sniping at those out of favour. Less difficult to predict for the working journalist, however, are those appeals which seem intended simply to avoid having the press expose blunders or incompetence in the military generally. Or splits within the ruling compact. Clashes between branches of the military, in fact any death by 'unnatural causes' or 'misadventure' involving military figures is unlikely to find its way into print.

However, for the Indonesian journalist or editor wanting to stretch the limits on media expression, the 'room to move' is ill-defined. In 1978, the year of the second sweeping attack by the New Order Government upon the nation's press, Nono Anwar Makarim, the former editor of *Harian KAMI*, one of the most vocal student papers to emerge in the 1960s and be closed down in 1974, wrote frankly that 'hard facts in government-press relations seldom emerge in an environment where a feeling for subtle hints and signals has proved more important for the continuation of a functioning press than open and formal statements, or even written law'.[35] Working journalists require a sensitivity to these 'signals' in order to remain employed. Working within these constraints takes journalistic dexterity and political tact which often means giving the government the first and last word. Common too is a 'unique form for criticizing the government, namely criticism by praise'.[36] For the newspaper-reading public, interpreting such articles takes a sensitive political instinct, a knack for reading between the lines (or 'reading between the lies' as former editor of *Sinar Harapan*, Aristides Katoppo, has claimed), and a healthy suspicion of government spokespersons so frequently the only legitimate source of comment on controversial issues! Both journalists and readers 'need to develop and learn "the grammar" of this "shadow language" for an active exchange of added meanings on the printed page'.[37]

Press analyst Daniel Dhakidae (who incidentally works as Research and Development chief at *Kompas*) has argued that, as journalists are drawn inexorably into a dependence on government bureaucrats as 'legitimate' sources of publishable information, the profession gradually adopts the linguistic behaviour of the bureaucracy, accepting its verbal subterfuge, euphemism, acronyms and slang.[38] The cautiousness and self-censorship exercised by journalists and their papers is rarely better exemplified than in what Ben Anderson has dubbed the 'determined boringness of *Kompas* – the

Orba [New Order] newspaper par excellence'.[39]

Compared with the free-for-all style of the early 1950s, the New Order press, particularly between the 1978 bans and the more recent period of vociferousness in 1993-4, adopted a cautious, measured, some would say cringing, way with words. Aristides Katoppo commented in 1993 that 'Among the established newspapers/magazines, there is an air of fear, resulting in the "wisdom of cowardice"'.[40] Crusading editor of the little gadfly *Indonesia Raya*, Mochtar Lubis has long accused the journalist profession of elevating euphemism to an art form. Under a regime which he regarded as dominated by neo-feudalist powerholders, Mochtar believed journalists succumbed to pressure to avoid expressing direct criticism, instead resorting to 'very subtle allusions to avoid hurting anyone's feelings, having to be like a snake, circling round and round without ever striking the target'.[41] Headlines never focus on negatives; articles bury any barbs in the final paragraphs. Criticisms are rarely written in the active voice, and circumlocutory passive form of speech disguises disapproval. Old crusaders like Mochtar Lubis continue to exhort the press to be constantly critical of those in power and influence, to expose corruption and malfeasance, to act within fear or favour as society's 'watchdog'. But contradicting this within weeks of his 1993 appointment as Chairperson of the government-regulated Indonesian Journalists' Association (PWI) was Sofyan Lubis who emphasised that 'our press is not a "watchdog"' and should only criticise within the constraints of the 'Pancasila political system'.[42] The role of the press, he believed, was to impart information.

Permits and government regulation

Apart from self-imposed censorship, linguistic restraint, warnings, bans and more brutal repression, the face of the press is fashioned by both personal whim and a range of other government regulatory measures. A government minister's pique may lead to certain papers being 'blacklisted', their journalists excluded from government press conferences and other official sources of information.[43] Occasionally 'carrots' as well as 'sticks' are used to influence the industry. In February 1980, the Department of Information commenced a program (called *Koran Masuk Desa*, or KMD) to introduce newspapers into villages and small towns. Initially 34, increased in 1981 to 43, press publications were subsidised under the scheme to produce special KMD village editions, featuring materials deemed relevant to such a readership.[44] The injection of government capital has thrown a life-line to several regional and pro-government papers since the government places substantial regular purchase orders with them for copies to distribute gratis in villages, ostensibly to stimulate the reading habit in the 80% of the Indonesian population who live in rural areas, largely unpenetrated by press products.[45]

More obvious perhaps than government efforts to stimulate press readership is the complex web of legislation and corporatist organisational structures (to be discussed in further detail in the following chapter) laid down by the government to regulate the press. For example, under guidelines set by the government-dominated Press Council (*Dewan Pers*), newspapers are subject to prevailing restrictions on advertising space (currently limited to 35% of total column space) and number of pages (currently 20 pages daily).[46]

More fundamentally, in September 1982 the 'transitional' 1966 Department of Information's requirement for a SIT (Surat Izin Terbit) Publishing Permit was replaced with a Press Publication Enterprise Permit (*SIUPP, Surat Izin Usaha Penerbitan Pers*).[47] The change is something of a sleight of hand, for publications are still subject to strict government regulation, however now it is based theoretically on the viability of the enterprises, that is, the press companies, rather than the individual newspaper's content.[48] Obtaining a SIUPP requires a raft of more than a dozen letters and preliminary permits, including letters of support from all relevant professional organisations (the Indonesian Journalists Association and the Press Publishers Association) at both the regional and national level, several permits from civilian and military authorities, together with supporting letters from the financing bank and the printing company.[49]

Once issued by the government, a SIUPP may not be sold (although 'joint management' agreements can effectively circumvent this restriction). Nor may the company deviate from the guidelines stipulated in their licence application governing content (e.g. financial or general news), physical size of the paper (e.g., tabloid or broadsheet), frequency of publication (e.g. daily or weekly), change their printing company, or senior editorial staff, without going through a similarly tortuous application process.[50] The inflexibility of the regulations makes it virtually impossible for a company to adhere to the letter of the government provisions. A minor change in senior personnel, office address, publication content and the like can technically breach the permit. Both *DeTIK* and *Editor* were officially closed in 1994 on the spurious grounds of such technical violations, despite wide acknowledgement within the industry that the root cause was their critical coverage of people close to the President.

The new legislation also obliged press companies to reserve for their staff a 20 per cent share holding, though the precise mechanism for this was not detailed. Generally, it seems, those companies that met their obligations did so by forming a staff cooperative which held the shares, which were not owned individually by employees and could not be taken if one decided to leave the company. (By 1993, of the 277 companies which held the SIUPP permits, it seems only 167 had actually met this requirement, the remaining 110 were merely 'reminded to immediately fulfil this requirement'.[51]) The government's aim was to instill in the staff a material interest in ensuring the success and longevity of their paper, in order that they would avoid rash political stands which might result in the paper being banned and the consequent loss of their share value. It appears frequently to have been a successful strategy for, as *Tempo's* editor Gunawan Mohamad pointed out, this condition tended to undermine rather than strengthen newspapers' editorial independence.[52]

While industry proprietors generally accepted the new legislation albeit with grumbling discontent, more controversial have been the Minister of Information's 1984 Regulations (known as *Peraturan Menpen*, No. 1/Tahun 1984) determining the implementation of the Act, and specifically those which refer to the withdrawal of the SIUPP. Senior editors and opposition political figures have pointed out that these regulations give the Minister (currently Harmoko, himself a major player in several press companies and founder of Jakarta's big-selling down-market *Pos Kota*) power to withdraw the SIUPP and thus ban any paper, without recourse to public defence or trial. It is argued by such editors as Teuku Yousli Syah of *Media Indonesia [Indonesian Media]*, that this contradicts the 1982 Act, which like the 1966 Act, stipulates that 'the national press is not subject to censorship or banning'.[53] Before a Parliamentary Commission in June 1991 Gunawan Mohamad asserted prophetically that, under Indonesian law a driver's licence had more legal authority than a SIUPP, since drivers charged with an infringement could defend themselves in court while newspaper proprietors could not. Opposition members of parliament agreed that provision should be made for companies threatened with a withdrawal of their SIUPP to defend themselves publicly against the Minister's accusations, but this has never happened.[54]

Nonetheless, this more open public discussion of ministerial power over the issuance and cancellation of the SIUPP, with only a nominal formality requiring him to seek limited counsel, has focused some attention on the anomalous position of the encumbent. While the SIUPP legislation was apparently the product of former Minister of Information and New Order intelligence strong-man, Lt.Gen. Ali Murtopo, it has been implemented by Harmoko, a civilian, who, on initial appointment was widely regarded as lacking in any political power-base. However, Harmoko, who has also secured the powerful position of Chairperson of the government's electoral organisation Golkar, has successfully entrenched himself as Information Minister, holding sway over this influential (and potentially lucrative) portfolio for a record three successive cabinets since 1983, suggesting something of the regard in which he is held by President Suharto.

Harmoko's personal position is a difficult one. He has been a working journalist and editor since 1960, with publications such as *Merdeka* and *Angkatan Bersenjata*, founding the commercially successful *Pos Kota* in 1970. He has occupied several key position in the Indonesian Journalists' Association (PWI). Yet despite such credentials, he is held in considerable suspicion and spoken of with some derision by many working journalists and editors who see his authoritarian treatment of the press as a betrayal. Journalists' ire over the implementation of the SIUPP legislation was not placated by Harmoko's personal style of self-promotion or suspicions of his increasing pecuniary interests in the industry.[55]

One of the most vocal opponents of the SIUPP provisions and particularly the Minister's 1984 Regulations has been press entrepreneur Surya Paloh, whose Prioritas was the second paper to have its permit withdrawn. In October 1992, for example, he wrote an open letter to the Parliament (People's Representative Council, DPR) requesting that during its 1993 session the decision-making house, the People's Deliberative Assembly (MPR), cancel all provisions and Ministerial Regulations governing the withdrawal of the SIUPP as contravening the guarantees of freedom of the press outlined in the 1945 Constitution, the New Order's 'Broad Outlines of State Policy' (GBHN), and the 1982 Basic Law on the Press. He called for press transgressions and penalties to be determined in public trial by the Supreme Court (*Mahkamah Agung*) rather than in secret negotiation by ministerial whim.[56] In November 1992, after attempting to galvanise support from senior editors of other publications such as *Kompas* and *Tempo*, he wrote directly to the Supreme Court requesting a judicial review to determine whether the

Ministerial regulations contravened the 1966 and 1982 legislation. Acting for him voluntarily were six of the country's most prominent lawyers, including office-bearers of the Indonesian Bar Association (IKADIN) and prominent leaders of the Indonesian Legal Aid Institute Foundation.

Ironically, support from other senior editors or from the Journalists Association (PWI) administration for Surya Paloh's crusade was disappointing. The Supreme Court apparently agreed to consider the issue at law, but stalled until the March 1993 session of the MPR, which was charged with the primary task of selecting the President and his Vice-President for the following five-year term. With Suharto predictably re-elected unopposed, and Harmoko reappointed as Minister for Information, the signal to the Supreme Court was clear: the President has full faith in his Minister. Some observers assumed, rather, that it would be appointments to the Supreme Court that would be re-considered should its legal determinations be critical of the government. The Court's eventual response in June 1993 was to reject Surya Paloh's request claiming appropriate procedure had not been followed (not surprising since this was the first such request in Indonesian legal history and no procedures had been laid down!). Surya Paloh's challenge forced the Court, however, to produce a ruling on the procedures for such an appeal against government regulation (below the level of Acts of Parliament), the ramifications of which extend far beyond the press into all aspects of government regulation. As one attorney claimed, the Supreme Court ruling 'is not only for the Press and the SIUPP, but many more regulations below the level of Acts which have been forced through by the government can now be questioned'.[57] Though unsuccessful, the precedent set by Surya Paloh is likely to be adopted by the three publications banned in June 1994. It certainly appears to be being considered as an option by *DeTIK*, at least, although the legal status of such appeals remains unclear.

Self-regulation

Despite the protests of people like Surya Paloh, 'survivors' of the bans of the 1970s have generally reached an accommodation with the New Order Government. Banning orders such as those against *Sinar Harapan* (1986), *Prioritas* (1987) and *Tempo*, *DeTIK* and *Editor* (1994) have become the exceptions rather than the rule since most major press groups have proved to be adequately 'self-regulating'. The *Monitor* case, mentioned above, is illustrative. Kompas-

Gramedia head Yakob Utama was chairing the extraordinary three-member executive meeting of the peak Press Council (of which he has been a member for 21 years) which recommended unanimously to the Minister of Information that *Monitor's* SIUPP be rescinded. He was also an adviser to the National Executive of the Indonesian Journalists Association, at the time the Jakarta chapter expelled Monitor editor, Arswendo Atmowiloto. Utama, who also held an executive position in the powerful Newspaper Publishers Association (*SPS, Serikat Penerbit Suratkabar*), then formally dismissed Arswendo from his positions in the Kompas-Gramedia Group. Arswendo's subsequent trial and five-year sentence for offending religious sentiments is a rare example of a journalist actually being taken to court over a breach of law.[58]

In a related episode following swiftly on the heels of the *Monitor* ban, on 2 November 1990 the Kompas-Gramedia Group voluntarily closed down and returned the SIUPP of another of its periodicals, the fortnightly *Senang [Happy]*, because the 21 September issue had published a reader's letter and illustration of the prophet Mohammad which may have given offence to Muslim readers. The management claimed it had taken this remarkable step after a period of 'introspection and self-correction'.[59] While this was a striking example of 'self-regulation' less dramatic gestures, such as sidelining staff who draw the ire of the government, are more common. For example, after senior government officials criticised feature reports on the November 1991 East Timor massacre in the weekly *Jakarta Jakarta* the Kompas-Gramedia Group re-assigned the staff responsible, in an effort to placate the authorities. While Yakob Utama's personal position, particularly in the cases of *Monitor* and *Senang*, was an unenviable one, the Kompas-Gramedia Group graphically displayed its preparedness to terminate publications and curtail staff to ensure compliance with government policy and to protect its other financial interests. Utama, head of the richest press and publishing empire in Indonesia, has said of the press generally, 'We are becoming less critical because we have to survive'.[60]

The case of *Senang* is rare, for generally a SIUPP is only surrendered to the government if the holder of the permit is unable to continue financing and publishing the newspaper. While differences of opinion remain regarding methods used by the government in withdrawing a SIUPP, a consensus operates between the Information Minister and the Newspaper Publishers Association (SPS) to limit the number of permits issued, totalling about 264 in April 1991.[61] This consensus, supported by calls from the Press Council for a moratorium on new SIUPP, excludes new players in the interests of the established members of the SPS and Press Council.[62] Christianto Wibisono has observed that this cosy relationship between the PWI, SPS and the Department of Information, enables established publishers to operate like a cartel, protected against outside competition.[63] Yakob Utama and Eric Samola, the financier behind the wealthy Tempo-Grafiti group, have both stated that they oppose 'deregulation' of the industry, since the status quo bars new competitors.[64] With such barriers against entry, other entrepreneurs who were increasingly keen to invest in the press in the late 1980s were forced to either take over, or buy into, existing enterprises as a way of obtaining a SIUPP.[65]

In the 1980s the focus of activity within the press industry seemed to shift from engaging in wide-ranging debate on government policy and its implementation, to ensuring financial survival through hard-nosed commercial expansion. As veteran editor Rosihan Anwar observed in early 1985, Indonesian press companies were splitting into two camps: those 'above the wind' which were economically strong and capable of reading the shifting political tide, and those 'below the wind' which had not adapted to changing management practices or established a viable economic base.[66] Some observers have argued that, in the struggle for financial security, the changing ethos of the industry has shifted attention away from concerns such as social justice, and human rights onto middle-class preoccupations with matters of life-style and individualism.

The 1980s were marked by an unparalleled surge in the total circulation of periodicals (including dailies, weeklies, fortnightlies and monthlies), from about 5 million (in 1978) to more than double that by the end of the 1980s, topping 11.7 million at the end of 1990 and rising to just over 13 million in 1991.[67] However, as the total circulation figures for the industry increased, there was a levelling off, indeed it could be argued, a relative decline, in the number of publications. From 283 in 1975, the number dropped to 256 in 1986, and was only marginally higher by 1991.[68]

Overall, with some startling exceptions such as the triple bans of June 1994, from 1978 it has generally been the marketplace rather than government bans which has determined those papers that survived. While some papers were curtailed by the government, overall the decrease in publications during the 1980s was due to the dynamics of capital accumulation. Since the SIUPP cannot officially be bought and sold, large expanding newspaper companies began forming 'joint management and capital investment' collaborations with newspapers whose fortunes were declining. In practice this meant smaller regional papers were collapsing or being absorbed within a limited number of metropolitan press empires, richest amongst them those empires centred on *Kompas*, *Suara Pembaruan*, *Tempo* and the relative newcomer *Media Indonesia*. After looking in more depth in the following chapter at the government agencies and professional organisations which deal with press matters, I shall return in Chapter 4 to examine the growth and expansion of these four press empires.

ENDNOTES

1. Slightly adapted from the official translation of Act No.21 of 1982 on Amendments to Act No. 11/1966 concerning Basic Provisions on the Press as amended by Act No.4/1967, found in Abdul Razak (ed.), (1985) *Press laws and Systems in Asean States*, Confederation of Asean Journalists Publication, Jakarta, pp.191-2 (with spelling corrected).

2. *Diskusi: Masalah Kebebasan Pers di Indonesia*, *(Tempo,* Jakarta, 1981), p.3. This is a pamphlet compilation of papers delivered at a seminar at the Aryaduta Hyatt Hotel on 11 March 1981, organised by the magazine Tempo to celebrate its first decade in print.

3. Atmakusumah (1980), 'Kasus *Indonesia Raya*' in Abdurrachman Surjomihardjo (ed.) (1980), Departemen Penerangan & LEKNAS-LIPI, Jakarta, (pp.181-245) particularly p.206; and Tribuana Said & D.S. Moeljanto (1983) *Perlawanan Pers Indonesia (BPS) terhadap* Gerakan *PKI,* Sinar Harapan, Jakarta, pp.106-11.

4. The following paragraphs are elaborated upon in David T. Hill (1988), 'Mochtar Lubis: Editor, Author, Political Actor', unpublished doctoral thesis, Australian National University, Canberra, pp.135-9, which provides more detailed referencing.

5. Ariel Heryanto (1990), 'Introduction: State Ideology and Civil Discourse' (pp.289-300) in Arief Budiman (ed.) (1990), State and *Civil Society in Indonesia*, Monash CSEAS, Clayton, quoted from p.298.

6. This law, promulgated on 12 December 1966, was signed by Sukarno, in his formal capacity as President. However, after 11 March 1966 effective control of the Parliament and the reins of power had transferred to General Suharto. Quotations are from the official English version, published by the Department of Information.

7. KAMI was a student action front organisation established by antiCommunist and anti-Sukarnoist students. In Indonesian, the word 'kami' means 'we, us, our', hence the newspaper's title plays on the double meaning 'our daily/KAMI daily'.

8. Enggak Bahau'ddin, editor of *Indonesia Raya* daily, in 'Pers dan "Appeal" Pemerintah', *Indonesia Raya*, 20 August 1973, p.4. For an overview of the press during this transitional period, see Roger Paget (1967a), 'Indonesian Newspapers 1965-1967', *Indonesia*, No. 4, October, pp.170210; and (1967b), 'Djakarta Newspapers 1965-1967: Preliminary Comments', *Indonesia*, No. 4, October, pp.211-26.

9. David Bourchier of Monash University informed me that Professor Umar Seno Aji, former Justice Minister (1966-74) and head of the Supreme Court (1974-81), pointed out that the source of this phrase was an American press publication from the 1950s. The term was popularised however by the New Order.

10. Peter Rodgers (1982), *The Domestic and Foreign Press in Indonesia: 'Free but Responsible'?*, Centre for the Study of Australian-Asian Relations, Griffith University, Nathan, Queensland, p.5.

11. Atmakusumah 1980:232 cites *Kritis Mengupas Suratkabar*, Cipta Loka Caraka, Badan Lektur Pembinaan Mental, Jakarta, 1970, pp.69-70.

12. For a list of major current newspapers, see Table 2.

13. For a comparative study of *Indonesia Raya* prior its 1957 and its 1974 bans, see David T. Hill (1987), 'Press Challenges, Government Responses: Two Campaigns in *Indonesia Raya*' in Paul Tickell (ed) (1987b), The *Indonesian Press: its Past, its People, its Problems*, CSEAS Monash, Clayton, pp.21-38. See also Ignatius Haryanto (1994), 'Hubungan Antara Pers dan Pemerintah di Indonesia: Studi Kasus *Indonesia Raya* Tahun 19721974', unpublished Sarjana thesis, Fakultas Ilmu Sosial dan Ilmu Politik, Universitas Indonesia.

14. For a more detailed discussion, see Hill 1988:152-8.

15. Rosihan Anwar (1983), *Menulis Dalam Air: Di Sini Sekarang Esok Hilang: Sebuah Otobiografi*, Sinar Harapan, Jakarta, p.250 cites *Suluh* Marhaen, 5/8/70 .

16. Sadono 1993:80-1.

17. For a discussion of the Malari incident see Junaedhie 1991:155-157.

18. For a detailed discussion of events and newspaper coverage, see Dhakidae 1991:301-23.

19. For an impressive study of student activism, see Laksmi Pamuntjak (1993), 'The Indonesian Student Movement in the 1980s/1990s: The development of resistance by a "marginalised minority"', B.A. (Honours) thesis, Murdoch University, Perth, unpublished.

20. Sadono 1993:83-4.

21. The Ministerial Decision (No. 03/SK/DITJEN-PPG/K/1987) is reproduced in Sadono 1993:142-45.

22. For a detailed analysis of the Monitor incident, see Andrew J. Rosser (1992), 'Political Openness and Social Forces in New Order Indonesia: The *Monitor* Affair', B.A. (Hons) Flinders University, Adelaide, unpublished.

23. This position was put to me with conviction by *Jawa Pos* editor Dahlan Iskan (personal communication, Perth, 3 June 1994) less than three weeks before the 21 June ban on three major newsweeklies.

24. For example, the *Bangkok Post* editorialised 'Jakarta's action has backfired. Many more people in Indonesia and abroad now know details of anti-government reports than if Information Minister Harmoko had left well enough

alone.' (Quoted in an AFP wire service report, 27/6/94.)

25. Quoted from the *Jakarta Post*, 23 June 1994, in Amnesty International's bulletin 'Indonesia: Free Speech Protesters Detained and Beaten', 29 June 1994, p.5.

26. Patrick Walters (1994), 'Jakarta toughens stance on protests', The *Australian*, 28 June 1994, p.7 (internet listing on apakabar@clark.net, 8 July 1994).

27. See, for example, 'Detik-detik terakhir TEMPO, EDITOR, DeTIK' in *Bisnis Indonesia* (26 June 1994) and 'In Memoriam: TEMPO, Editor, DeTIK', Sentana weekly (week four, June 1994).

28. 'Magazine threats', the *West Australian*, 27/7/94, p.19.

29. See, for example, reports in Amnesty International's bulletin 'Indonesia: Free Speech Protesters Detained and Beaten', 29 June 1994.

30. Mr Luhut Pangaribuan, director of the Jakarta branch of the Legal Aid Institute, quoted in Patrick Walters, 'Indonesian court fines 20 censorship protesters $1', the *Australian*, 29/6/94, p.10.

31. These minimum fines follow other surprisingly light prison sentences of six months given by the Central Jakarta District Court in May 1994 to 21 students involved in peaceful demonstrations critical of the President in December 1993. They had been charged with publicly insulting the Head of State. Only after the prosecution appealed to the High Court were these sentences extended to between 8 and 14 months. See Amnesty International's bulletin 'Indonesia: Update on Student Prisoners of Conscience', July 1994.

32. 'Yang Ditunggu Massa Merdeka', Tempo, 5 May 1984, p.52. *Topik* ceased publication in 1987, and had its licence (SIUPP) withdrawn for failure to appear regularly in 1991.(See 'Daripada Menganggur Lebih Baik Terkubur', *Tempo*, 13 April 1991, p.82.)

33. USIS 1992, Vol. 1, p33.

34. The letters of the mnemonic refer in Indonesian to: Menghasut, Insinuasi, Sensasi, Spekulasi then Suku, Agama, Ras, Aliran. For a discussion of the range of issues and events that cannot be published, see David Hill (1990), 'Publishing within Political Parameters', *Inside* Indonesia, (Melbourne) No.23, June, pp.16-7.

34. Nono Anwar Makarim (1978), 'The Indonesian Press: An Editor's Perspective' (pp.258-81) in Karl D. Jackson and Lucian W. Pye (ed.) (1978), *Political Power and Communications* in *Indonesia*, University of California Press, Berkeley. *Quotation* from p.258.

35. Don Michael Flourney (ed.) (1992), *Content Analysis of Indonesian Newspapers*, Gadjah Mada University Press, Yogyakarta, p.2 (introduction).

37. Heryanto 1990:294.

38. 'Language, Journalism and Politics in Modern Indonesia', a paper presented at the 'Indonesian Democracy, 1950s and 1990s' conference, Monash University, 17-21 December 1992.

39. 'Rewinding "Back to the Future"', a paper delivered at the 'Indonesian Democracy 1950s and 1990s' Conference, Monash University, 17-21 December 1992, p.16.

40. 'Current Trends in the Indonesian Printed Media', paper presented at the 'Indonesian Paradigms for the Future' conference, Asia Research Centre, Murdoch University, 23 July 1993, unpublished.

41. The quotation is translated from the diary written by Mochtar Lubis during his two-and-a-half-month detention in 1975 while under suspicion of complicity in the January 1974 riots *(Malari)*. The original manuscript, *Nirbaya: sebuah buku harian dalam tempat tahanan* (in Indonesian and English) has not be published, but there is a Dutch translation, *Kampdagboek* by Cees van Dijk ~ Rob Nieuwenhuis, (A.W. Sijthoff, Alphen aan den Rijn, 1979, see p.39).

42. Compare Mochtar Lubis 1993:536 with the interview with Sofyan Lubis in 'Pers Indonesia Bukan Watchdog', *Forum Keadilan*, 23 December 1993, p.28.

43. Justice Minister Ismail Saleh reportedly blacklisted journalists from Media *Indonesia, Pos Kota*, Berita Buana and *Tempo*. *(See* 'Blokade Ismail Saleh', *Tempo,* 23 February 1991, p.22.)

44. For example, since 1979 the Armed Forces paper Angkatan *Bersenjata* has had a government contract to supply 20,000 copies to villages and about 16,000 to the Army, totalling more than half its daily circulation of 52,000. Similarly 10,000 copies of *Berita Yudha*, a paper regarded as close to the military intelligence network, have been distributed under this scheme. The government also assists the Yogyakarta paper *Kedaulatan* Rakyat publish an eight-page Javanese-language weekly called *Kandha Raharja* as part of this Newspapers for the Village program and the *Bali Post* also has a special weekly edition assisted by this program (See USIS 1992 Vol. 1, pp.6, 9, 46 & 62).

46. Till July 1986 the maximum was 12 pages daily, which was then increased to a permissible 16 twice-weekly, raised again to four times weekly from January 1990. In March 1991, 16 pages could be published daily (See USIS 1992 Vol. 1, p.19, and 'Lebih Tebal Lebih Makmur', *Tempo*, 16 March 1991, p.30). In January 1992 the Press Council called for the limit to be raised to 20 pages in 1994 ('Diberi Kesempatan Pada Media Cetak Terbit 20 Halaman', *Suara Pembaruan* 12/1/92).

47. Although the SIUPP legislation was introduced in 1982, it was not enacted formally until 1985.

48. On 3 May 1977 Kopkamtib had abandoned the SIC (permit to print), obliga-

tory since the early 'New Order' period (see 'Kronologi Perkembangan dan Pembreidelan Pers di Sekitar 'Malari' Januari 1974' in Abdurrachman Surjomihardjo (ed.) 1980:247-253, esp. p.253).

49. The formal 1984 'Decision of the Minister of Information concerning the Procedure and Conditions for obtaining a SIUPP' (No.214A/KEP/MEN-PEN/1984) actually lists 16 major forms and documents, plus an additional three or four depending on whether it is a private limited company, a non-profit foundation or a cooperative which is applying for the SIUPP. Not all documents are necessarily required in all SIUPP applications (see Anon. 1989:85-97.)

50. So reluctant are press companies to go through the formal process of altering SIUPP details that changes in key senior staff are not formalised. In December 1993, for example, the twice-monthly magazine *Majalah Film*, was still listing as Editor-in-Chief responsible for the publication 'Chaidir Rachman (1934-1989)'!

51. The 'reminder' was included in the Decision of the 37th Plenary Session of the Press Council, held in Surakarta on 22-23 January 1993 (and published in *Reporter*, No. 26/V/April-May 1993, pp.41–44).

52. See Goenawan Mohamad (1992), 'Masalah intervensi modal - dan kebebasan editorial', *Bisnis Indonesia*, 29 October, p.6.

53. Gunawan Mohamad, founder-editor of *Tempo* provides a thoughtful discussion of the SIUPP and Ministerial Regulations in 'SIUPP', *Tempo*, 22 June 1991, p.26.

54. The opposition position was put during a June 1991 meeting of a Parliamentary Commission (DPR Komisi 1), which deals with foreign affairs, defence and security, information and intelligence, with the Minister of Information, broadcast in the *Parlementaria* television program on the government television network, TVRI, 28 June 1991. For press reports, see 'Pengadilan atau Dewan Pers?' Berita Buana, 13 June 1991.

55. Numerous senior editors have stated off the record that, in return for authorising publication permits, Harmoko routinely requires that shares be allocated to his nominees. It is obviously impossible to verify such rumours.

56. 'Siapa Mengapa', Reporter, 24/IV December 1992-January 1993, p.34.

57. 'Silakan Menggugat Peraturan!', DeTIK, 23-29 June 1993, p.24. The ruling is known formally as the Supreme Court Decision Regulation (*Peraturan Penetapan Mahkamah Agung*) No. 1/1993.

58. 'Menggelar Monitor Tanpa Amarah', *Tempo*, 2 February 1991, pp. 30–31 and 'Kasus Angket Tabloid "Monitor"', *Reporter*, No. 12, Vol. II 1990–1991, p.36.

59. See 'Majalah "Senang" Ditutup', *Kompas*, 4 November 1990, p.1 and

'Kejakgung dan Deppen Adakan Koordinasi', *Kompas*, 5 November 1990, p.1.

60. See Michael Vatikiotis, 'Masses of Media', *Far Eastern Economic Review*, 26 July 1990, pp.46-7.

61. A total of about 275 SIUPP have been issued, while about 11 of them have been withdrawn for various reasons; some banned, others for failing to publish on a regular basis. 'Daripada Menganggur Lebih Baik Terkubur', *Tempo*, 13 April 1991, p.82.

62. The Press Council's 6 July 1986 plenary decision, reiterated on 22 September 1988, is detailed in Dewan Pers (1992) Undang-undang *Republik* Indonesia Nomor *21* Tahun *1982* tentang *Perubahan* atas Undang-undang Nomor *11* Tahun *1966* tentang *Ketentuan-ketentuan Pokok Pers sebagaimana telah diubah dengan Undang-Undang Nomor 4 Tahun 1967* (and related documents including *Hasil-hasil* Keputusan *Sidang Pleno Dewan Pers sejak Tahun 1980 sampai dengan Tahun 1991*), Direktorat Publikasi Ditjen Pembinaan Pers dan Grafika, Departemen Penerangan RI, Jakarta, pp.123 & 166-7.

63. Christianto Wibisono (1994), 'Media Massa dari Politik ke Bisnis', *Tempo*, 11 June 1994, p.102.

64. On their opposition to de-regulation and the issuing of new SIUPP, see 'Yang Senang di Regulasi', *Tempo*, 17 June 1989, p.28.

65. 'Ekspansi dalam Keterbatasan', *Tempo*, 20 October 1990, p.32.

66. Comments made at a seminar, The Social Responsibility of the Journalist, in Jakarta on 6-7 February 1985, as reported in Junaedhie 1991:206-7.

67. The figure of 11.7 million was given by Subrata, the Director-General of the Department of Information's Press and Graphics section [Dirjen PPG] (See 'Dari Soal Bredel sampai Saham', *Tempo*, 1 December 1990, p.88.) while the 1991 statistic is found in Data *Oplah dan Peredaran IPPPN Tahun 1991*, Proyek Pembinaan Pers, Departemen Penerangan, Jakarta,1991/1992, p.i.

68. Dhakidae (1991) illustrates this point graphically, providing statistics in Table i (p.551) in addition to graphs comparing circulation increase and number of publications (Figures 1.12 and 1.13, pp.66 & 67). While this trend may continue in the longer term, in 1991 there was a marginal increase officially to 270 (see Data *Oplah dan Peredaran IPPPN Tahun 1991, p.i)*, although several of these were highly irregular or ceased publication in that year.

CHAPTER 3
Government Agencies and Industry Bodies

The Indonesian Press is a Pancasila Press in the sense that it is a press whose orientation, attitude and behaviour is based on the values of the Pancasila and the 1945 Constitution... The essence of the Pancasila Press is a healthy press, namely a press which is free and responsible in carrying out its function as a disseminator of information which is correct and objective, a channel of the people's aspirations and constructive control by the society.

Press Council Declaration
25th Plenary Conference
December 1984

Much discussion of the role and function of the press in Indonesia has been couched in the terminology of American social science theories of the press, dominant in the 1950s and 1960s. Influential texts asserted broadly that there were four kinds of press systems: libertarian, authoritarian, communist, and socially responsible.[1] It has been argued and accepted by government policy makers and industry bodies alike that the Indonesian press falls into the final category, and 'is committed to free and social responsible journalism'.[2] The New Order Government condemns 'libertarianism' and points to the fact that there is no pre-publication government censorship of the press as proof that there is no 'authoritarian' control. The government's strategy is geared to fostering a sense of 'responsibility' in journalists and editors, a professional loyalty to a common community interest in political stability and security.

Despite considerable legal and extra-judicial regulation of the print media in Indonesia a diversity of interests have been permitted expression in the mainstream print media. Apart from periods of severe government crack-down and banning, discussion on non-taboo topics can often be boisterous and colourful. While there are semi-government and military organs, the majority of newspapers are not government-affiliated. Competition between them produces often lively open debate, despite the often-heavy hand of the authorities. It is evidence of the talent and commitment of many in the journalists' profession that much of the Indonesian press retains such verve under a mass of regulation and corporatist control.

The 1982 'Law No. 21 Concerning Changes to Law No. 11, 1966' is the most recent major legislation governing the Indonesian press. Because it details the differences between the earlier 1966 pre-New Order law and the new 1982 law it succinctly juxtaposes the rights and obligations of the pre- and post-1966 press.[3] Article (*Pasal*) 1 encapsulated the contrast between the politically active, often partisan press of the early years of nationhood, and the moderated media of the New Order, by listing changes in the terminology.

Many of the keywords of the Indonesian radical nationalist political lexicon which were sprinkled through the previous legislation were struck out. For example, in the legislation signed by President Sukarno in December 1966 the press had been 'a tool of the revolution'. In September 1982, Suharto's legislation altered that simply to 'a tool of National Struggle'. Yet even the term 'struggle' (*perjuangan*), so integral to the formation of the Indonesian nationhood since the early 'struggle' movements against colonialism, was not much mentioned elsewhere in the document. The exhuberance and dynamism of the early 1960s was replaced by a carefully modulated and qualified 'responsibility' to some unstated entity. The press was no longer 'an activator of the *masses*' but 'an activator of *national development*'; no longer a 'guardian of the *revolution*' but a 'guardian of the *Pancasila ideology*'; no longer a 'Pancasila *Socialist* Press', simply a 'Pancasila Press' (emphasis mine). In short, political activism and revolution were out and national development and the Pancasila (as conservatively re-interpreted by the New Order) were in.

While several matters in the 1966 legislation were to be determined by 'the Government together with the Press Council', by 1982 the authority was held by 'the Government after listening to the judgement of the Press Council'. While in 1966 the National Press was obliged to 'struggle for honesty and justice upon the basis of press freedom', it was now 'responsible press freedom'. The obligation to be a 'channel for constructive, and revolutionary progressive public opinion' was replaced by a 'positive interaction between the Government, press and society' aimed at 'broadening communication and community participation and implementing constructive control by the society (*kontrol sosial*)' (Article 1.6).

Holding authority for the government in all press dealing is the Minister of Information, who oversees the powerful Department of Information, and particularly its Directorate-General of Press and

Graphics, which monitors and ensures compliance from a variety of nominally 'independent' and 'professional' press organisations, whose operations provide the appearance of participation in decision-making by workers within the press industry.

Department of Information (*Departemen Penerangan*)

Daniel Dhakidae has argued convincingly that the Department of Information 'more than any department within the State apparati, is the locus of the interchangeability of the repressive and ideological role of the State apparatus, precisely because of its double role as an information apparatus and an economic apparatus'.[4] From the point of view of the economics of the industry, the Department is crucial, since it both controls the newsprint monopoly, that is the basic material of newspaper production, and controls the various permits required for the production and distribution of printed materials. These controls are used explicitly to influence the nature of information produced by the press. Not surprisingly, of the twelve Ministers of Information in Cabinets since 1960 half have been either military or Golkar figures, the longest-serving of which is the incumbent, Harmoko, appointed in 1983 and elected General Chairperson of Golkar in 1993.

As outlined by presidential decrees in 1974, the fundamental duty of the Department of Information (known widely by its Indonesian abbreviation 'Deppen') is to 'carry out part of the general duties of Government and of development in the field of information'. The Information Minister, responsible directly to the President, oversees the department's various official functions, including 'building the Pancasila national spirit', 'making a success of National Development through the Five Year Development Plans', laying a base of national security and stability, and ensuring the success of the five-yearly general elections, and other such national duties.[5]

Structurally the department is divided into a variety of units, with the Directorate General of Press and Graphics (*Direktorat Jenderal Pembinaan Pers dan Grafika*) being the most directly relevant to the print media. The Directorate General consists, in turn, of a secretariat, and separate directorates for the Press, Journalism, Graphics and Publications. The Press Directorate handles, among other matters, press publication permits (the SIT and subsequent SIUPP), arranging supply of newsprint (and related levies and taxes), statistical data collection, the 'Newspapers for the Villages' (*Koran Masuk Desa, KMD*) program, monitoring of foreign publications, monitoring advertising revenues, and professional press organisations (mentioned in more detail below). The Journalism Directorate arranges various professional training and education programs and seminars, journalist accreditation (for nationals and foreign correspondents) and monitoring overseas press reports about Indonesia. The Graphics Directorate is concerned primarily with associated technical and print industry skills development. Finally the Publications Directorate functions like a State Publisher coordinating the production and distribution of such publications as official speeches, legislation, State documents, and public education and information materials.

For working publishers and journalists, the 'Dirjen PPG' (as the Director General of Press and Graphics is often referred to) is one of the most powerful and influential bureaucrats with whom they have to deal, for it is largely through this channel that they interact with the government. For example, the Director General sits on the Advisory Board (*Dewan Pembimbing*) of the Antara National News Agency, is Vice-Chairperson of the peak 'consultative' body, the Press Council (*Dewan Pers*) (discussed in detail below), and determines, or at least formally recommends to the Minister, the issuance of publishing permits (SIUPP).

The organisational and supervisory structures of Antara illustrate the convergence of the State bureaucracies and intelligence agencies in managing press affairs. According to a 1962 Presidential Decree, Antara is directly under presidential authority. While operationally the Agency is notionally autonomous, in structural and administrative terms it comes under the State Secretariat, which has provided Antara's government subsidies since 1977. (In 1987-88 for example, these amounted to Rp 600 million per annum or around 11% of its Rp 5.7 billion production costs.) Yet, Antara also falls within the Department of Information's coordination responsibilities. Indicative of the forces which regulate the press, under the New Order Antara's three-person Supervisory Council (Dewan Pembimbing) overseeing its operations has been chaired by the Cabinet Secretary, with the Director-General of Press and Graphics from the Department of Information, and the Deputy Chief of the State Intelligence Coordinating Body (BAKIN) as members.[6]

In its dealings with the press industry the New Order Government has adopted a corporatist approach. For each particular interest group, the government has determined which 'professional organisation' or body would be its sole authorised voice. In some cases, prior organisations existed. In others, the government fostered the establishment of 'peak industry bodies' through which it could operate. This corporatist structure of the industry's organisational bodies is based on the New Order principle of 'basic family values' (*asas kekeluargaan*), that is, that the various sections of the industry are required to work together harmoniously as members of a single press 'family' towards the common goal of national economic development. An understanding of the functions and roles of these various organisations contributes to an appreciation of the mechanisms by which the State and the print media interact.

The Press Council (*Dewan Pers*)

In addition to the variety of Department of Information administrative units the Government regulates the press through intermediary institutional structures, most notably the Press Council. This Council is intended as a meeting point between the Government and the various organisations representing press interests, namely the Indonesian Journalists Association (PWI), the Newspaper Publishers Association (SPS), the Press Graphics Association (SGP), the Advertising Companies Association of Indonesia (PPPI) together with hand-picked community representatives. It is this Council which most evidentally embodies the supposedly 'positive interaction between the Government, press and society' outlined in the 1982 legislation.

In theory the Minister of Information is advised on matters to do with the withdrawal of SIUPP by the Press Council. In practice, the Council is dominated by government members with the Minister of Information (as Chairperson), the Director-General of Press and Graphics, the Secretary-General of the Department of Information, the Junior Attorney-General for Intelligence, and the Director-General for Social and Political Affairs (in the Department of Internal Affairs), all heading the list of members. The weight of the military (either serving or retired) too is heavy. In the 1990-93 Council, for example, there were four Brigadier-Generals, a Colonel and a Rear Admiral. One of the Brigadier-Generals, Nurhadi Purwosaputro, head of the Armed Forces Information Centre (Puspen ABRI), seemed at pains to emphasise that he was not formally representing the Armed Forces, but was there 'as a member of the society, a community representative'.[7]

In recent years, it has been rumoured that civilian members of the

Council privately hope that the Government may permit future Councils to be less government- and military-dominated and more representative of public and industry interests. There have been no public statements to that effect however. Yet industry observers believe that the civilian members are looking overseas for appropriate models for a new-style Press Council, while having no guarantee that any such liberalisation will be permitted.

But it is not always the predominant influence of military and government figures on the Press Council which concerns newspaper editors and staff. The Council represents the interests of the older established newspapers, like Kompas, rather than the newer, bolder, expansionist and entrepreneurial enterprises like *Media Indonesia* (discussed in more detail below), which are viewed with some suspicion and scepticism by the old guard. *Media Indonesia*, seen as the successor to *Prioritas* (which had its publication permit withdrawn in June 1987) has been highly critical of the workings of the Council (which has to recommend formally to the Minister when a ban is being considered). In an editorial about the withdrawal of permits where papers no longer reflect a press which is 'healthy, free and responsible', *Media Indonesia* implicitly questioned the independence and competence of the Council, by asking 'How does the Press Council assess this? What measurement does it use? What are its considerations? What of its freedom to decide? Questions such as these cannot yet be answered openly'.[8]

The fact that the Press Council plays a role in advising the Minister for Information on the allocation of new publication permits (SIUPP) enables it to constrict access by newcomers, protecting the position of established businesses, should it wish to do so. At the Plenary Congress in September 1988, for example, the Press Council reiterated its call to the government made two years previously to withhold the issuing of any further publication permits, arguing that the market place was saturated, particularly in the Jakarta area. Such calls have been interpreted by analysts as defending the status quo of a highly regulated industry rather than accepting the inevitable pressures to loosen up entry requirements and accept more cut-throat commercial competition between press companies. Recent investors (such as the Ika Muda business group's Sutrisno Bachir, who had been investing in press enterprises since 1986) have argued that, to foster a healthy press industry, the market, not the government or its agencies, should determine the number of publications.[9]

The Indonesian Journalists Association (PWI)

Under a 1969 Department of Information ministerial decree (No.02/PER/MENPEN/1969, chapter 1, article 3) 'Indonesian journalists are obliged to become members of an Indonesian Journalists Organisation which is recognised [*disahkan*] by the Government'. Only one organisation, the Indonesian Journalists Association (PWI) is so recognised. Founded in Solo in February 1946 during the Republican resistance against the returning Dutch colonialist power, the PWI began as an attempt to mobilise professional journalists in the nationalist struggle at a time when the press was regarded as a potent tool in fashioning domestic and international opinion. The Association became a site for considerable ideological conflict, particularly during the early 1960s when groups associated with various political parties (particularly the PSI and the PKI) vied for control.

Since 1966, like many key professional organisations and all labour unions, the PWI has been tightly regulated and directed by the New Order Government. A close look at the key office-bearers during the period 1988-93 is instructive. Until his death in September 1991, the chairperson of the PWI's Education Committee was a retired brigadier-general, M. Hilny Nasution. The PWI's executive chairperson similarly was a retired brigadier-general (described somewhat disparagingly by one of Indonesia's most respected senior editors as 'a general who never writes a line'), Sugeng Wijaya, editor of the Army's *Berita Yudha* daily, and chairperson of the Executive Board of the government's political organisation, Golkar. He was a long-time functionary in the field of government information, propaganda and psychological 'guidance'. He was formerly deputy head of KOPKAMTIB's Information and Public Relations Service during one of the most strained periods of government-press relations (1974-76), after which he became deputy chief, then finally chief, of the Armed Forces/Department of Defence and Security (*Dephankam*) Centre for Mental Guidance (*Pusbintal* ABRI) (1976-80). It is not surprising then that the PWI leadership expressed concern about the perils of increasing political liberalisation and 'openness'. As PWI's central executive chairperson Sugeng Wijaya was quoted as telling the Parliamentary Commission which deals with information and press affairs (Komisi 1 DPR) in September 1989, although the 'political climate for exercising control by the society [over the government] (*kontrol sosial*) had improved with the existance of openness..."If openness continues, the results could be destabilising."'

Occasionally, throughout its existence under the New Order, PWI membership has rejected office-bearers unacceptably tainted by behind-the-scenes government machinations. In October 1970, for example, at the PWI 24th Congress in Palembang, government operatives (widely believed to be from the OPSUS Special Intelligence Operations branch) attempted to secure the election of a pliable executive board, under B.M. Diah, founding editor of *Merdeka* daily and briefly a Minister of Information in Suharto's 1968 Cabinet. Members' suspicions led to Diah being narrowly defeated by *Pedoman*'s Rosihan Anwar, who made a last-minute run for the post of General Chairperson and was regarded as more independent of the government. Diah's supporters claimed the election had been rigged, convened a rival meeting (between midnight and 4 a.m. the night after the formal close of the Congress), to form a rival executive. The authorities suppressed details of the Rosihan Anwar board from press reports and the Minister of Information, Air Vice-Marshall Budiarjo (who had replaced Diah as Minister of Information in 1968) formalised the Diah panel. The brawl between the two rival executive committees nonetheless became public knowledge, with Anwar seeking to take the Minister and the Diah committee to court. A face-saving settlement was reached on 6 March 1971 with the complete integration of the two parallel bodies, resulting in there being two bearers in each of the offices. In a pyrrhic victory for the PWI membership the government had been forced to acknowledge the formally elected Anwar executive.[10]

Generally, however, such indelicate government intervention in the PWI has been unnecessary since the leadership is usually selected from the more moderate senior members of the profession, who already have cordial working relations with the Government, without significant challenge from critical opponents. The current executive (elected in December 1993 for a five-year term) is headed by Sofyan Lubis, editor-in-chief of the 'blood-and-guts' crime daily *Pos Kota*, established by the current Minister of Information Harmoko. Lubis' victory had been predicted since he became chairperson of Golkar's Department of Information, Publications and Mass Media in October 1993, when Harmoko became Golkar's General Chairperson. The new PWI Secretary-General is Parni Hadi, Editor-in-Chief of *Republika*, the pro-government daily, sponsored by the Indonesian Muslim Intellectuals' Association (ICMI) and backed by B.J. Habibie, the powerful Minister for Research and Technology and executive chair of the presidium of Golkar's policy-formulating Guidance Council. Some observers have suggested that the Sofyan

Lubis - Parni Hadi partnership in the PWI mirrors the powerful combination of their patrons Harmoko and Habibie in the Golkar hierarchy.[11]

The allegiance of the PWI Board has been widely questioned. Adnan Buyung Nasution, one of the human rights lawyers who formulated Surya Paloh's request to the Supreme Court for a Judicial Review of the Minister of Information's regulations on the withdrawal of a paper's publication permit, described as 'tragic' the PWI's failure to support Paloh's campaign. In fact, to add insult to injury, the PWI declared its 'concern' that Paloh was taking up the issue, leading Nasution to bemoan 'so I am left wondering, whose interests does the PWI really represent now?'[12] Similarly, when maverick editor Eros Jarot sought to circumvent the June 1994 ban on his weekly tabloid *DeTIK* by taking over the languishing *Simponi* weekly in October, it was the central administration of the PWI (under a protege of Information Minister Harmoko) and the pro-government Newspaper Publishers' Association (under a retired brigadier-general) which colluded with the Director-General of Press and Graphics to block the revamped *Simponi* after a single edition.[13]

For the rank-and-file journalist however, a PWI membership card is theoretically essential and rejection by (or in the case of *Monitor*'s editor Arswendo Atmowiloto, expulsion from) the Association, for whatever reason, is likely to close the door formally on a press career. Hence, the PWI executive has the power to act as a gate-keeper for the government in controlling professionals seeking access to the industry. In November 1989, the organisation formalised this role by declaring that only it had the authority to issue any form of press identification card for journalists, declaring invalid any authorities issued by individual publishers and urging that any other form of journalist identification be disregarded and invalid.[14]

Obtaining full PWI membership is a prolonged process. All applicants are required to submit 'a letter certifying good behaviour from a police precinct chief' and 'a letter certifying non-involvement in the Indonesian Communist Party/G-30-S treachery [of 30 September 1965] from the responsible authority, if the applicant was born before 1955'.[15] After a candidature of least three years while working continuously as a journalist with national press companies, an applicant can apply for 'junior membership', open to Indonesian nationals over 19 years of age. 'Ordinary members' must pass a PWI test after two further years as a 'junior member'. For those associated with the profession but not working as active journalists with commercial publications, or those with the electronic media, there is an 'extraordinary' membership category. Finally, there is a special 'honorary membership' for those whose life-long contributions to the profession warrant special recognition. In 1992, according to PWI records, there were 3,983 members: 2,290 candidates, 497 juniors and 1,196 ordinary members.[16] There are currently branches in all 27 provinces, as under the organisation's charter a branch may be established with a minimum of ten ordinary members if authorised by the PWI Central Office.

Despite government provisions which require all practising journalists to be members of the PWI, in fact of the 5,359 journalists whose details are routinely provided to the Department of Information by their employers, only 3,164 are actually listed as members of the PWI.[17] In the words of former Tempo editor Gunawan Mohamad, 'the curious thing about this organisation is that it has no genuine support from the reporters. The government thinks that when it controls the leadership the reporters will follow the line, but it never works that way... The association contributes nothing to the freedom of the press, or the unfreedom of the press. It has no relevance at all, in my opinion'.[18] While membership does entitle a journalist to some benefits, such as certain welfare support and access to subsidised housing, these have been inadequate to stem disaffection with the organisation from within its constituency. In many cases such benefits are more generously provided directly by the newspaper companies to their employees, together with a raft of other incentives (like interest-free loans and medical assistance), thus superseding the PWI provisions.

The small, often collegial, working style which typified papers from pre-Independence through to the mid-1970s, exemplified in dailies such as *Indonesia Raya* and *Abadi*, which were pervaded by an ethos of intense company loyalty, shared commitment and ideology, is the exception rather than the rule today. The boom in the number of new or revamped, expanded publications has introduced 'headhunting' into the labour market stimulating intense competition for experienced staff, improving pay and conditions, with attractive fringe benefits and transfer fees being offered to key personnel. Such improved conditions have, to a degree, reduced the long-standing financial dependence of many practising journalists, particularly in the small-circulation marginal papers, upon outside supplementary payments, known as 'envelopes' (*amplop*). It has been commonplace for journalists, often receiving only subsistence wages, to expect payment from those deemed to benefit from any stories they wrote. So a company issuing a press release or a government department seeking to have its views publicised, for example, would distribute money in envelopes to journalists attending press conferences or briefings. While the amounts varied, often substantial sums could change hands to ensure favourable coverage. Individuals newspapers usually developed their in-house policies regarding the recipt of 'envelopes'. Some routinely pooled the money and divided it equally amongst all staff. Some publicly donated it to charities. Some threatened to sack any employee who pocketed an 'envelope'. But journalists and analysts alike have generally argued that, in the long term, only a marked improvement in the salaries and working conditions of journalists would wipe out the practice of 'under the counter' payments.

While the raising of the financial stakes in print media companies and the increasing competitive pressures have in many ways improved the working conditions and bargaining power of staff, for some the volatility has resulted in mass sackings. Such was the case with employees in *Pelita*[19] when in July 1991 one fifth of the newspaper's staff was sacked without warning. The delegation that approached the DPR for re-instatement claimed that 'the provisions of the SIUPP are apparently not strong enough to protect journalists and press workers'. Those dismissed were not entitled to protection from the All-Indonesia Workers Union (*Serikat Pekerja Seluruh Indonesia,* SPSI) according to the SPSI's General Chairperson, Iman Sudarwo, because press companies held a special status and were not covered by labour union policy. New Order official discourse has frequently been at pains to emphasise that journalists are not 'workers' but 'professionals' and, as such are not eligible to 'labour union' protection through the government-controlled SPSI.

For its part, the PWI adopts the position, under government directive, that it is not a trade union or labour organisation protecting workers in such disputes, but rather a 'professional association' expressing the aspirations of the profession as a whole. Instead of labour unions, the SPSI policy is that each press workplace is entitled to establish a Staff Council (*Dewan Karyawan*) to negotiate on labour's behalf, an arrangement which, in the Pelita case at least, left staff with little legal recourse and exposed the risk this represents for unprotected journalists.[20]

The idea of journalists participating in an independent labour organisation is as anathema to those heading press empires as it is to the government. When four journalists in *Kompas* (regarded as one of the most 'liberal' and 'democratic' papers) attempted to set up a labour union within the company in March 1988, the paper's management moved firmly either to dismiss the ring-leaders or 'transfer' them to other parts of the *Kompas* group's empire. Rather than support the rights of journalists to act collectively in this manner, in a strongly worded letter the central leadership of the PWI (dominated by newspaper editorial/management staff rather than rank-and-file journalists) backed the *Kompas* management's action and condemned the concept of the labour union.[21] Similar attempts within other publication companies, such as the Tempo-Grafiti group, have reportedly faced staunch opposition from the management. Some companies attempt to undermine representatives on the Staff Council by offering them comfortable positions in the Personnel Section.

Broad dissatisfaction with the PWI among rank and file journalists has generated considerable pressure from within the industry for the establishment of a rival professional body or trade union. According to Gunawan Mohamad in early 1993, there was an 'informal' network of young journalists disgruntled with the PWI 'but they have no power at all in influencing the course of events in the Indonesian media yet'.[22] Pressure for an alternative professional organisation was mounting, however. In mid 1993 a number of young journalists in Bandung and Yogyakarta established a rival journalists' network. The forming of the Yogyakarta Journalists' Discussion Forum (*Forum Diskusi Wartawan Yogyakarta*, FDWY) and counterpart groups elsewhere, caused the authorities some consternation, and the movement was quickly regarded as a potential threat to State regulation of the profession. The shock banning of three weekly news publications in June 1994 provided a dramatic stimulus for such unofficial workers' organisations. In the wake of the bans, a variety of lobby groups emerged, some community based, such as the SIUPP (*Solidaritas Indonesia untuk Pembebasan Pers*, Indonesian Solidarity for Press Freedom), and others formed by workers within the industry, like the Alliance of Independent Journalists (*Aliansi Jurnalis Independen*). On 7 August 1994, about 60 journalists, including such leading figures as Gunawan Mohamad, Fikri Jufri, Bambang Harymurti (from *Tempo*), Eros Jarot (of *DeTIK*), Aristides Katoppo (formerly of *Sinar Harapan*), Christianto Wibisono (media analyst and columnist) and Arief Budiman (academic and columnist), established the Alliance by signing the Sirna Galih Declaration, which stated 'we reject all kinds of interference, intimidation, censorship and media bans which deny freedom of speech and open access to information' since 'freedom of speech, access to information and freedom of association ... [are] the basic right of all citizens'.[23] Ironically, it appears the triple banning has only triggered a greater militancy amongst industry professionals and intensified interest in alternative organisations to the PWI.

Groups like the FDWY provided the nucleus for such militancy. The FDWY initially consisted of only a couple of dozen young, energetic journalists from local and national papers, together with some academics and press commentators. Yet when it attempted to organise a seminar on 'Press Offences' in Yogyakarta in September 1993, the local PWI chapter appealed to the police to prohibit the event on the basis that the FDWY was an 'illegal' organisation.[24] The police permit was only issued after the local branch of the Bar Association, Ikadin, agreed to take responsibility for the gathering. Nationally, the in-coming PWI executive made it clear that the government restriction recognising only one professional journalist association would be strenuously maintained.[25] It is highly unlikely that government permission for any rival would be forthcoming although pressure to open labour markets generally to competing representative organisations and trade union increases.

In analysing the clash between the PWI and the FDWY, Ariel Heryanto[26] noted the recent rapid expansion in the numbers of young, highly-trained, professionally-oriented journalists now finding a place in the industry, some of them eagerly courted by expansionist entrepreneurs seeking new talent for growing press empires. Such journalists had a sense of their own professional worth, economic power and political influence. They matched this with a high commitment to a modern, principled, rational work ethic. They resent the restrictive regulations and the corporatist organisations that govern their working lives. Like the student activist groups (whose history many of the young journalists share), they are organising to assert themselves. Like the students, in Heryanto's opinion, these young journalists too are part of an expanding and potentially politically assertive Indonesian middle class, starting to flex its muscles.

The Newspaper Publishers Association (SPS)

Less flamboyant and controversial than the PWI, yet equally as influential is the Newspaper Publishers Association (*Serikat Penerbit Surat Kabar*, SPS), which represents the newspaper companies and plays a significant role in determining such policies as newsprint import levels and prices.[27] Ironically perhaps its origins are in the Journalists' Association. As an official history of the SPS declares: 'The SPS and the PWI are siblings! ... not only are they siblings. They are even more than that. The SPS and the PWI are Siamese Twins. Born of the same father and mother, at the same moment.'[28] At the 9-10 February 1946 meeting which founded the PWI in Solo, some of the 300-odd participants raised the idea of establishing a newspaper publishers' grouping. A 10-member working party was set up to examine the possibility, recommending the formation subsequently of the SPS, which took place in June 1948 under the sponsorship of the PWI.

This close 'familial' relationship between the PWI and the SPS continues to the present, with many SPS members holding influential positions in the PWI. Like the PWI, the office-bearers of the SPS often come with the imprimatur of the government just as since 1975 the SPS itself has been the sole professional publishers' body recognised by the Government. The June 1989 election of Zulharmans (a former Executive Chairperson of the PWI) as Executive Chairperson of the SPS, for example, was regarded openly by a large number of delegates as 'already determined from above'.[29] This election, too, highlighted another irony in the operations of these press organisations. While the SPS is the closest thing in Indonesia to an employer confederation whose interests may be interpreted as antithetical to those of the PWI which ostensibly represents wage-earning journalists employed by these press companies, nonetheless several of the key leadership of the PWI also sit on SPS executive committees. Apart from Zulharmans (former editor of *Harian KAMI*, then editor-in-chief of *Neraca* economic daily, and chairperson of Golkar's Mass Media, Publications and Information Department), overlapping members in the 1989-94 Board included Yakob Utama (Kompas-Gramedia chief) and Atang Ruswita (from the Bandung daily *Pikiran Rakyat [Thoughts of the People]*) while Brigadier-General (retired) Sugeng Wijaya chairs the SPS Advisory Council.[30] While such a close arrangement between the PWI and the SPS may smooth communication between the two bodies, it could be seen to weaken any advocacy role of the PWI in supporting non-managerial employees in press companies.

The potential for a conflict of interests has not escaped notice. For example, Mara Karma, a senior journalist who formerly worked for the oft-banned campaigning daily *Indonesia Raya* recently called publicly for a clear division of interests and personnel between these two professional organisations. Expressing concerns felt by many rank-and-file journalists he observed that 'It is not right to have media owners, editors and reporters all sitting as members of the Indonesian Press Association [presumably referring to the Indonesian Journalists' Association]. They should all have separate organisations.'[31] Many of the interests of press company owners could be regarded as inimical to those of their journalist employees, as the Arswendo sacking during the *Monitor* incident (discussed earlier) exemplifies.

The Press Graphics Association (SGP)

In 1974 an association was formed to bring together all printing companies which were primarily producing press publications. The resulting Press Graphics Association (*Serikat Grafika Pers*, SGP) was endorsed as the sole press printing body recognised by the government in a 1978 ministerial decree. Its role is less significant and less public than that of the powerful publishing body, SPS. The relative importance attached by the government to the various press organisations can be gleaned from their representation on the Press Council. While the Journalists Association has eight, and the Publishers Association six, the Press Graphics Assocation and the Advertising Companies Association (mentioned below) have only one seat each.

The Indonesian Advertising Companies Association (PPPI)

As the economic and political climate for foreign investment in Indonesia began to improve in the early years of the New Order, international advertising conglomerates started to take an interest in the country. The injection of foreign expertise, which really only became noticeble after 1970, gradually transformed the rather sleepy domestic advertising industry into an offshoot of the international marketplace.[32] With the metamorphosis of the industry came the transformation too in December 1972 of the old Indonesian Advertising Bureau Association (*Perserikatan* [later *Persatuan*] *Biro Reklame Indonesia*, PBRI), established in September 1949, into the sole recognised advertising peak body, the Indonesian Advertising Companies Association (*Persatuan Perusahaan Periklanan Indonesia*, PPPI).

Its charter, like so many of the professional bodies mentioned, declares the organisation to be 'based on the Pancasila and the 1945 Constitution and directed towards full, responsible participation in pursuing the duties of national development' and specifically 'improving the world of advertising enterprises'.[33] In the 1982 Press Law and associated documents, the advertising industry organisation was included as a member of the national 'press family' of organisations, along with the PWI, SPS and SGP. While commercial and financial aspects of the advertising industry would be overseen by the Department of Trade and Cooperatives, the codes governing the suitability and appropriateness of advertising materials were under the scrutiny of the Department of Information.

The economic and political significance of advertising in the media industry was flagged not solely by its incorporation into the 'press family' and by the government's allocation of a seat on the peak Press Council to the PPPI, but also with the earlier establishment in July 1981 of the related Body for Equalising the Distribution of Advertisements, (*Badan Penyalur dan Pemerataan Periklanan*, BPPP). The explicit catalyst for its establishment was the President's National Budget speech before the DPR in 1981 when he announced the government's ban on national television advertising (then entirely in the hands of the sole network, the government TVRI), and his subsequent speech at the 35th PWI Congress in Banjarmasin noting that he believed the resultant flow-over of advertising to the print media could best be directed to benefit the small weaker papers through an intermediate 'equalisation' agency. The concept was endorsed by the Press Council, despite some private reservations, and the BPPP was born.

Industry analysts are divided over the success and efficacy of the Body, with several editors arguing that advertisers would prefer the high tariffs and long wait to place ads in the large-circulation capital city dailies or prestige weeklies rather than direct their clients to weaker or regional outlets. Statistics for 1991 indicate the considerable discrepancy in advertising tariffs between the major national dailies and smaller regionals: Jakarta's *Suara Pembaruan* charges Rp 6,000 per millimetre column for film ads while *Fajar*, in South Sulawesi charges Rp. 50 for a comparable film ad. While *Suara Pembaruan's* circulation of about 340,000 is about 20 times *Fajar's* 17,500, it charges 120 times more for the ad.[34] While this enormous contrast may be an extreme example, invariably the most expensive papers (considering circulation and price) are *Kompas* and *Suara Pembaruan* in all categories for which official Department of Information statistics are available.

Department of Information statistics also show that while in rare cases the BPPP provides up to 25% of the advertisements for dailies, and even up to 50% for struggling weeklies (for example, in Jambi, West Nusa Tenggara or North Sulawesi), in most cases the figure for BPPP ads is insignificant, with the vast majority of advertising revenue flowing from non-BPPP sources such as advertising agencies or companies. Any chance of the BPPP equalising advertising revenues was largely scuttled by the government's backdown and re-introduction of television advertising. Press advertising revenues were slashed as money was sucked into private television when it began 'free-to-air' broadcasts in the capital in 1990, spreading quickly to other major cities, such as Surabaya, Bandung and Denpasar. Finally commercial broadcasts went nationwide on the Indonesian Educational Television (*Televisi Pendidikan Indonesia*, TPI) network in early 1991, offering TV advertisers a reach unmatched by the press.

Nonetheless, Christianto Wibisono, of the Indonesian Business Data Centre (PDBI), has argued that PWI and SPS collusion with the Department of Information to restrict the number of publication permits (SIUPP), together with the extraordinary level of protectionism surrounding the industry, and the government's strict limits on advertising ratios has driven print media advertising rates in Indonesia up to amongst the world's most expensive. Such advertising income has launched successful press conglomerates, and funded lavish expansion into non-press businesses. Let us look now at some of these company success stories and the trend towards the increasing concentration of ownership in the domain of a limited number of press empires.

ENDNOTES

1. For recent discussions suggesting the influence of such theories, largely disseminated in Indonesia through the work of Fred S. Siebert, Theodore Peterson and Wilbur Schramm (1956), *Four Theories of the Press*, University of Illinois Press, Urbana, see Sadono 1993:21 and Abdul Razak (1992), 'Analysis of Press Freedom in Editorial Context' (pp.122-45, particularly p.144) in Don Michael Flournoy (ed.) (1992), *Content Analysis of Indonesian Newspapers*, Gadjah Mada University Press, Yogyakarta.

2. Razak 1992:144. As an example of how such categories have become accepted wisdom, see their use in statements by the Golkar parliamentary faction of the DPR concerning proposed changes in press legislation, 7 September 1982, as published in JCT Simorangkir (1986) *Ketentuanketentuan mengenai pers, SIUPP, Wartawan dan beberapa komentar*, Gunung Agung, Jakarta, pp.76-90, esp. p.78.

3. Numerous publications by the Department of Information contain these laws and their accompanying 'explanations', e.g., *Pedoman Pembinaan Isi Pers*, Direktorat Jenderal Pembinaan Pers dan Grafika, Direktorat Pembinaan Kewartawanan, [1987?], pp.63-98. English translations of the major legislation and regulations can be found in Razak 1985:188-252.

4. Dhakidae 1991:432. Italics in original.

5. Junaedhie 1991:48, and Departemen Penerangan RI (1982), *Pedoman Pembinaan Pers, Grafika dan Penerbitan Pemerintah*, Deppen, Jakarta, p.7.

6. On Antara, see Atmakusumah's entry in *Ensiklopedi Nasional Indonesia*, Vol. 2, PT Cipta Adi Pustaka, Jakarta, 1988, pp.132-7, and Departemen Penerangan RI (1982), *Pedoman Pembinaan Pers, Grafika dan Penerbitan Pemerintah*, Direktorat Jenderal Pembinaan Pers dan Grafika, Jakarta, pp.89-93.

7. 'Dari Soal Bredel sampai Saham', *Tempo*, 1 December 1990, p.88.

8. 'Stop Breidel Pers', *Media Indonesia*, 3 October 1990.

9. Soetrisno Bachir (1992), 'Bisnis Pers di Tengah Arus Globalisasi', *Kompas*, 10/2/92.

10. On the Diah-Anwar dispute, see Peter Polomka (1971), *Indonesia Since Sukarno*, Penguin, Harmondsworth, pp.200-1; and Soebagijo I.N., Abdurrachman Surjomihardjo, & P. Swantoro (1977), *Lintasan Sejarah P.W.I.*, PWI Pusat & Departemen Penerangan, Jakarta, pp.39-40 & pp.112-4.

11. On Lubis and Hadi, see 'Duet Baru Selepas Magrib', *Tempo*, 11 December 1993, p.81 and 'Pers Indonesia Bukan Watchdog', *Forum Keadilan*, 23 December 1993, p.28.

12. Adnan Buyung Nasution (1993), 'Menggugat Peranan Pers di Indonesia' (pp.509-21) in Hotman M. Siahaan & Tjahjo Purnomo W. (eds.) (1993), *Tajuk-Tajuk dalam Terik Matahari: Empat Puluh Tahun Surabaya Post*, Yayasan Keluarga Bhakti, Surabaya. Quotation from p.517.

13. Sofyan Lubis of the Central PWI and Sugeng Wijaya of the Central SPS confronted *Simponi* editor-in-chief Syamsu Hadi in the office of Director-General Subrata, forcing Hadi to suspend publication 'temporarily' (see 'PWI Pusat Cabut Rekomendasi Pemred 'Simponi'' *Kompas*, 7/10/94, and 'Simponi [Sementara] tadak terit', *Jawa Pos*, 8/20/94, both on internet's apakabar network).

14. 'Hanya Kartu PWI untuk Tugas Jurnalistik', *Kompas*, 6 November 1989, p.9, & 'Identitas PWI', *Kompas*, 25 January 1990, pp. 1 & 8.

15. This provision is quoted from the English translation of the PWI 'Rules and Procedures', Chapter II, in Tribuana Said (1986), *Indonesian Journalists' Association*, Persatuan Wartawan Indonesia, Jakarta, pp.44-6.

16. USIS Vol 2 1992: 94.

17. According to *Data Kewartawanan IPPPN Tahun 1991*, Proyek Pembinaan Pers, Departemen Penerangan, Jakarta, 1991/1992, p.i. A 1984 ministerial decree obliged press publications to provide such statistics as part of the Inventory of the Growth and Development of the National Press (IPPPN).

18. Comment made at the conference Indonesia: Paradigms for the Future, Murdoch Asia Research Centre, Perth, July 1993.

19. For further details on *Pelita*, see David T. Hill (1992), 'The Press in a Squeeze: Operating Hazards in the Indonesian Print Media', *Southeast Asian Journal of Social Science* (National University of Singapore), Vol. 20 No. 2, pp.1-28.

20. 'Pijar-pijar Pelita', *Prospek*, 10 August 1991, p.29.

21. For details of the membership of the PWI executive, see USIS 1992, Vol.2, pp.94-5. The letter was signed by Zulharmans, General Chairman (editor-in-chief of Neraca economic daily, formerly with Harian Kami) and Atang Ruswita, Secretary General (General Chairman and editor-inchief of *Pikiran Rakyat*). Both were concurrently office-bearers in the Newspaper Publishers Assocation (SPS), Zulharmans as General Chairperson of the Executive Board, and Atang Ruswita as Vice-Chairperson of the Advisory Council. As such, these Editors-in-Chief of substantial papers might be seen as more likely to act in the interest of Yakob Utama *Kompas*' Editor-in-Chief, rather than those of the rank-and-file journalists. For a detailed discussion of the *Kompas* incident, see Dhakidae 1991:404-13.

22. Comments made at the Murdoch Asia Research Centre conference Indonesia: Paradigms for the Future, Perth July 1993.

23. 'Journalists' union set up in Indonesia', *West Australian*, 8/8/94, p.22; and internet listing about AJI on apakabar@clark.net, which included the full text of the Declaration in English and Indonesian made at Sirna Galih, near Puncak, West Java. The Indonesian text appears in Ayu Utami, Imran Hasibuan, Santoso, Liston P. Siregar (eds.) *Bredel* 1994: *Kumpulan Tulisan tentang Pembredelan TEMPO, DETIK, EDITOR,* Aliansi Jurnalis Independen, Jakarta, pp.122-5

24. The incident is described in Ariel Heryanto (1993), 'Demokratisasi Kelas Menengah?', *Kompas*, 3 September.

25. 'Pers Indonesia Bukan Watchdog', *Forum Keadilan*, 23 December 1993, p.28.

26. Heryanto 1993.

27. For a detailed discussion of the role of the SPS, see Dhakidae 1991:492–516.

28. SPS [c.1971] *Garis Besar Perkembangan Pers Indonesia*, SPS, Jakarta, p.13.

29. 'Dari PWI, Zul Kini Mengemudikan SPS', *Editor*, 15 June 1989, p.57. Zulharmans died in office in 1993.

30. USIS 1992 Vol. 2, p.97.

31. Mara Karma quoted in 'Study urged on impact of big capital on media industry', *Jakarta Post*, 28/9/92.

32. On this transformation, and the advertising industry in Indonesia in general, see Michael H. Anderson (1984), *Madison Avenue in Asia: Politics and Transnational Advertising*, Fairleigh Dickenson University Press, London/Toronto (particularly Chapter 6), which was based on his earlier study 'The Madison Avenue Connection: A Study of Transnational Advertising and Political Development in Malaysia, Singapore and Indonesia', PhD thesis, University of Hawaii, Honolulu, 1979. Other useful information can be found in Razif & Bambang Saptono (eds.) (1993), *Sejarah Periklanan Indonesia 1744-1984*, Persatuan Perusahaan Periklanan Indonesia, Jakarta; and Baty Subakti h Ernst Katoppo (eds.) (1993), *Media Scene 1992-1993 Indonesia: The Official Guide to Advertising Media in Indonesia*, PPPI, Jakarta.

33. Junaedhie 1991:217.

34. These statistics are derived from *Data* Periklanan *Pers IPPPN Tahun 1991* (p.i), and *Data Oplah dan Peredaran IPPPN Tahun 1991* (pp.12 & 46), both published by Department of Information, Direktorat Jenderal Pembinaan Pers dan Grafika, Proyek Pembinaan Pers, 1991/1992.

CHAPTER 4

The Rise of Press Empires

Whoever deliberately and in a way opposed to law uses press publications for his personal or group interests, causing deviations or obstructions to the task, function, rights and duties of the press ... shall be liable to a prison sentence to a maximum period of 4 (four) years and or fine to a maximum amount of Rp 40,000,000.00 (forty million rupiahs).

Indonesia's Press Act No.21/1982, Article 1.17 (1)[1]

The press companies which survived the mass anti-left bans of 1965-66 and those that appeared in the ensuing years were small struggling enterprises living hand-to-mouth in a chaotic economy. They were dependent on government subsidised allocation of erratic supplies of imported newsprint. Generally, proprietors were only able to raise pin-money from advertising in a country with virtually no significant advertising industry until the early 1970s. Technologically, they were hamstrung. Even to import out-dated machinery donated by Western sympathisers required specific ministerial exemption from blanket bans on foreign interference in the industry.[2] The industry lacked the capital to upgrade and was an unattractive investment because, by its very nature the press was seen to be a likely victim of broader political volatility. Papers lived with the ever-present possibility of bans, under the shadow of the anti-press actions of the previous decade.

But some were able to translate political and public support into capital. Those that survived the 1970s frequently adopted a new pragmatism and commercial discernment, accumulating capital and strategically re-investing it, while diversifying to insure against potential losses in vulnerable areas of their publication empire. By the late 1980s, shrewd management and a tempering of the 'perjuangan' ethos had led to a high degree of stability and consequent expansion of the media as a whole. The press industry was bouyed by a growing economy, restructuring after the 1970s' oil booms. The media came to represent an increasingly more attractive investment by the beginning of the 1990s.

By highlighting the history and development of the four major press empires to emerge in the New Order this chapter attempts to sketch the changing nature of the press industry, particularly the decline of the small-scale independent single paper company and the rise of press empires.[3] The first two of these empires were based on daily newspapers founded during the early 1960s, associated initially with the numerically small but politically influential Catholic and Protestant communities. One stands apart as the most successful media company in Indonesian history, while the second has only survived the rigours of New Order bannings by dint of metamorphosis. Nonetheless, together they represent those press companies which successfully managed the transition from 'old' to 'new' Orders. The third conglomerate was the earliest to break the nexus which had required a successful press publication to be dependent on sectional or party political connections. It symbolises the erratic and unpredictable fate of press companies, having had its flagship, the most financially successful weekly magazine in Indonesian history, banned without warning in June 1994. The fourth and final enterprise, whose founder's first newspaper was also banned, exemplifies the benefits of building a commercially-oriented national syndicate, linking smaller formerly independent papers with a strong central flagship, particularly if the network enjoys close connections with some of the most powerful economic and political interests within the New Order.

Taken together, the intersecting stories of these four endeavours demonstrate something of a shift of power from within the New Order State apparatus to elements outside it. The rise of these press giants illustrates a capacity for independent capital accumulation in an industry fraught with political and financial risks, constantly facing the possibility of uncontestable bans. Despite the continuing importance of both capital and a public perception of editorial independence, it may still be impossible for press companies to insulate themselves from the dangers of political vagaries. Nonetheless, pressure is increasing on the State to follow legal process and demonstrate public accountability for actions taken against the press.

The chapter concludes by documenting the recent interest and involvement in the press by key New Order entrepreneurs, not the least amongst them members of the presidential family and their associates. The discussion highlights the case of the President's son, Bambang Trihatmojo, whose involvement as financier of a press company focuses attention on his shift from an earlier dependence on presidential largesse and State power to his increasing reliance on capital, financial management and market forces. The contradictions this situation throws up are demonstrated by the fact that the newspaper group with which he is associated has been one of the most vociferous in challenging the State's arbitrary exercise of power over the press. But if the press conglomerates are mobilising their resources to challenge the power of the State, there is a growing concern amongst the public that the emerging oligopoly of press giants poses its own threat by monopolising information flows for its own interests.

Kompas-Gramedia Group

The morning newspaper *Kompas* is Indonesia's most prestigious and largest selling daily (reaching sales of 525,000 in 1991 with 50,000 more for the Sunday edition) and is generally regarded as the largest quality newspaper in Southeast Asia (although it is outsold by the sensationalist *Thai Rath* in Bangkok with its 900,000). In July 1994 it claimed in its advertising that it was 'read daily by 3,120,00 educated people all over Indonesia [making it] the highest reach newspaper in this country'.[4]

Kompas was established in 1965, by Chinese and Javanese Catholic journalists on the initiative of the Catholic Party in an attempt to present a Catholic voice in the cacophony of 1960s Indonesian politics, at a time when, in the words of one of the founding editors, Yakob Utama, 'a number of newspapers labelled as BPS [anti-Sukarnoist] and having an anti-Communist tone had been closed down'.[5] In some senses, *Kompas* filled this gap. It succeeded in riding the political storms of 1966 and generally supported the emergence of the New Order, at a time when certain right-wing Catholics played significant behind-the-scenes roles as intellectuals and ideologues (such as in the Military Intelligence-aligned think-tank, the Centre for Strategic and International Studies). During this transition period Christian political figures and intellectuals tended to wield an influence disproportionate to the modest size of the Christian communities, which constituted only about 9% of the population.[6] *Kompas*' proximity to the Catholic Party continued till 1971 by which time generally the links between newspapers and political parties were slackening as the government tried to dilute sectional loyalties. The early jibe that the name 'kompas' had been selected for the paper because it represented the 'KOMando PAStor' (the pastors' commandoes) continued to be heard, but any substance it once may have had evaporated. Two years later the government acted to erode long-standing party identities and allegiances (thereby strengthening its own position) by forcing all political parties (except the ruling quasi-party Golkar) into two amalgams: the Islamic-oriented Development Unity Party (*Partai Persatuan Pembangunan*, PPP), and the nationalist-Christian Indonesian Democracy Party (*Partai Demokrasi Indonesia*, PDI).[7]

Kompas began with a modest circulation of 5,000 but sales rose consistently as it earned a solid reputation for its analytical depth and polished style. One of the two founders, P.K. Oyong, had long experience as chief editor of *Star Weekly* in the 1950s till it was banned in the early 1960s, while the other, Yakob Utama, was editor of a Catholic weekly *Penabur* [*The Sower*]. Under Utama's influence as editor-in-chief, *Kompas* became synonymous with a style of subtle, indirect and implicit criticism, often dubbed typically 'Javanese'. Characterising its style as 'determined boringness' and implying that this may contribute to its authority, Ben Anderson recently described *Kompas* as the New Order newspaper par excellence.[8] By virtue of its caution and self-moderation in its coverage of sensitive political issues, *Kompas* weathered the mass bans of the 1970s, albeit somewhat traumatised and conscious of its vulnerability. The paper, which dominates the middle- and upper-class market, established a strong and loyal subscriber base (unlike the down-market *Pos Kota* which sells a massive 80% of its print run through street sellers[9]). Some analysts argue that even though *Kompas* subscribers may also now be reading racier rival papers they remain extremely reluctant to kick the *Kompas* habit and cancel their subscription. *Kompas* remains the country's prestige 'paper of record'.

P.K. Oyong died in 1980, but under the direction of Yakob Utama the *Kompas* enterprise determinedly pursued a strategy of massive diversification and reinvestment through the 1980s. By the beginning of the 1990s *Kompas* had become the parent of an interlocking empire of around 38 subsidiaries - known collectively as the Kompas-Gramedia Group. The group included not only Gramedia book publishers and a printery, but also a radio station, offshoots in the travel agency, hotel, heavy equipment, supermarket, insurance, leasing, banking and advertising industries (to name just a selection).[10] Yakob Utama still heads the empire, which has generated for him an enormous personal wealth warranting his listing as the 120th largest personal tax-payer in 1991.[11] The expanded Kompas-Gramedia Group dominates the publishing industry and has been one of the top forty conglomerates in the nation.[12] *Kompas* newspaper itself regularly commands the largest share of the nation's print advertising revenues, and that percentage is rising. In 1989 it earnt 26.8% (amounting to Rp 50,258 million) of all advertising spent on newspapers, a figure expected to increase to around 32.2% (or Rp. 85,916 million) by 1993.[13]

Since 1989, the Kompas-Gramedia Group has drawn in a clutch of regional papers, via capital injection, editorial and managerial collaboration. These include *Serambi Indonesia [Indonesian Porch]*, formerly known as *Mimbar Swadaya* (Banda Aceh), *Sriwijaya Post* (Palembang), *Mandala [Circle]* (Bandung), *Berita Nasional [National News]* (Yogya), later known simply as *Bernas*, and *Surya [Sun]* (Surabaya). A Regional Press Bureau unit was established within the empire to coordinate and manage this aspect of its expansion. The Kompas-Gramedia Group's market diversification produced a miscellany of targeted specialist publications: children's reading (*Bobo, Hai [Hi], Kawanku [My Friend]*); music and youth culture (*Citra Musik [Musical Image], Nova, Monitor, Senang [Happy]*); lifestyle, popular psychology and health (*Tiara, Sigma,*); environmental issues (*Suara Alam/Voice of Nature*); photography, computers and aeronautics (*Foto Media [Media Photos], Info Komputer [Computer Info], Angkasa [Sky]*), as well as sports (*Bola [Ball]*), the 'Reader's Digest'-style *Intisari [Essence]*, and the lower-middle class pictorial entertainment weekly *Jakarta Jakarta*.

The success stories have been legion, with *Monitor*'s meteoric rise (and fall) a shining example. In November 1986 when the group took over *Monitor*, formerly a tabloid published by the government television network TVRI, it had been unpublished for two years because of its unprofitability. Kompas-Gramedia totally revamped it, targeted a middle- and lower-class readership, and launched it with 200,000 copies. Although sales later dropped to around 500,000, by July 1987 *Monitor* claimed a circulation of 720,000, becoming the first Indonesian publication ever to exceed the 700,000 barrer.[14] When combined with its spin-off publications *Monitor Minggu [Sunday Monitor]* and *Monitor Anak [Children's Monitor]*, the weekly circulation reached an astounding 1.2 million copies prior to the withdrawal of its SIUPP.[15] The enormous success of *Monitor* is but one achievement of the enterprising entrepreneurial editor Arswendo Atmowiloto who spearheaded much of the group's expansion into magazines. He was rumoured to have controlled 22 SIUPPs prior to his expulsion from the group.

With the considerable barriers to newcomers, in the form of government SIUPP restrictions and massive capital required, the

Kompas-Gramedia group, with its cautious editorial and management styles, is regarded by most in the industry as being in an unassailable position at the pinnacle of the print media sector, and unlikely to relinquish its dominance in the market in the foreseeable future. Of all the media groups to be mentioned in this chapter, the Kompas-Gramedia Group is the one which has demonstrated most explicitly its preparedness to operate within the constraints imposed by the New Order Government. The flagship *Kompas* has the longest publishing history of any commercially successful daily and has only very rarely been banned, even temporarily. It continues to expand circulation steadily and consistently. The Kompas-Gramedia Group as a whole maintains cordial professional working relations with the relevant government media institutions, generally keeping pressures from particular journalists or publications for greater boldness in news coverage in check. The group's management, particularly in the person of founder Yakob Utama, is not adverse to disciplining journalists or even closing down particular publications rather than risking a government or public backlash, which may disadvantage the group as a whole.

Sinar Kasih Group

The original flagship of what is now known as the Sinar Kasih Group was the afternoon newspaper, *Sinar Harapan*. '*Sinar*', as it was commonly known, was established by Protestant Christian interests in 1961 at a time when several anti-Communist right-leaning papers, such as *Indonesia Raya [Greater Indonesia]*, *Pedoman [Compass]* and *Abadi* had either been banned or had closed voluntarily. Its expressly Protestant tone in the early years was moderated as the Church-affiliates declined in influence under challenge from those with greater professional journalistic experience. With an initial circulation of 7,500 in 1961, *Sinar Harapan* survived the 1960s, was amongst the bolder of the papers during the press crises of the 1970s, and moved into the 1980s targeting an expanding middle-class readership. Since the 1970s, *Sinar Harapan* was generally Indonesia's second highest selling daily, and, prior to its demise, was the second largest recipient of newspaper advertising revenues (1982-86) after *Kompas*. Its style was rather more explicit, assertive, sometimes even combative in its challenges to the government.

In September 1986 it had the dubious honour of being the first newspaper permanently closed down under the newly-implemented SIUPP regulations.[16] Its avatar, *Suara Pembaruan*, arose four months later but is yet to fully recover from the financial blow of the ban. With official 1991 sales of about 340,000, *Suara Pembaruan* became the fourth largest selling daily, after *Kompas* (525,000), *Pos Kota* (500,000) and *Jawa Pos* (350,000).[17] Nonetheless, its prestige reputation and high profile in Jakarta attract advertising revenue, and it remains the newspaper advertisers' second choice after *Kompas*, albeit trailing at some distance with 10.5% of the total newspaper advertising expenditure (in 1992).[18] Despite the demise of *Sinar Harapan* daily the expansion of the Sinar Kasih Group overall continues, led by the rather more muted reincarnation, *Suara Pembaruan*.

The Sinar Kasih Group had actually begun its diversification in 1971, with a printery (Sinar Agape press) and, in addition to its newspaper and magazine publishing branches (producing such successful popular magazines as *Mutiara [Pearl]*), it grew to control companies in transportation, tours and travel, advertising, book publishing, a private radio station, and to hold shares in a bank, the Ina Perdana. Through cooperation agreements, it co-publishes several Jakarta magazines, including a weekly sports magazine *Tribun [Tribune]* (produced with the Ministry for Youth and Sports), the specialist monthlies *TSM [Military Technology and Strategy]* and *Higina [Hygiene]* (on popular medicine). In 1989 the group began a management agreement with the Jakarta morning daily *Jayakarta [City of Jakarta]*, whose shareholders included Ponco Sutowo (son of the disgraced former head of the state oil company Pertamina, Ibnu Sutowo) and a foundation formed by the Jakarta Military Command (*Kodam Jaya*).[19] The advantage to the group of having interests in such auxiliary publications as a buffer against political and economic vagaries was evident in 1986 when *Sinar Harapan* was banned, for many staff simply shifted temporarily to *Mutiara* magazine, also produced in the group's East Jakarta headquarters.

In the non-metropolitan regions, the Sinar Kasih Group was one of the first major national papers to diversify by cultivating collaborative agreements with smaller papers. When government regulations forced *Sinar Harapan* to cut back from 20 to 12 pages and to reduce its substantial advertising to only 30% of total space, it lost about a quarter of its advertising revenue. It then embarked on a policy, described by a key strategist in the group, as 'growing together', in which the paper would provide editorial and managerial expertise to regional papers, without requiring majority shareholding.

It was generally financially unsuccessful and most of the regional papers which drew up agreements with *Sinar Harapan* eventually cancelled them, locking into deals with other national networks. For example, *Sinar Harapan* initiated a cooperation agreement with the north Sulawesi daily, *Obor Pancasila* [*Flame of the Pancasila*] (which later changed its name to *Cahaya Siang* [*Midday Light*]). This liaison broke down and the paper subsequently cooperated with several other major press groups, most recently moving into the *Media Indonesia* group. In the early 1980s, the Sinar Kasih group collaborated with the *Suara Indonesia* business daily in East Java (now in the *Jawa Pos* group), and later the weekly *Suara Timor Timur* [*Voice of East Timor*] (which became a daily in the Kompas-Gramedia Group in February 1993). While *Sinar Harapan* in some ways pioneered such collaborations, it proved reluctant or unable to bind together a workable national network of publications. The 1986 ban, and the paper's resultant re-structuring as *Suara Pembaruan* forced the enterprise to make a virtue out of necessity, concentrating on the 'main game' of revivifying the capital city afternoon paper rather than diversifying into either other industries or other regional papers.[20]

Tempo-Grafiti/Jawa Pos Group

At the time of writing this section, the future of *Tempo*, the nation's premier weekly news magazine, was dismal. Having been banned on 21 June 1994, its founding editor, Gunawan Mohamad, declared '*Tempo* is now consigned to the glorious dustbin of history'.[21] The public position of *Tempo*'s leadership was that the magazine would not reappear unless the government agreed to rescind the withdrawal of the publication permit (SIUPP) and permit the magazine to appear in its original form. As negotiations with the government faltered a split developed in the staff with approximately one-third of the journalists accepting an offer from timber magnate and presidential ally Bob (Mohammad) Hasan[22] to establish a new publication, *Gatra*. Most *Tempo* staff however, have indicated they will cash in their shares in the *Tempo* Employees Prosperity Foundation to raise the 4,000 million rupiah needed to launch an independent new weekly, *Opini* [Opinion]. After the government rejected their initial application for a permit, they quickly re-applied. As spokesperson Bambang Harymurti has stated, 'We basically want to open almost the same kind of magazine. *Tempo* has proven to be the leading news weekly magazine in Indonesia, so why change the winning formula?'

Tempo has had a long and distinguished history. It was established in 1971 when a contingent of highly creative young journalists and literary figures, who had worked in the student paper *Harian KAMI*

[*Indonesian Student Action Front Daily*] and B.M. Diah's *Ekspres* [*Express*] magazine, gained funding from a collection of Jakarta business people to produce a quality weekly modelled on *Time* magazine.[23] Its founders regarded this as the country's first experiment with venture capital in the press industry, with practising journalists contributing their labour and investors contributing capital, and dividing profits in equal measure.[24] *Tempo* immediately pioneered a blend of well-paced articulate and informative articles, written in a fresh, crisp language style, setting the benchmark against which all subsequent news magazines have been measured. With its motto 'Pleasant reading, and essential' (Enak dibaca dan perlu), its style was 'de-politicised', non-party journalism, with a dash of literary flair, consciously targeted at the urban middle-class reader, who had an interest in politics and economics, but no strong party loyalty. It was a strategy that led Ben Anderson to ask rhetorically 'Is *Tempo*'s mannered knowingness exactly what is required of a non-oppositional opposition?'.[25] In effect, *Tempo* was a journalistic by-product of a New Order which had emasculated explicitly 'political' Opposition newspapers as well as Opposition political parties. The magazine dominated the market and consistently managed to attract the largest total advertising revenue for magazines since 1982 (amounting to 24.2% or Rp.20,879 million in 1992).[26]

The company behind *Tempo*, PT Grafiti Pers, is driven by a forceful Minahasan business person, Eric F.H. Samola, treasurer of the ruling Golkar political organisation, together with Ciputra, the group's major financier, a real estate entrepreneur and director of the Pembangunan Jaya company. Following the success of the magazine, Grafiti moved into book publishing, then established a string of related magazines (including *Zaman* [*Era*] which was later reshaped as up-market *Matra* [*Dimension*], *Humor* and *Medika* [*Medical*]). Grafiti also cooperates in the publication of others in the same group (such as *SWAsembada* [*SELF-Sufficient*] and a 'magazine of law and democracy' called *Forum Keadilan* [*Justice Forum*]). In July 1993 a co-publication agreement between Grafiti and the foundation which publishes the long-established, independent *Horison* broke down after a single issue. Grafiti Pers then decided to go it alone and in early 1994 launched a glossy quarterly literary and cultural magazine entitled *Kalam* [*Quill/Word*], to rival *Horison*. Despite the strength of these associated publications, the empire has been significantly weakened by the 1994 banning of *Tempo*. One early casualty is likely to be *Kalam*, yet to establish a readership, which may close to minimise losses.

Tempo itself has undergone several previous periods of instability. In 1986, in a conflict largely over conditions and management style, a large number of staff at all levels left *Tempo* to establish a rival newsweekly, *Editor*, with the apparent financial backing of real estate businessman Mohammad Sulaiman Hidayat[27] reportedly together with a daughter of then Vice-President Sudharmono. While closing the gap on its predecessor during the early years, *Editor* was unable to topple *Tempo*. In 1991, for example, it managed sales of 90,000, barely half of *Tempo*'s 171,000.[28] In 1992, it commanded less than 4% of total magazine advertising earnings compared to *Tempo*'s 24.2%.[29] By 1993 *Editor* was reportedly struggling as it sought new investors to help cover sustained losses. When it was banned together with *Tempo* in June 1994, it was reportedly in financial difficulties. *Tempo*, on the other hand, recovered from the 1986 split to retain its place as the soundest magazine in the Indonesian marketplace.

Coincidentally, in April 1982, the month *Tempo* was temporarily banned for its coverage of the general election campaigning, Grafiti gained control of Surabaya's *Jawa Pos [Java Post]* daily, originally established as a family concern in 1949. Dahlan Iskan, then head of *Tempo*'s Surabaya bureau, was selected to revamp the paper, a task he conducted with a success undreamed of by his Jakarta backers. Within a decade this insignificant company had become one of the top 200 in Indonesia, ranking 188 in the list of company tax-payers in 1990.[30] By 1992 the *Jawa Pos* was the third largest newspaper in Indonesia with an estimated circulation of about 350,000, a 'regional' capable of taking on the 'nationals' and winning. This paper was quickly used by Tempo-Grafiti as a base to expand into the regions, thus spawning its own regional 'family' headed by Dahlan Iskan.

This *Jawa Pos* group bought controlling shares in *Manuntung* in Balikpapan and *Cahaya Siang [Afternoon Ray]* in Manado, North Sulawesi (although *Cahaya Siang* subsequently joined the *Media Indonesia* group, discussed below). It then developed cooperative associations with (and became major shareholder in) the dailies *Akcaya* in Pontianak, *Mercusuar* in Palu, *Fajar [Dawn]* in Ujungpandang, *Manado Post* in North Sulawesi, *Suara Maluku [Voice of the Moluccas]* in Ambon, *Suara Nusa [Island Voice]* in Mataram, Lombok, *Riau Pos* in Pekanbaru, *Cendrawasih Post* in Jayapura, the *Batam Post* in Batam, *Independent* in Jambi, the *Palangkaraya Pos* (later designated the *Kalteng Pos [Central Kalimantan Post]*) in central Kalimantan, and a new Bengkulu daily (established with the support of the rival to *Jawa Pos*, the *Surabaya Post*) *Semarak [Lustre]*.

In Surabaya it also runs the business daily *Suara Indonesia [Voice of*

Indonesia], and has drawn into its group the thrice-monthly sensationalist entertainment magazine *Liberty*, the children's magazine *Mentari Putera Harapan [Sun of the Children of Hope]* and the papers *Karya Darma [The Product of Duty]* (a rural development daily), the weekly *Dharma Nyata [Clear Duty]* and in Surakarta the Javanese-language tabloid *Jawa Anyar* (established in 1993). For what editors described as 'social reasons' it also advises the management of a pro-Golkar paper, *Bhirawa*, although it was stated there is no direct financial stake in that publication.[31] In October 1991 it initiated a weekly sports paper, *Kompetisi [Competition]* and in July 1992 drew the deeply indebted Surabaya daily *Memorandum* into its fold taking a 50% share.[32]

More recently it has commenced the tabloids *Agribis [Agribusiness]*, and *KOMPU-Tek [COMPUTER-Technology]*. In fact, by January 1993, it appeared that the *Jawa Pos* had collaborative arrangements with more than 20 smaller regional papers as well as a broad range of publications covering most sectors of the market in East Java.[33] In addition it owns several of the printing companies associated with the newspapers and formerly own Radio FM Strato in Surabaya and the motor magazine *Mobil Indonesia [Indonesian Car]* (until it transferred this to the Jakarta *Tempo* branch of the concern). Of all the newly emerging major conglomerate groups, the *Jawa Pos* group created by Tempo-Grafiti seems to be coping best with the challenges of the 1990s.

The conglomerate decided to consolidate rather than expand in 1994, using the year to plan several new projects for 1995, including anticipated ventures in Palembang, Jambi and Lampung. By 1995 too, provided it succeeds in obtaining a publication permit, it hopes to be launching an English-language morning daily, the *Surabaya Daily News*, targeted at markets in Bali and eastern Indonesia with an opening circulation of 10,000. More ambitiously, it has declared 1995 to be the year of its diversification overseas. Boss Dahlan Iskan has been actively pursuing plans to invest in several regional Australian papers.[34]

Media Indonesia/Surya Persindo Group

The three empires discussed thus far were all founded prior to the government's policy of economic deregulation of the 1980s. They were based on existing publications, established and run by working journalists (in the case of the youngest, *Tempo*, collaborating with successful business people) and diversified gradually as they adjusted to the changing economic environment. All were strongly identified in the public mind with key individual personalities, editors who had stamped their own identity upon the group's flagship. The mid-1980s saw another breed of press empire emerging. The Media Indonesia/Surya Persindo Group provides an example of how a major entrepreneur with no prior experience in journalism invested in the press industry, with a clear investment strategy of regional diversification.

Surya Paloh, the Acehnese-born son of a police officer in North Sumatra, was a founder and chairperson of the local Medan branch of the anti-Communist and anti-Sukarno Indonesian Secondary School Student and Youth Action Front (KAPPI) in 1966. He became a Golkar activist prior to the 1971 election and was coordinator of the Golkar campaign in North Sumatra and Aceh in the 1977 elections, during which time he drew close to several senior Golkar figures, including the then Vice-President Adam Malik. After the 1977 election he was appointed member of the People's Consultative Assembly (MPR) and moved to Jakarta, becoming chairperson of the Association of Young Indonesian Entrepreneurs (*Himpunan Pengusaha Muda Indonesia*, HIPMI) within months of his arrival in the capital. As a founder of the influential military-aligned lobby group, Communication Forum for the Sons and Daughters of Retired Members of the Armed Forces (*Forum Komunikasi Putra-Putri Purnawirawan ABRI*, FKPPI), he was in close contact with some of the nation's most powerful families. His early fortune derived mainly from a successful food catering business, PT Indocater, but influential connections did his ventures no harm.[35] Surya Paloh came to be seen frequently in the company of the President's son, Bambang Trihatmojo, boss of the powerful Bimantara conglomerate.[36] Surya Paloh is also a relation by marriage of Rosano Barack, a director of Bimantara.[37]

In 1985 the Acehnese entrepreneur expanded from catering to establish PT Surya Persindo, a publishing holding company, to produce the controversial straight-talking, rather flashy daily *Prioritas*. Initially the paper was printed at PT Sinar Agape Press, owned by *Sinar Harapan*, which provided some technical assistance with layout. Surya Paloh also poached two senior *Sinar Harapan* journalists, Panda Nababan and Derek Manangka, to become Deputy General Editor and Managing Editor of the new *Prioritas*.[38] That changes were taking place in the industry was signalled when *Prioritas* became the first Indonesian daily to feature regular colour photos on its front and back pages.

Close friendships with the political elite did not stop *Prioritas* becoming the second paper to have its SIUPP revoked (the first being *Sinar Harapan*), on 29 June 1987. The revocation order stated that *Prioritas* had published 'reports which are not true and are not based on facts, and which are cynical, insinuative and tendentious', and that it had deviated from its SIUPP provisions to publish 75% economic news and only 25% general news. However, it was widely believed that the paper met its demise because of its outspoken discussion of various corruption cases and its ability to 'anticipate' government economy policy in an embarrassing manner.[39] Unsubstantiated claims by interests associated with the paper suggested Minister of Information Harmoko had initially been keen to obtain shares in *Prioritas* but had been refused by Surya Paloh, causing the Minister to take a somewhat jaundiced view of the paper and its publisher.

After applying for a new SIUPP for another paper tentatively named *Realitas [Reality]* in August 1987, Surya Paloh was refused on the dubious grounds that the market would not sustain another 'general daily'. From documentation held by the Newspaper Publishers' Association (SPS) it would appear that his application was still officially 'being processed by the Department of Information' more than five years later. In the intervening period licences have been issued for other 'general dailies' (such as the Islamic *Republika*), to the consternation of those involved in *Prioritas*.

Unperturbed, in January 1988 Surya Paloh initiated a cooperative arrangement with the publishers of a modest 12,000 circulation entertainment magazine, called *Vista*. After injecting a massive Rp. 11.5 billion and about 40 former *Prioritas* staffers, Surya Paloh visually revamped and expanded the periodical, later re-christening it *Vista TV*, and including a detailed program guide to the private television station owned by Bimantara, *Rajawali Citra Televisi Indonesia* (RCTI).[40] The glossy colour magazine concentrates on television, film, video and music news, and now includes program guides to more than a dozen Indonesian and international satellite television stations.

About twelve months after acquiring *Vista TV*, with still no SIUPP for a new paper, Surya Paloh obtained access to an existing SIUPP for a daily paper by becoming co-publisher of lack-lustre *Media Indonesia*, established in 1969 by Teuku Yousli Syah.[41] Paloh breathed new life into it, injecting funds from PT Surya Persindo and employing a large number of former *Prioritas* staff. After its launch on 11 March 1989 with a logo reminiscent of *Prioritas*, its popularity rose steadily. Visually, *Media Indonesia* was a breath of fresh air: its layout and design was innovative, its typeface easy on the eye, and its regular features varied and attractive. It challenged the established promotional strategies of the market leaders, which generally depend on a secure base of regular subscribers, by instead aggressively courting the impulse reader who buys a newspaper on the street rather than having it home delivered. Another innovation agreement with taxi companies meant free copies of *Media Indonesia* were placed in cabs for customers to browse. The paper passed its 'break-even point' within a rapid 20 months, when its daily circulation hit 85,000, despite (or perhaps because of) a 'final stern warning' (the penultimate notification prior to a revocation of SIUPP) from the Department of Information for a 23 March 1990 article comparing President Suharto with Pharaoh.[42]

By February 1991, *Media Indonesia* was advertising a circulation of 300,000, 72% of whom were holders of bank accounts (an implied measure of middle-class status), a 'market which really possesses a very high "disposable income"' (the English term was used).[43] The ad glossed one of the company's shrewdest promotional stategies to bump up circulation: that of offering gift subscriptions to customers holding bank accounts with the Bank Central Asia (BCA), which was partially financing Surya Paloh's press venture.

Paloh and Surya Persindo quickly diversified into regional publishing. In 1989-90 he invested in editorial and management assistance (often regarded as euphemisms for 'take-overs') reaching a total of ten regional publications in Banda Aceh (the weeklies *Peristiwa* [*Event*], *Aceh Post*), Medan (daily *Mimbar Umum* [*Public Forum*]), Padang (daily *Semangat* [*Spirit*]), Palembang (*Sumatera Express*), southern Sumatra (daily *Lampung Post*), Bandung (daily *Gala*), Yogyakarta (daily *Yogya Post* formerly *Masa Kini* [*These Times*], affiliated with the Islamic Muhammadiyah organisation[44]), Pontianak (*Dinamika Berita* [*News Dynamics*]), Manado (*Cahaya Siang* [*Midday Light*]) and in Denpasar (*Nusatenggara*, known as *Nusra*, in collaboration with the Bali regional military command). While he has obtained some flagging regional papers at fire-sale prices (the *Aceh Post*, for example was obtained for only Rp 1 million or US$543, while Medan's *Mimbar Umum* required a Rp 500 million initial investment), the stable of papers was estimated to be costing him about Rp 100 million per month in early 1990.[45] His target in these ventures was to reach 'break-even point' within a year, a goal which appears generally to have eluded him.

Surya Paloh's goal of fusing a national chain of newspapers was pursued with more zest than the expansion of the previous press groups mentioned. Papers in the family tended to adopt a common 'Surya Persindo' block-style lay-out and similar typeface, modelled on *Media Indonesia* and its predecessor *Prioritas*, as if to demonstrate their shared progenitor. Some observers have suggested that this, and the tendency for *Media Indonesia* daily and the group's regional partner publications to aim for similar market segments, may have hampered the overall sales growth of the group. They argue that newspaper readers in the regions regard *Media Indonesia* and its local affiliated paper as looking too similar to warrant purchasing both. By contrast, regional papers affiliated with the Kompas-Gramedia Group retained their separate styles, and were generally targeted at a lower socio-economic readership than the parent *Kompas* so as not to draw sales away from it.[46]

Surya Paloh's aggressive marketing strategy often generated friction and resentment with older proprietors (particularly of smaller regional papers). For example, he 'temporarily' closed down his two Aceh papers *Aceh Post* and *Peristiwa* at the end of 1990 and instead began selling *Media Indonesia* on the local Aceh market at only Rp 100 [about $AUD 0.07 cents], well under the Jakarta cover price of Rp 300, in an attempt to undercut and woo readers away from competing local publications.[47] The North Sumatra branch of the Newspaper Publishers Association (SPS) protested strongly about this practice, termed 'dumping', to which the Jakarta magnate responded that his strategy was prompted by the altruistic motive of raising the level of public knowledge, and the more pragmatic goal of increasing circulation to attract greater advertising, the life-blood of any newspaper, and a commodity in increasingly short supply.[48] 'Dumping' and other such pressures from the major national conglomerates exacerbated the declining fortunes of the unaffiliated regionals, forcing them to either close or to seek a sympathetic financier.

More than the three previous conglomerates mentioned, Surya Paloh's empire was hit hardest by the economic difficulties of the 1990s which forced a streamlining of the corporate family. By the end of 1992 several other of his regional papers had been forced to close (like *Semangat*, *Yogya Post* and *Nusa Tenggara*) or down-grade from dailies to weeklies (like *Gala*). The flagship *Media Indonesia* struggled to maintain a real circulation of 100,000, although a cover-price increase to Rp 500 helped offset the declining sales. Its share of advertising revenue, too, seemed to be dwindling from

6.7% (Rp 17,927 million) of newspaper advertising expenditure in 1991 to a projected 3.4% (Rp 9,367 million) in 1993.[49] Industry observers suggested that a significant proportion of *Media Indonesia*'s advertising was placed by companies financing the paper, which could suggest the business was in poor financial shape and inadequately attracting outside advertising.

Despite such setbacks the Surya Paloh group appears to be consolidating partially. In late 1992 interests associated with Surya Paloh successfully revamped the low-circulation Jakarta weekly *DeTIK [Moment]*, established in 1977. Within 18 months *DeTIK* was spectacularly converted into the capital city's most outspoken and sought-after newsweekly, boasting an impressive circulation of about 215,000 in early 1994 (and a rather dubious 450,000 when banned in June). With such indications of *DeTIK*'s success it appeared the Surya Persindo Group had modified its initial strategy of zealous regional expansion in order to consolidate and concentrate on the more lucrative (and politically critical) Jakarta market. Billed as a 'News and Opinion Tabloid Weekly' (although officially holding a publication permit as a 'crime' magazine), *DeTIK* sold for Rp 1200, or one-third that of glossy rival news weeklies like *Tempo* and *Editor*. Under energetic Deputy Chief Editor (and award winning film-maker) Eros Jarot, *DeTIK* captured the imagination particularly of younger politically active readers with its long topical interviews, racy columnists and 'action' photographs. Its style was reminiscent of bolder campus papers, not surprising since many of its forty journalists were young graduates from Gajah Mada University in Yogyakarta.

In February 1994, Jarot acknowledged that the spirit of political 'openness' being fostered by the government in the early 1990s assisted his paper, stating 'I have some strong supporters in Government. Some people genuinely want to see change'.[50] With such tacit support, *DeTIK* appeared to lead a charmed life, broaching subjects previously unthinkable, such as the banned book manuscript *Primadosa*, which challenged Suharto's role in the events of October 1965, and tensions between senior military officers and civilian proteges of the President. For example, in an interview published in 1993 Major General Sembiring Meliala, deputy leader of the Armed Forces contingent in parliament, castigated Minister Habibie, whom some in the military feared Suharto was grooming for the presidency in 1988. Among Jarot's supporters were progressive elements within the military, who were seeking to prepare for the post-Suharto period by fostering non-violent reform.

DeTIK's commercial success underlined the financial logic of the mass media: that news is a commodity, and that credible and investigative journalism can generate high circulation and sales. The political significance of *DeTIK* was as a measure of the latitude available to shrewdly managed and well-targeted newspapers. It brought back a spirit of political risk-taking into an industry, somewhat more preoccupied with commercial consolidation since the 1978 bans. Of the three weeklies shut in June 1994, its staff were the most independent and assertive, and its rise most meteoric. *DeTIK* was also the first of the banned publications to circumvent the ban (if only fleetingly) by taking over the name and publication permit of a lacklustre weekly broadsheet *Simponi* [Symphony], established in 1972. In the first week of October 1994, the new look *Simponi*, staffed by ex-*DeTIK* journalists, sold out its inaugural print-run of 130,000, with driving-force *DeTIK* editor Eros Jarot officially listed only as 'consultant' to the original editor-in-chief, Syamsu Hadi. Within days the government had manoeuvred Hadi into 'temporarily' suspending publication after officials identified minor contraventions of his publication permit. Irrespective of whatever efforts by Jarot to re-float a *DeTIK* avatar are sucessful, *DeTIK* has demonstrated graphically that the marketplace will enthusiastically support incisive critical newspapers prepared to challenge the government and advance the public debate towards democratisation.

New players

Neither Surya Paloh's aggressive style nor his entry as one of the potential big players in the industry is unique. Other indigenous Indonesian (*pribumi*) entrepreneurs have invested heavily.[51] For example, Sutrisno Bachir from the Ika Muda business group established a management and editorial cooperation agreement in November 1990 with *Berita Buana [World News]*, effectively becoming the paper's publisher, although legal title still lay in the hands of General Chairperson and Editor-in-Chief Sukarno Hadi Wibowo, a pro-military figure who collaborates with the State Intelligence Coordinating Agency (BAKIN) in publishing the country's only Chinese language daily. About 20% of the print run of this new-style *Berita Buana* was initially distributed free, door to door, to targeted suburbs or housing complexes as an inducement to subscribers. The more vibrant younger staff latched quickly onto an attractive, eye-catching format, backed by straight-talking reports. Circulation was gradually improving.[52] However, a split developed over its handling of the Dili Massacre in November 1991 and general coverage of the military, as newcomers confronted resistance from the formal owner and his old staff who were anxious lest the paper be banned over its critical coverage. By January 1992 many of those brought in by Sutrisno Bachir had left the paper, together with the entrepreneur.

Berita Buana, however, was only one of Sutrisno Bachir's press ventures. Since 1986 he and another entrepreneur Dali Sofari, had been funding *Mode Indonesia [Indonesian Fashion]*, and a sister publication, the short story magazine *Aneka Ria [All Kinds of Fun]*, although ownership later shifted to their partner, Nuniek H. Musawa. Sutrisno Bachir, as management chief with 40% of the shares, was the effective publisher of the monthly banking magazine, *Infobank* (in collaboration with former president directors of two sizeable banks, Bank Duta and Bank Bukopin[53]). He was also Management Adviser and effective publisher of *Prospek [Prospect])* economic weekly, in cooperation with publisher of *Pos Kota*. His takeover (with Nuniek H. Musawa) of *Anda [You]* 'pop' psychology monthly, which he re-named *Anda Bos [You, the Successful Person's Barometer]*,[54] was unprofitable however, with the magazine closing in early 1991. Bachir was rumoured to be paying the journalists he recruited highly, but was unable to turn a profit in his press companies, declaring in June 1993, 'I have failed in the media business, but I still love it!'. By 1993, the national credit squeeze had forced the Ika Muda Group to restructure its debt load, withdraw significantly from its publishing enterprises and concentrate on its main business in fisheries, to stave off the threat of bankruptcy.[55] By mid-1994 *Prospek* was reportedly in the hands of a major bank which was trying to find a buyer for it. The involvement of leading bankers in *Infobank* may have been a factor in the surfacing earlier of unconfirmed rumours that the funds behind the Ika Muda Group's *Prospek* magazine came from Bank Duta, controlled by three foundations headed by the president.[56]

Another prominent 'pribumi' entrepreneur, Aburizal Bakrie,[57] President Director of PT Bakrie Brothers and currently head of the Indonesian Chamber of Commerce (KADIN), has invested in *Popular*, an entertainment monthly, and *Pelita* (of which he is a Vice-Chairperson). Company director of *Pelita* is Muslim entrepreneur Fadel Muhammad, the President Director of the Bukaka business group, who, though a relative newcomer to the press industry, also holds the largest share of *Warta Ekonomi [Economic News]* weekly.[58] In January 1993 Bakrie Brothers expanded from print into electronic media when the conglomerate was granted the fourth commercial TV licence for *Cakrawala Andalas Televisi* (ANTEVE). After the banning of *DeTIK*, there were rumours that Bakrie Brothers were intending to launch a new *DeTIK* clone as part of their continuing push into the mass media.

The capacity of younger entrepreneurs like Aburizal Bakrie and Fadel Muhammad to invest in the press in the 1980s was largely due to their successes in other enterprises. Policies, such as Presidential Decision No. 10 in 1980 requiring the vetting of government purchases over Rp 500 million by a special team, benefited indigenous entrepreneurs who were given preference. Many were further helped by support from Ginanjar Kartasasmita, the Minister for Increasing the Utilisation of Domestic Production, who was keen to build up a strong domestic entrepreneurial base.[59] With their footing in lucrative non-press businesses, an increasing number of fast-rising entrepreneurs were prepared to risk slow returns in the print media industry. Reportedly included amongst those investing from outside the industry from the mid-1980s were Bambang N. Rachmadi, Mohamad Suleiman Hidayat (in *Editor*), Nirwan Bakrie and Ponco Sutowo (in *Jayakarta*). More established capitalists such as the Suharto associates Liem Siu Liong, Sukamdani Sahid Gitosarjono (in *Bisnis Indonesia*) and the President's half-brother Probosutejo (in Semarang's *Kartika* and Yogyakarta's *Kedaulatan Rakyat*) were also part of this trend.[60]

The Palace enters the press

While several such entrepreneurs had invested heavily in the press during the boom years of the 1980s, on the surface the industry did not then seem to have attracted interest from members of the Suharto family. This contrasted starkly with the television industry in which the three pioneering private channels, initially in Jakarta, Bandung, and Surabaya (but now carried nationally on Palapa satellite) were effectively monopolised by companies associated with President Suharto's family. Son Bambang Trihatmojo owned RCTI, issued with the first commercial television license in 1987.[61] Foster brother Sudwikatmono gained the second commercial license in 1990, heading *Surya Citra Televisi*, SCTV. In August 1990 TPI (*Televisi Pendidikan Indonesia*, Indonesian Educational Television), controlled by President Suharto's daughter H. Hardiyanti Indra Rukmana (known affectionately as 'mBak Tutut') through her holding company Cipta Lamtoro Gung Persada, gained the third license.

After the 1986 banning of *Sinar Harapan* Sudwikatmono had attempted to obtain the paper, but this did not eventuate.[62] However in March 1991 a foundation headed by Sudwikatmono (and including *Tempo* backer Ciputra) began publishing a 24-page weekly tabloid, *Bintang Indonesia {Indonesian Star}* devoted to television, video, radio and film news, and purporting to 'meet society's need for light reading'.[63] Sudwikatmono and Ciputra reportedly invested about ten billion rupiah and, in an attempt to capture the market identified by Kompas-Gramedia's lucrative *Monitor* magazine banned only months previously, enlisted 20 staff from *Monitor*.[64] *Bintang Indonesia* commenced with a print run of 200,000 and ambitions of topping 500,000 by the end of the year, though this appears not be have been achieved.[65]

Following this success, in September 1993 Sudwikatmono launched a 'development newsweekly', cheekily called *Sinar [Ray]* to evoke memories of the defunct *Sinar Harapan* daily which he had attempted to obtain in 1986. Sudwikatmono was financier, president of the board of directors of the magazine's publishing company and the publication's 'Pembina' (Founder). The magazine's hands-on 'editorial adviser' was Abdul Gafur, former Minister for Youth Affairs and Golkar activist. More down-market than *Editor* or *Tempo*, *Sinar* was clearly targeted at the ethnic Chinese community and included such features as a one-page Chinese horoscope (*hokkie*). By early 1994, the magazine was in dire straits, with a circulation that had plummeted from 30,000 to 12,000, well below the illusive 50,000 break-even point. During the first six months, Sudwikatmono reportedly had poured more than Rp 4,000 million (approximately $AUD 2.5 million) into the fledgling magazine.[66]

In April 1994, Sudwikatmono withheld the publication for several weeks to assess its future; a future undoubtedly made more rosy with the removal of the three major rival weeklies the following June. As the sole remaining newsweekly magazine, *Sinar* is best-placed to capitalise on the elimination of all competitors. With the market-leaders now banned, it would be surprising if Sudwikatmono could not improve *Sinar*'s fortunes miraculously. He can readily tap the proven market of about 550,000 magazine purchasers now going begging, and absorb advertising revenue flowing from the three defunct weeklies. *Sinar*'s mediocre personnel could be upgraded with imports from the hundreds of highly skilled newspaper staff now unemployed.

Whatever its ultimate fortunes, *Sinar* is notable as the first public step into the high-profile newsweekly market by a member of the

Suharto family. Public acceptance of any publication associated so transparently with the presidential family, however, may be slow. However, once papers like *DeTIK* have demonstrated the market demand for investigative, politically critical publications, it would not be surprising if *Sinar* attempts to capture the current floating readership, by encreasingly bold reporting of events of public interest. For example, *Sinar* was one of several publications which incurred stern Department of Information warnings in the weeks after the bans of *Tempo, Editor* and *DeTIK* for their reporting of the bans and subsequent demonstrations.[67]

The coalescence of interests in television and print media appears to have been beneficial, too, for another member of the Suharto clan. In 1989 Hardiyanti Rukmana, as General Chairperson and publisher, established a 32-page weekly tabloid for women, *Wanita Indonesia* [*Indonesian Woman*], which devotes eight pages to TPI programs. By 1991 the colour paper claimed an impressive circulation of around 240,000.[68] After the June 1994 ban of *Editor* newsweekly, it was rumoured that Hardiyanti Rukmana was attempting to gain control, through a third party, of any transmuted offspring magazine. In return, she would provide political patronage and influence to acquire the necessary new publication permit. If any such negotiations actually did take place, they were certainly not made public and can not be independently confirmed.

Also more a matter of industry speculation rather than public knowledge was the relationship between Surya Paloh's Surya Persindo company and Bambang Trihatmojo's Bimantara Group. The *Far Eastern Economic Review* reported that as early as 1988 (the year he had revamped *Vista* magazine) Surya Paloh had required a capital injection from Bimantara.[69] At the close of 1991 when an economic downturn was beginning to bite hard, the Surya Persindo group was partially restructured to give major shareholders, including representatives of the Bimantara Group, a greater say in executive decisions. These new arrangements were extremely discrete.[70] While numerous journalists and several highly-placed editors were convinced of the connection, which was widely acknowledged within press circles, it was not something about which they felt they could write publicly given the delicate nature of the Bimantara's political connections.

A link between the two organisations did become public however, when in April 1992, Harry Kuntoro, former Deputy Director of the Bimantara's Central Control Unit and its corporate secretary, became the Vice-President of the Surya Persindo Group, the number two office-bearer after Surya Paloh himself.[71] However, little detail was released regarding the precise relationship between Bimantara and Surya Persindo. One unnamed source in a reliable Jakarta newsweekly claimed that 'Bimantara does not hold shares in [Surya Persindo]. Even if there are some, they are only private shares held by Bimantara executives'. Kuntoro, who was the President Director of a Bimantara real estate and housing development company, PT Bimantara Siti Wisesa, said of the arrangement with Surya Persindo, 'It is a management cooperation between SP and Bimantara. Meaning that SP pays a management fee to Bimantara, not to me'. This 'cooperation' is for an unspecified period.[72]

That such a link was emerging publicly seems to have been partly due to Surya Persindo's grave need for financial restructuring. Its national syndicate was extensive but expensive. Facing economic constraints in the 1990s it responded by shedding staff and cutting costs. Bimantara too was being forced to trim its operations, tightening strings to subsidiaries, presumably seeking a clearer return on investment, and, in June 1992, 'de-activating' about 26 unprofitable associated ventures in the conglomerate.

That Bimantara remains coy about the precise nature of its relationship to Surya Persindo is not unusual since it customarily preferred a low profile. Similarly, *Media Indonesia* certainly sought to maintain a reputation as a politically independent, financially autonomous publication. Politically-aligned newspapers had not fared well during the New Order. Readers, it might be surmised, tend to buy papers which are not obviously sectarian or associated with known political interest groups, papers which are prepared to write about contentious issues (even if, in the case of *Kompas* for example, in a measured style). During its period of growth *Media Indonesia* newspaper had gained a reputation as being bold in its coverage of such controversial events as the November 1991 Dili massacre and was cautioned by the authorities for its critical political coverage on more than one occasion.

Journalists with the publication argue strenuously that the editorial and news policy is not determined by the financiers. However, Surya Paloh himself takes a close interest in such policy and has reined in his staff on several occasions when their coverage was likely to reflect poorly upon members of the First Family, companies associated with financial backers of the newspaper, or, in the case of the trial of East Timorese independence leader Xanana Gusmao, likely to inflame military antagonisms. Overall, his journalists point out that Surya Paloh has employed and devolved responsibility to a young, idealist and energetic staff, many of whom were activists from the campus press. He is regarded by them as friendly, approachable and generally supportive. They are proud that Surya Paloh has been one of the most outspoken critics of the legislation and ministerial regulations governing press licences, to the extent of approaching the Supreme Court in late 1992 requesting a Judicial Review of the ministerial provisions for banning newspapers. That such a challenge to ministerial authority should come from someone so closely associated with an influential member of the presidential family suggests something of the complexity of State-press relations in contemporary Indonesia.

Nonetheless, some industry figures view with concern the involvement of Bimantara in PT Surya Persindo, which together with Sudwikatmono's *Bintang Indonesia* and *Sinar* and Hardiyanti Rukmana's *Wanita Indonesia*, may represent a calculated move by members of the presidential family to establish a foothold in the print media, after their success in the electronic media. Michael Vatikiotis, the *Far Eastern Economic Review*'s correspondent in Jakarta for four years in the 1980s, asserts that 'one way in which Suharto appeared to be trying to curb the press by early 1990 was by having members of his own family buy into the media. All three of the commercial television stations, and a major publishing group, "Media Indonesia", were controlled by family members.'[73] Apprehensive that such 'newcomers' as Surya Paloh have considerable financial backing and political connections, one leading editor whose paper had been banned several times, expressed concerns that the industry was 'not a level playing field' any longer.[74] If the motivation of such entrepreneurs was solely financial, he argues, they would make greater profits with less risk in other sectors of the economy. The driving intention must logically be to strengthen their political position.

Adherents of the old 'pers perjuangan' school, like Mochtar Lubis, question the ethics of the new press investors and are vehemently opposed to the spread of conglomerates into the press, warning 'it is certain that they will use their publications to protect and promote their own interests. If necessary, papers will lie to the community for their own interests.'[75] In an allusion perhaps to the investments of people like Harmoko and the presidential family, Lubis pointed to the 'dangers' of large papers consuming small regional ventures, 'even more so, if it is actually the high-level government officials themselves who own these press publications; that is clearly not right'. This apprehension was endorsed by Christianto Wibisono, head of the influential Indonesian Business Data Centre (PDBI), who has stressed his belief that the conglomerates were entering the industry both for financial and political advantage.[76]

With the President deemed unlikely to continue beyond the end of current five-year term in 1998 by which time he will be 77, it seems likely that new entrants to the press industry are seeking a niche in preparation for a post-Suharto era, when access to a newspaper-reading public may enhance both commercial interests and political leverage. While the 1982 Press Act provided stiff penalties for 'Whoever deliberately and in a way opposed to law uses press publications for his personal or group interests', there was clearly nothing illegal about press acquisitions as part of this shrewd economic and political strategy.

Concern over the increasing concentration of press outlets in the hands of a decreasing number of major capital city syndicates goes beyond apprehension at the growing influence of the presidential family. The Code of Ethics of Press Companies, formulated in September 1968, had explicitly declared its opposition to industry concentration which it regarded as unhealthy. The code states, 'attempts leading to a concentration in or monopoly of the press world by any group, or attempts by Indonesian Press companies to exert control over one another are not permitted'.[77] As the power of the press empires has grown since the mid-1980s critics have reiterated the code's warning.

At a press seminar in Solo in February 1985 B.M. Diah, a founder of the Republican flagship *Merdeka* daily in 1945 whose financial interests grew to include several related publications and the Hyatt Aryaduta Hotel, but who had not been able to compete with the major press conglomerates, predicted that what was to be feared in Indonesia was not the government, but the increasing concentration of press ownership in a few hands, which would give rise to a monopoly over public opinion.[78] It was a concern which did not diminish. In September 1992, Mara Karma, a senior journalist formerly with the crusading *Indonesia Raya* daily, called on the House of Representatives (DPR) to set up a commission to study the impact of increased capital investment in the media, together with the impact of the 1982 Press Law. At a seminar at the prestigious University of Indonesia, he argued that 'It is dangerous to let large media companies grow larger by taking over smaller ones'. Once again, the fear was expressed that this may lead to the danger of 'monopolising public opinion'.[79] It was a concern felt particularly by weaker sections of the press to whom I turn my attention in the following chapter.

ENDNOTES

1. Quoted from the translation in Razak 1985:194.

2. For example, Mochtar Lubis's *Indonesia Raya* was offered printing and setting machinery from the *Manila Times*, the *Straits Times* in Kuala Lumpur and the Australian *Mirror* Group when it re-opened in 1968, but the importation required official clearance given by Adam Malik, then Senior Minister for Social and Political Affairs *(Indonesia* Raya, 30/10/68, p.5).

3. Dhakidae (1991) has superbly documented this process of capital accumulation by *Kompas, Sinar Harapan* and *Tempo,* and it is from this source that much of the following discussion is drawn.

4. Quotation taken from an advertisement placed in *The Australian* newspaper's special survey supplement on Indonesia, 15 July 1994, p.14.

5. Jakob Oetama, 'Berkat Kemurahan Tuhan' (special brochure, no date, published by *Kompas* June 1988) quoted in Dhakidae 1991:239. Despite its disingenuous name the BPS *(Badan Pendukung Sukarnoisme)* or Body for the Support of Sukarnoism, formed in September 1964 to oppose Communist influence in the press industry, was highly critical of President Sukarno and particularly his proximity to the political Left. Sukarno banned the organisation in December 1964, after which time the Minister of Information closed down two dozen pro-BPS newspapers and the PWI expelled members sympathetic to the BPS. For a pro-BPS interpretation of these events, see Tribuana Said & D.S. Moeljanto (1983), Perlawanan Pers Indonesia *(BPS)* terhadap Gerakan *PKI,* Penerbit Sinar Harapan, Jakarta.

6. The 1980 Census figures on religion reported 87% Muslim, 9% Christian, 2% Hindu and 1% Buddhist (cited in G. Hugo, T. Hull, V. Hull & G. Jones (1987), *The Demographic Dimension in Indonesian Development,* Oxford University Press, Singapore, p.24.

7. On the forced amalgamation of (1978), *The Army and Politics* in *Indonesia,* Cornell University Press, Ithaca, pp.245-72.

8. Benedict Anderson (1994), 'Rewinding "Back to the Future"': The Left and Constitutional Democracy' (pp. 128-42) in David Bourchier and John Legge (eds.) (1994), *Democracy in Indonesia: 1950s and 1990s,* Monash CSEAS, Clayton, particularly p.140. A useful study of *Kompas* (concentrating on selected editorials and the coverage of particular political and social issues) is Tjipta Lesmana (1985), 20 *Tahun Kompas: Profil Pers Indonesia Dewasa Ini,* Erwin-Rika Press, Jakarta.

9. See Ari Satriyo Wibowo (1993), 'Mencari Harga yang Benar', *SWA,* November 1993, pp.92-3.

10. Not all the group's endeavours have been successful. Their film company went

bankrupt, the shrimp culturing concern was closed down, and their Grasera supermarkets are apparently not particularly remunerative. An orange plantation was a slow starter, as was a tissue paper factory. (See 'Seperempat Abad Oom Pasikom', *Tempo*, 30 June 1990, pp.80-1.) The figure of 38 companies is given in Michael Vatikiotis 'Masses of Media', *Far Eastern Economic Review*, 26 July 1990, pp.46-7.

11. "Daftar Perusahaan dan Perorangan Penerima Piagam Pembayar Pajak", Editor, 26 Januari 1991, pp.80-1. While the accuracy of such a listing is clearly open to question, since the President's extraordinarily affluent relative Probosutedjo only appears behind Utama at 127th position, Utama's appearance in such company indicates something of the financial success generated by the Kompas-Gramedia empire.

12. The *Kompas* parent company, PT Kompas Media Nusantara was listed as the 32nd largest tax-payer in 1990, down from its 28th ranking in 1989 (see 'Seperempat Abad Oom Pasikom', *Tempo*, 30 June 1990, pp.80-1). It fell to 46th place in 1991, with the book publishing wing, PT Gramedia ranking 151 ("Daftar Perusahaan dan Perorangan Penerima Piagam Pembayar Pajak", *Editor*, 26 Januari 1991, pp.80-1). In 1988, when the group included only 19 companies, total assets were estimated by Christianto Wibisono's authoritative Pusat Data Bisnis Indonesia to be in excess of Rp.200 billion (see 'Oom Pasikom Terbang Tinggi', *Tempo*, 26 August 1989, p.27).

13. See Table 3. Katoppo makes the point elsewhere that such calculations of advertising revenue (as used here and elsewhere in this essay) are based on 'gross advertising expenditures, meaning it is advertising space used converted into rupiah based mainly on the officially known advertising rates as published by the media'. In fact, space may often be given away or sold at less than listed rates. This is highly likely to occur with companies associated with a particular media group. See Ernst Katoppo (1994), 'Advertising industry enjoys healthy growth', *The Jakarta Post*, 14/1/94.

14. USIS 1992 Vol.2, p.14 gives these figures. Dhakidae (1991) gives only 500,000 for 1987 and 570,000 for 1988. Nonetheless, the acceleration since 1986 was unparalleled.

15. Junaedhie 1991:170.

16. Ostensibly the ban was because the paper had published speculative reports on the economy and devaluation likely to cause 'restlessness' among the population. Some observers believe a more likely reason was the paper's editorial jousts at business monopolies, which might have been interpreted as business interests of President Suharto and his family. See Max Lane (1986), 'Why Sinar Harapan was silenced', *Inside Indonesia*, No. 9, December, pp.6-7.

17. These figures are rounded off from those given in *Data Oplah dan Peredaran IPPPN Tahun 1991*, pp.12 & 32. Such statistics must be regarded as of questionable accuracy, particularly since an inflated figure is in the newspapers' own interest. Nonetheless, the general ranking is widely acknowledged as accurate.

18. Table 7.5 in Subakti & Katoppo 1993:51. This table indicates however that *Suara Pembaruan's* percentage of newspaper advertising expenditure has been declining from 15.2% in 1989 to a projected 10.3% for 1993.

19. See 'Bang Jaya, Adik Baru SP', *Tempo*, 9 September 1989, p.40.

20. Details from interview with Aristides Katoppo, a senior member of the Sinar Harapan group (5/2/93); USIS 1992 Vol 1, p.36; Dhakidae 1991:32533; and 'Suara bukan Sinar', *Tempo*, 14 February 1987, p.25.

21. Quoted in Patrick Walters and Lenore Taylor, 'Jakarta cautions leading editors amid clampdown on media', *The Australian* (23 June 1994), reported in apakabar@clark.net 24 June 1994.

22. The other businessperson close to the palace who was reportedly involved in early discussion for control of *Tempo*, was Hasyim Joyohadikusumo, the older brother of Prabowo Joyohadikusumo and son of technocrat Prof. Sumitro Joyohadikusumo. Prabowo, a fast-rising military officer, is married to one of President Suharto's daughters. Bob Hasan, one of Indonesia's wealthiest entrepreneurs, apparently has a financial interest in the sports magazine *Sportif*, and maintains a high public profile on the executive of the All Indonesia Athletics Association and in sports entrepreneurial ventures (see the underground publication, *Kompak*, 4th Week, July 1994).

23. On *Tempo*, see Dhakidae 1991:255-269 & 351-62.

24. See Christianto Wibisono (1991), 'Transformasi Pers dari Profesi ke Bisnis?' in Pet Parmono (ed.) (1991), *Peringatan Hari Pers Nasional 1991: Reorientasi Pers Nasional Menjelang Tahun 2000*, Panpus HPN 1991, Jakarta, pp.30-4, particularly p.32.

25. Anderson 1994:16.

26. See Table 3.

27. For background information on M.S. Hidayat, see Ohiao Halawa (1992), *Pahlawan Wiraswasta: Profil Sepuluh Pengusaha Indonesia*, Nyiur Indah Alam Sejati, Jakarta, pp.119-30.

28. Departemen Penerangan (1992), *Data Oplah dan Peredaran IPPPN Tahun 1991*, pp.15-6.

29. Subakti & Katoppo 1993:51.

30. 'Daftar Perusahaan dan Perorangan Penerima Piagam Pembayar Pajak', *Editor*, 26 Januari 1991, pp.80-1.

31. I am indebted to a group of senior staff and reporters at the *Jawa Pos* offices (20/1/93) who spent several hours clarifying my ideas in a discussion of a draft of this section.

32. Details in the preceding paragraph compiled from USIS (1992) (various sections); 'Ekspansi dalam Keterbatasan', *Tempo*, 20 October 1990, p.32; and 'Memo di Tangan Jawa Pos', *Editor*, 1 August 1992, p.16.

33. 'Pasar Besar, Oplah Turun', *Tempo*, 15 February 1992, p.33.

34. Interview with Dahlan Iskan, Perth, 3 June 1994.

35. Information on Surya Paloh from Halawa 1992:149-65 and 'Dia yang Tak Kunjung Kapok, *Prospek*, 28 March 1992, pp.50-1.

36. On the enormous holdings of Bimantara, see, e.g. Adam Schwarz's articles 'All is relative' and 'From oil to aircraft', in *The Far Eastern Economic Review [FEER]*, 30 April 1992, pp.54-7, plus related articles in the same issue. Schwarz writes, 'Of all the businesses owned by President Suharto's children, Bambang Trihatmodjo's Bimantara Group is the largest and has moved furthest along the path to becoming a sustainable corporate enterprise. But like other companies linked to the presidential family, Bimantara continues to depend heavily on preferential trading arrangements' (p.56).

37. 'MI Dikelola Bimantara', *Prospek*, 21 March 1992, p.18.

38. On the establishment of *Prioritas*, see 'Berwarna, dengan Kaca Rayban', *Tempo*, 10 May 1986, p.74.

39. On the banning of *Prioritas*, see 'Batalnya Sebuah SIUPP', *Tempo*, 4 July 1987, p.63.

40. On *Vista* (also known as *Vista FMTV*), see USIS 1992 Vol. 2, p.67 and Junaedhie 1991:274.

41. Material on Paloh and Surya Persindo is drawn pp.24-6 and 'Ekspansi dalam Keterbatasan' *Tempo*, from USIS 1992 Vol 1, 20 October 1990, p.32.

42. The two Executive Editors deemed responsible, Jasso Winarto and Elman Saragih Siadari, were technically fired, but in practice remained with the company.

43. See the advertisement for *Media Indonesia* in *Warta Ekonomi*, No. 36/II/4 February 1991, p.34. While official figures for 1991 list *Media Indonesia's* sales at just a fraction over 300,000 (Data *Oplah dan Peredaran IPPPN Tahun 1991*, p. 12), some industry observers are highly sceptical of this (with USIS 1992 Vol. 1 p.24 stating only 150,000).

44. On Surya Paloh's conflict with the former Muhammadiyah owners of *Masa Kini*, see 'Sengketa Selembar SIUPP', *Tempo*, 30 December 1989, p.21.

45. Michael Vatikiotis, 'Profits from regional papers', Far Eastern *Economic Review*, 26 July 1990, pp.46-7 and 'Dari Jakarta Turun ke Daerah', *Tempo*, 14 October 1989, p.40.

46. For a discussion of these contrasting editorial and marketing strategies, see Octarina 1991:179-183.

47. For a useful study of relationships between newspaper conglomerates and their regional affiliates, including *Media Indonesia, Aceh Post* and *Peristiwa*, see Joke Octarina (1991), 'Kerja Sama antara Surat Rabar Nasional di Daerah dengan Grup Penerbitan Pers Jakarta', unpublished thesis in the Fakultas Ilmu Sosial dan Ilmu Politik, Jurusan Ilmu Komunikasi, Universitas Indonesia, Depok.

48. See 'Jor-joran Menembus Pasar', *Tempo*, 22 December 1990, p.101.

49. See Table 3.

50. Much of this detail on *DeTIK* comes from Patrick Walters (1994) 'Feisty tabloid shakes up Indonesia', *The Weekend Australian*, 12-3 February, p.15.

51. For details of such investments by newcomer entrepreneurs, see Michael Vatikiotis, 'Masses of Media' and 'Profits from regional papers', both in *Far Eastern Economic Review*, 26 July 1990, pp.46-47; 'Muka-Muka Baru', *Tempo*, 10 March 1990, p.86; and also 'Jor-joran Menembus Pasar', *Tempo*, 22 December 1990, p.101. Other details from USIS 1992, various sections.

52. See 'Jor-joran Menembus Pasar', *Tempo*, 22 December 1990, p.101.

53. Respectively Abdulgani (as General Chairperson) and Muchtar Mandala (as Editor-in-Chief). Both are now non-active. See USIS (Vol. 2) 1992:27.

54. In the magazine's name, 'Bos' stood for 'Barometer Qrang Sukses', that is, the Successful Person's Barometer.

55. 'Dulu 'First Class', Kini Cukup Kelas Ekonomi', *DeTIK*, 30 June-6 July 1993, pp.8-9.

56. See Michael Vatikiotis, 'Masses of Media', *Far Eastern Economic Review*, 26 July 1990, pp.46-7.

57. For background biographical details on Aburizal Bakrie and others, see *Tempo* (1986), *Apa & Siapa Sejumlah Orang Indonesia 1985-1986*, Grafitipers, Jakarta.

58. For background information on Fadel Muhammad see Halawa 1992:91-116.

59. On the benefits such entrepreneurs gained from government regulations and encouragement from Ginanjar, see 'Mencetak Pengusaha Tangguh', *SWA*, November 1993, pp.46-9.

60. According to 'Peluang Besar, Uang Kurang?', Prospek, 23 February 1991, pp.9-10. Probosutejo's interest is *Kartika (partly* owned by the Diponegoro Regional Military Command) is noted in 'Chris Kembali ke Media', *Prospek*, 26 January 1991, p.27 and his name began appearing as the Adviser *(pembina)* of Yogyakarta's *Kedaulatan Rakyat* in November 1991, although he claimed he had 'no plan to buy it' (USIS Vol.1992:47).

61. Bambang's Bimantara Group reportedly invested US$ 80 million in developing RCTI, the nation's first private television network. ('Makin Dewasa di Usia Sebelas?', *Warta Ekonomi*, No.4, IV, 22 June 1992, pp.147, see particularly p.17).

62. Dhakidae 1991:526-7.

63. The foundation was called *Yayasan Tujuh Dua*. See '"Bintang Indonesia" Segera Beredar', *Kompas*, 2 March 1991, p.12.

64. USIS (Vol. 2) 1992:11

65. See 'Mengintip Gaya dan Harta', *Tempo*, 23 March 1991, p.98. The official 1991 sales figures in *Data Oplah dan Peredaran IPPPN Tahun 1991*, p.13 remain 200,000.

66. 'Demik Tiras dan Titik Impas', *Tempo*, 2 April 1994, p.89.

67. See 'Magazine threats', *The West Australian*, 27/7/94, p.19.

68. USIS (Vol.2) 1992:69, however, only gives the figure of 100,000.

69. See Michael Vatikiotis, 'Masses of Media', *Far Eastern Economic* Review, 26 July 1990, pp.46-7.

70. It was widely believed by informed industry observers that Tony Salim, of the Salim Group, was also financing Surya Persindo and was also represented on the new executive (confidential interviews on 5/12/91 and 18/12/91).

71. 'Makin Dewasa di Usia Sebelas?', *Warta Ekonomi*, 22 June 1992, pp.14-7, particularly p.15. For biographical background on Harry Kuntoro, see Ciptawidya Swara (ed.) (1992), *TOP Eksekutif Indonesia*, Ciptawidya Swara, Jakarta, pp.313-23.

72. 'MI Dikelola Bimantara', *Prospek*, 21 March 1992, p.18.

73. Michael R.J. Vatikiotis (1993), *Indonesian Politics Under Suharto: Order, development and pressure for change*, Routledge, London & New York, p.108.

74. Confidential interview, 5/12/91.

75. Mochtar Lubis (1993), 'Menangislah, Wartawan Indonesia' (pp.535-8) in Hotman M. Siahaan & Tjahjo Purnomo W. (eds.) (1993), *Tajuk-Tajuk dalam Terik Matahari: Empat Puluh Tahun Surabaya Post*, Yayasan Keluarga Bhakti, Surabaya. Quotation from p.537.

76. 'Pasar Besar, Oplah Turun', *Tempo*, 15/2/92, p.33.

77. Document published in Anon. 1989:241.

78. Junaedhie 1991:136.

79. Mara Karma is quoted in 'Study urged on impact of big capital on media industry', *Jakarta Post*, 28/9/92.

CHAPTER 5

Marginal Presses

The regional press needs to be developed in harmony with the principle of pluralistic information flows. To achieve this, obtaining a publication permit should be made easier. The development of specialist press publications and those by associations needs to be supported.

*Formulation of Outcomes from
PWI Seminar on the
Social Responsibility of
Indonesian Journalists*[1]

Clearly dominating the Indonesian press industry are the major Jakarta-based newspapers, frequently with their associated magazines and extending regional tentacles. However, also contributing substantially to the industry, albeit frequently marginalised, are a miscellany of other types of publications. It is to these that I now turn, to focus on the non-commercial periodicals dubbed 'special publications', campus newspapers, and newspapers produced in regional areas (in Indonesian and regional languages). Increasing secularisation of the media has tended to marginalise, too, explicitly religious publications, although, as the chapter notes, one Islamic paper has challenged this overall trend. Finally, a signficant, if less visible, economic and political role played by domestically produced newspapers in various foreign languages is examined.

'Special publications'

Most of the preceding discussion has focused on the commercial press. However, apart from those commercial publications which require the government SIUPP, there is another, frequently ignored, category of printed matter, which appears to be on the increase. These are the non-commercial, restricted circulation 'special publications' (*penerbitan khusus*). These periodicals, which only require a 'Registration Permit' (*Surat Tanda Terdaftar*, STT) rather than a publication permit, include materials as diverse, for example, as campus broadsheets, non-government organisations' brochures, or in-house company publications.

These Registration Permits are less problematic to obtain than the publication permits (SIUPP). They are governed by a separate 1975 regulation,[2] but are still liable to cancellation if the publications run material which deviates from the terms of the permit, or if they fail to appear for 6 months (or 18 months in particular circumstances). Formally, such 'special publications' should not carry general news, nor engage in 'practical politics'. Since they are non-profit, they should be managed and structured differently from the SIUPP publications. For example, they are not supposed to use terms such as *Pemimpin Umum* (General Chairperson) or *Pemimpin Redaksi* (Editor-in-Chief) but instead *Ketua Pengarah* (Coordinating Chairperson) and *Ketua Penyunting* (Editorial Chairperson). Staff working on such special publications may not describe themselves as 'journalists' (*wartawan*) nor carry press cards.[3]

According to the Director-General of Press and Graphics, Subrata, while there were about 275 SIUPP at the close of 1991, there were about 1,825 STT, although approximately 45% of these were not active.[4] While their individual circulations may be insignificant and their appearance infrequent, the sheer multiplicity of titles, still numbering over 1000, warrants some comment. Moreover, since 1975, included in the STT, or 'special publications' category, has been the campus press (to which I shall return below).

Theoretically such non-profit STT publications are for 'internal' distribution and may not be sold publicly. Their advertising content is limited to a maximum of 10% of total space, and should only be included to cover printing and production costs, not to generate profit. In practice, such advertising may be extremely glossy and professional, and the more 'entrepreneurial' of these publications are relatively indistinguishable from their commercial cousins. In fact, many can be bought on the streets, just like ordinary SIUPP publications, but the cover price is explicitly designated as a payment to cover publication costs (since these STT publications cannot be profit-making ventures). On a casual stroll down Jakarta's Sabang Road, near the Thamrin Boulevard commercial district, one can pick up more than a dozen simply by paying the 'pengganti ongkos cetak' (print production cost).

Some of these might be clearly in-house publications of government departments, or non-government organisations. For example, the Central Council of the All-Indonesia Worker's Federation (*Dewan Pimpinan Pusat Serikat Pekerja Seluruh Indonesia*, DPP SPSI) publishes the monthly *Media Pekerja [Workers' Media]*. The *pribumi* entrepreneurs' association HIPPI (*Himpunan Pengusaha Putra Indonesia*) publishes a business and economics bi-monthly *Pengusaha [Entrepreneur]*. The University of Indonesia's Faculty of Economics' Management Institute is publisher of the monthly *Manajemen & USAHAWAN Indonesia [Management and the Indonesian ENTREPRENEUR]*. Such STT publications seem to cover much of the same ground staked out by commercial business weeklies like *Warta Ekonomi* or *InfoBank*, a situation which raises the hackles of some editors of SIUPP publications.[5] The economic expansion of the 1980s stimulated numerous large private companies to produce their own 'in-house' magazines.[6] Some STT publications, such as the two-monthly 'journal of science and culture', *Ulumul Qur'an*, published by the Institute for the Study of Religion and Philosophy (*Lembaga Studi Agama dan Filsafat*) together with the Association of Indonesian Muslim Intellectuals (*Ikatan Cendekiawan Muslim Indonesia*, ICMI) under Editor-in-Chief Dawam Raharjo, are quite influential highly regarded publications.

In some cases, it would appear that STT publications might be testing the market response for latter SIUPP ventures. For example, when Hardiyanti Rukmana, President Suharto's daughter, launched her weekly tabloid for women, *Wanita Indonesia [Indonesian Woman]*, in February 1989 it was initially a STT publication; its SIUPP was only issued eight months later. Up-market specialist magazines seem particularly likely to evaluate the market initially with an STT before attempting to get a SIUPP. The magazine, *Golfer*, which began appearing in early 1992 (before even its STT was fully processed!), demonstrated the viability of such a sports publication by achieving a circulation of about 20,000 by the end of 1993. However, in November 1993 a competitor, *Progolf*, emerged complete with a SIUPP to take advantage of direct public sales, which pressured *Golfer* to seek its own SIUPP in 1994 to maintain its market share.[7]

Using the STT to test the waters can have other risks. A magazine on interior design, gardens and environment *Asri*, was initially published under an STT when it appeared in February 1983, but the permit was cancelled by the Information Minister in January 1986 because it was being circulated commercially. Three months later it re-appeared with a SIUPP.[8] Official rebukes are not always so mild, and the authorities throughout the country periodically threaten people producing unregistered 'illegal' publications.[9] Opposition groups suffer particularly. The environmental activist group

SKEPHI had its *Berita Hutan {News of the Forest}* closed in March 1989, while the *Indonesian Human Rights Monitor* was banned in February 1990, both ostensibly for failure to obtain the required permits.[10]

Perhaps the most significant single category of 'special publications' since the introduction of the relevent 1975 legislation is now the campus newspaper.

Student press

Student newspapers emerged with the nationalist movement in the early decades of this century. *Jong Java [Young Java]* was published by a nascent nationalist organisation in 1914, while *Indonesia Merdeka [Free Indonesia]*, published by Indonesian students in the Netherlands ten years later, was regarded as one of the most controversial and influential expressions of nationalism of the period. Once independence was achieved and tertiary institutions multiplied after the turbulence of the physical struggle for independence (1945-49), the campus press emerged even more vociferously than before.[11]

By 1955, reflecting the political diversity of the liberal democracy period, there were at least 35 student-generated publications produced by all kinds of faculty, university and student political and religious groups, reflecting much the same multiplicity and vitality that existed in the commercial press.[12] In that year ten student publications sent representatives to a national conference in Kaliurang, Central Java, which established two student press organisations, the Indonesian Student Journalists' League (*Ikatan Wartawan Mahasiswa Indonesia*) and the Indonesian Students' Press Association (*Serikat Pers Mahasiswa Indonesia*) subsequently merged in 1958 into the Indonesian Student Press League (*Ikatan Pers Mahasiswa Indonesia*, IPMI).

The political and economic constraints of the 1959-65 period made it difficult for the campus press. It became *de rigueur* for papers to align themselves with a particular political party and to declare this affiliation publicly, making 'independent' campus papers a rarity. Those that attempted to maintain neutrality were frequently accused of tacitly supporting the conservative forces of the Indonesian Socialist Party or the Islamic Masyumi, and hence regarded as anti-Communist.

From their bases on university and college campuses, those student newspapers which had not been banned as sympathetic to the Indonesian Communist Party were amongst the most stridently critical of President Sukarno and the political left-wing during the transitional years between 1965 and 1967. Their impact upon the ethos and style of the New Order press has been marked. Several of today's senior editors, politicians and political analysts gained their formative experience with crusading student papers like *Harian KAMI* or *Mahasiswa Indonesia*, which spilled out of the campuses and into the streets along with the student demonstrators so keen to bring down the 'Old Order'.[13] Not surprisingly, such papers, seen as willing collaborators in the New Order mission, were amongst the earliest to gain the obligatory publication permits required after 1966. Within the context of the time they maintained a technical and journalistic standard equal to that of most of their off-campus commercial competitors. For example, the Bandung-based *Mahasiswa Indonesia* established a reasonably solid market on the streets of Jakarta and attracted contributions from some of the major intellectuals and political figures of the time.[14] The Jakarta-based *Harian KAMI* claimed peak daily sales of 70,000 in 1974, making it then one of the largest-selling papers in the country.[15]

At their 1971 Congress the Indonesian Student Press League (IPMI) adopted a policy of 'back to campus', urging member publications to choose between being student newsletters or public media (like *Harian KAMI*). Those in the latter category were urged to withdraw from the organisation. The split weakened the IPMI and the student-produced press as a whole. It was followed by a period of hiatus.

By early 1974 however, student papers were again stirred to criticise what they saw as the regime's betrayal of its initial rhetoric. Yet unlike the dozen commercial papers which had their permits withdrawn in the aftermath of the January 15 incident, *Malari*, campus papers tended to avoid closure. For several, the heated political climate together with the removal of their bolder commercial papers appeared to have combined to stimulate an increase in their circulation. Several new student periodicals appeared in the main cities of Java. Such publications became eligible for university subsidies of at least half their production costs, establishing a financial dependence on the university administration.

Once more in 1978 it was often through the mouthpiece of the student press that the most explicit attacks on the broken promises and corruption of the government were expressed. Public sales were healthy, with the Bandung Institute of Technology's *Kampus* [*Campus*] and University of Indonesia's *Salemba* (named after the campus's location), for example, claiming sales of 30,000 at their peak in 1978, leading up to the General Assembly of the MPR to (re-)elect the president.[16] But the authorities moved on these partially university-subsidised newspapers as the political crisis broke. In Yogyakarta, both the University of Gajah Mada's *Gelora Mahasiswa* [*Student enthusiasm*] and the Teacher Training College's *Derap Mahasiswa* [*Student march*] were suspended by their respective Rectors. The Minister of Information cancelled the permits of *Almamater* (Bogor Agricultural Institute), *Airlangga* (Airlangga University, Surabaya), *Salemba* (University of Indonesia) together with *Kampus* and *Media* (both based at Bandung Institute of Technology). Several of the students tried for subversion after the 1978 crackdown were active on their local campus papers.

The Information Ministry claimed that these student papers were closed for contravening their STT permit, by circulating to the general public off campus. The then Minister for Education and Culture, Daud Yusuf, however, made it clear that the bans were part of the government's policy of 'normalising' (that is, de-politicising) campus life. This policy, known as NKK (*Normalisasi Kehidupan Kampus*), involved the banning of student councils and suppression of independent student publications. The Department of Education and Culture established its own 'student magazine' *Majalah Mahasiswa*, to promote a moderate campus press and garner support for NKK. While the majority of students may have been rather apathetic about the changes, there was nonetheless signficant student opposition to the NKK policy.[17] It introduced detailed monitoring of any publications produced on campus. It is now rare, if not virtually impossible, for radical student papers to be sold publicly off campus. Permits are required from within the university, usually from the Rector (Vice-Chancellor) and the advice of the local security body (*Bakorstanasda*) is apparently sought routinely by the university administration, at least in an informal manner. In 1993, for example, a total of ten campus papers were closed for publishing political reports regarded as beyond their 'legitimate interests'.[18]

Campus papers still thrive, but they tend to be tame organs for university public relations rather than an expression of student discontent. Some campus publications have adapted by claiming the political middle ground, displaying commercial nous and journalistic sophistication in both content and lay-out. Gajah Mada University's *Balairung*, for example, produced a special edition to celebrate its eight-year (*windu*) anniversary in 1994. The 128-page glossy magazine was slick and well-produced, marketed through major bookshop chains such as Gramedia, for Rp.3,000. It included a lengthy article about, and interview with, prominent leftist author Pramudya Ananta Tur, seventeen researched essays by student leaders on their vision for Indonesia's future, together with a student analysis of the election of the university's new Rector. The magazine listed on its advisory board not only Amir Effendi Siregar, who in addition to lecturing in the university's highly-regarded journalism program is also a director of *Warta Ekonomi* economic weekly, but also *Kompas'* chief Yakob Utama. Part of the university administration's rein on all publications, however, was the obligatory presence on the advisory board of the third Deputy Rector, who under the 'Campus Normalisation' program, has responsibility for campus 'security' matters.

On occasion, students resist a university administration's attempts to regulate their media, but in such cases the military authorities are likely to intervene. At Surabaya's Airlangga University, for example, in January 1993 students in the Faculty of Social and Political Sciences produced 200 copies of an eight-page tabloid *Dialogue*, despite the university's refusal to permit a rival to the existing publication *Retorika*. Half the print run sold at Rp 300 in two days. The paper, which included an article concerning pressure on the East Java Governor to resign, stirred a swift response. The local military commander telephoned the Deputy Rector to ensure that the paper had no university fiat. Although no one was detained, students involved were questioned by the local police, all unsold copies were seized, and the Rector declared his intention to discipline the students severely.[19]

Despite such constraints upon the student press, underground publications, staffed largely by students, continue to provide a limited alternative to the mainstream media, in a country where ready availability of photocopiers means unauthorised printed materials may circulate widely amongst groups within the broad opposition, irrespective of official government controls. Groups critical of the government are often in contact with sympathisers abroad. In some cases 'foreign' Indonesian-language magazines actually contain material written entirely within Indonesia and sent to the overseas publishing group using computer and telecommunications technology. The resultant publication can then be sent back to Indonesia, with the appearance of being a 'foreign' publication, thereby deflecting suspicion from local groups which actually write the copy. In some cases, such as the publication *Indonesian Mobilisations*, a Dutch postal address masks a domestically-produced magazine. In other cases, the precise relationship between the overseas and domestic organisations is secret. Recent technological strides, particularly facimile machines, but to a lesser extent the use of modems, e-mail and international computer information networks have the potential to enable small opposition groups, particularly students, to work around many of the contraints placed upon their predecessors in earlier decades. Nonetheless, given that critical 'alternative' publications would never be issued with the obligatory publication permit, there is little possibility of establishing a viable readership or obtaining enough income to ensure any longevity.

Regional press in Indonesian language

It has long been regarded as accepted wisdom in Indonesia, at least since 1966, that the press industry was, and would inevitably be, dominated by large 'national' newspapers based in Jakarta and distributed throughout the major towns of the archipelago. It is these papers about which people normally speak when discussing the 'Indonesian press'. Such papers employed the most highly paid staff, the most sophisticated technology used by the country's press and commanded the lion's share of the nation's readership. A multitude of modest regional newspapers in the national language of *Bahasa Indonesia* did exist, but they survived on the crumbs left from the national print media cake.

By the late 1980s, this prevailing assumption had been challenged by the emergence of some regional tigers, capable to taking on the nationals and winning. It was part of a substantial capital realignment in the print media industry, which, combined with the expansion of regional economies more generally, enabled some of the peripheral papers to re-write the rules, staking out new market territories and beating the Jakarta-based 'nationals' at their own game. As we have noted when discussing the *Jawa Pos* empire in the preceding chapter, this has been the case most noticeably in East Java.

Official statistics for 1991 provided by the Indonesian Department of Information illustrate the magnitude of the national press market and the concentration of press publishers.[20] Of the 270 newspapers, magazines and periodical publications throughout the archipelago, 126 were based in Jakarta. The national total circulation per edition was just over 13 million copies of which nearly 8.77 million were produced in the nation's capital, with only 3.8 million being consumed there. The only other province (or special administrative region) to produce in excess of 560,000 copies was East Java with just over 1 million from 17 publication titles.

Despite this dominance by Jakarta-based newspapers, Indonesia has had a long history of viable independent regional papers publishing in the national language. Media analyst Christianto Wibisono has identified eight major successes, which he dubbed the 'Wali Songo' (Eight Saints), after the eight revered missionaries credited with bringing Islam to Java. He grouped together *Waspada {On Guard}* and *Mimbar Umum [Public Forum]* (in Medan), *Haluan {Direction}* (in Padang), *Suara Merdeka [Voice of Freedom]* (in Semarang) *Kedaulatan Rakyat [People's Sovereignty]* (in Yogyakarta), *Pedoman Rakyat [People's Guide]* (in Ujungpandang), *Surabaya Post* and *Bali Post* as having been established around the time of Indonesian independence and having remained independent, usually under same management, throughout this period.[21] Some have expanded with modest subsidary publications to form a regional 'family'. As a measure of such successes, a recent advertising industry guide to print media penetration in the six largest cities in Indonesia noted that, of the ten largest circulation daily papers, five were regionally-based.[22]

However, such successes are rare. Faced with the burgeoning expansion of Jakarta-based press empires, together with an exponential increase in the investment required to keep abreast of the rapidly changing technologies of the press industry at a time when advertising revenues are being sucked off to television accounts, many of the smaller regionally-based newspapers are struggling. For many their choice is either to be incorporated into one or other of the contending empires, or to struggle independently with limited capital, circulation, staff training levels and technologies, inevitably falling further and further behind their networked rivals.[23]

Nonetheless, by providing a different blend of news and information, focusing competently on local events unnoticed in the national media, a market niche may be secured by a small paper. In some locations poor transportation and communications provide a buffer for the locally produced product. For example, if capital city papers do not arrive until the following day, then the more modest local publication may maintain a market share. But in many cases the natural exigencies of climate and terrain also make it difficult for a local paper to be marketed much beyond its immediate surrounds. As one editor of the major Surabaya afternoon daily pointed out, the rainy season's afternoon downpours may decimate evening street sales of papers.[24] Flooded roads may slow down distribution in the hinterland or may even become impassable, simply exacerbating a world-wide trend against afternoon papers. There are still no daily papers at all, for example, in Central or Southeast Sulawesi, partly because of what has been called a lack of a 'reading habit'. But L.E. Manuhua, the founding editor of the Ujungpandang daily *Pedoman Rakyat*, has argued that geography and demography collude, ensuring that these provinces' dispersed and isolated market poses an enormous difficulty for the swift distribution and viable circulation of a daily. Furthermore, such factors equally impeded the expansion of papers produced in neighbouring provinces from securing a firm market in such outlying regions.[25]

For nearly a decade now there has been periodic discussion within the Press Council and other professional bodies regarding the impact of 'long distance printing', whereby, using computerised satelite technologies, simultaneous editions of a leading daily could be printed throughout the archipelago. Though long since technologically feasible, 'long distance printing' (sistem cetak jarak jauh) has not be permitted in Indonesia. The Department of Information and the Press Council have been convinced by the argument that this would, in one stroke, eliminate most of the struggling regional papers, which would be unable to compete with simultaneous productions of the capital city dailies in their market place. Nonetheless, confident of an eventual relaxation in this prohibition, some of the large networks already have invested in the technologies. In January 1993 Dahlan Iskan, head of the *Jawa Pos* network, declared for example that, although his company already had the 'long distance' technology and was capable of commencing publication 'long distance' at three weeks' notice, he believed that the widespread use of such sophisticated technologies will not be the winning industry strategy of the future, nor would it eliminate the well-targeted local paper, which could continue to provide unique coverage of local events.[26]

While nonetheless facing a squeeze from the conglomerates, the regional press looks like continuing to meet a need. The Newspaper Publishers Association (SPS) is even collaborating with regional governments to assist in the establishment of local papers. When the regional government of Bengkulu on the coast of southern Sumatra approached the SPS for assistance in founding a daily, independent of the major press conglomerates and staffed by locals, the organisation sought the help of the *Surabaya Post*, which had maintained such an independent position despite tight encirclement by press empires. In August 1991 the daily *Semarak* began publishing 6,000 copies in Bengkulu with a local staff fully trained by the *Post*. Capital of about Rp 200 million came from the SPS which maintained 49% share, with the remainder held by the regional government. The venture proved a success, but the pull of the conglomerates appears to have been too strong. By mid-1993, *Semarak* has been drawn into the *Jawa Pos* group. Nonetheless, the precedent of such SPS-regional government collaboration was apparently so successful it was being followed in East Timor in February 1993 with the Armed Forces Headquarters joining as a third sponsoring organisation.[27]

Symbolically, the future for the regional papers of Indonesia is epitomised by the battle being fought out in East Java. Four names highlight the competition.[28] There are two burgeoning offshoots of the Jakarta-based national press empires. The achievements of the *Jawa Pos*, a satellite of the Tempo-Grafiti Group and now the country's third largest daily paper, have been detailed earlier. *Surya* was set up as a new venture by the sensationalist Jakarta *Pos Kota* paper in 1986. With an initial circulation of about 50,000, it slid back badly until rescued by incorporation into the *Kompas*-Gramedia Group in 1989.[29] It now competes strongly for the upper end of the market and, after initially printing about 160,000 copies (many distributed free), seems to have maintained a second place circulation of 127,000. Behind them comes the *Surabaya Post*, established in 1953 by a founder who had been in journalism since working with a Dutch paper in Surabaya in the 1940s. The *Surabaya Post* is a strong regionally-oriented daily, with no pretensions of going 'national'. It maintains a high standard of professionalism, an achievement recognised by the SPS's decision to invite it to join as consultant in the establishment of the daily paper in Bengkulu (discussed above). Its facilities are modern and computerised and its circulation is about 100,000, but despite the optimism and talent of its editorial staff and its strong habitual readership, in the long term it will be difficult for it not to continue to fall further behind the two high-fliers, since it too targets the middle (though perhaps more the lower-middle) classes.

Emblematic of the fate of small-scale 'independent' regionals was *Memorandum*. From its roots as a student weekly in the provincial town of Malang, *Memo* (as it is generally known), moved base to the regional capital of Surabaya in 1982 and struggled to find a niche. It tried an Islamic orientation till about 1987, when it became first more sensationalist, then more 'news'-based. At the end of 1991 it had an estimated circulation of 25-35,000 but like so many smaller provincial papers, it was swallowed by well-financed high-tech competitors. When the 1991 Gulf War erupted, the limitations of the small, often family-owned, medium-technology regional papers were starkly evident in their sparse coverage. Like many smaller regional press companies, *Memo* lacked the capital and the professional expertise to seize new initiatives for expansion, despite the belief of *Memo*'s Editor-in-Chief, Agil H. Ali, that, with a 1991 ratio of one paper to 40 inhabitants in East Java, the province could still absorb the aspirations of the smaller dailies.[30] In early 1992 *Memorandum* was incorporated into the *Jawa Pos* empire. The paper, printed at the *Jawa Pos* printery, had been falling deeply into debt until *Jawa Pos* took control under a management agreement. They have since used *Memorandum* as the wedge to penetrate East Java's vast lower-middle and lower class readership which had previously been out of range of the up-market *Jawa Pos*.

An element in the success of the *Jawa Pos* empire has been that, rather than promoting the *Jawa Pos* daily across all socio-economic sections of the reading public, it has diversified and directed different, smaller publications at these various groups. In the words of Dahlan Iskan, the head of the empire, 'With lots of papers, we can enter all levels of the market', adding that they were particularly keen to capture readers in the public service, business sectors and the lower class to expand the group's overall sales.[31] With an interest in five out of the seven Surabaya daily newspapers — *Jawa Pos*, *Suara Indonesia* (12,000), *Memo* (35,000), pro-Golkar *Bhirawa* (75,000) and lower-class rural-oriented *Karya Darma* (30,000) — together with its sports, agri-business, computer and children's publications, the group has virtual blanket cover of the various socio-economic layers of the market in East Java, to a lesser extent radiating out into Central Java and Eastern Indonesia, making the *Jawa Pos* group the unassailable Colossus of the country's regional press enterprises.

What is telling about the achievements of the *Jawa Pos* group is that, after some testing of the Jakarta market in the early years after the *Tempo* involvement, the group's marketing strategy was to regard success in Jakarta as insignificant and to target by preference the untapped newspaper markets of Central and East Java and eastern Indonesia. In 1991, of the 350,000 copies of *Jawa Pos* sold, only about 1,500 were in Jakarta, about 290,000 were in East Java, and in declining order Central Java (17,000), East Kalimantan (12,000), South Kalimantan (7,800), Bali (5,000), Maluku (3,250), South Sulawesi (2,300), East Nusa Tenggara (2,250), with even Irian Jaya taking nearly 1,300 copies (or almost as many as that sold in Jakarta). When sales from the group's numerous Outer Island regional papers are added to these, it is clear that the *Jawa Pos* Group proved that national credibility and prosperity could be achieved even if Jakarta was ignored.

Regional language press

In striking contrast to the proliferation of vociferous vernacular publications in that comparable multi-ethnic country India, there is virtually no press published any of the approximately 250 regional languages of Indonesia. The few exceptions are several weeklies or cultural magazines in the dominant languages used on Java which survive from past glories. In the Javanese language, for example, there are the weeklies *Penyebar Semangat* (57,000), *Jaya Baya* (55,000), *Kandha Raharja* (part of the government's 'Newspapers for the Villages' program, KMD) and *Mekar Sari [Blooming Pollen]* (42,360).[32] Similarly there are several other tenacious Sundanese-language weeklies, including *Galura* (45,000) and *Mangle* (17,000), circulating in West Java. But these are insignificant compared to the national language press in the same distribution regions. Such publications tend to be more a 'labour of love' of an ageing editor striving to maintain a venue for regional language literature rather that commercially competitive 'news' or 'current affairs' media.

Some have illustrious pasts. The Javanese language weekly *Penyebar Semangat*, published in Surabaya, was established in 1933 by Dr Sutomo, one of the founding figures of the nationalist press in Indonesia. *Penyebar Semangat* is actually the oldest commercial publication in Indonesia, having appeared for 60 years with only a brief break from 1942 till 1949 after being banned by the Japanese occupation forces. The magazine was a continuation of an earlier Javanese daily *Suara Umum*, established by the leadership of the Budi Utomo nationalist organisation in 1931, initially appearing bi-lingually in Indonesian and Javanese. *Penyebar Semangat*'s initial circulation of 3,500 copies rose to a peak of about 85,000 during the 1950s and 1960s, but by 1991 had declined to around 57,000, which still makes it the largest circulation Javanese and regional language publication.[33]

The cultural and entertainment publication *Mangle*, the only current Sundanese language magazine, was established in October 1957 with a circulation of just 500. Based in Bandung, it expanded strongly through the 1960s, peaking in 1985 with a circulation of 70,000 each fortnight. By the end of the decade it had become a weekly, with sales apparently falling significantly to around 63,000 according to some claims. Official statistics suggest they are actually closer to about 17,000.[34] Financially the business appears to be reasonably sound, with its own offices and printery, although it faces considerable difficulties in competing with the more flamboyant entertainment magazines emerging from Jakarta. One of *Mangle*'s main strengths has been the vitality of its entertainment and short story columns, which have sustained a small but committed circle of regional language writers.[35] *Sipatahunan*, a Sundanese weekly established in 1923, failed to apply for the new publication permit (SIUPP) when the 1982 legislation was introduced. Its fortunes had been flagging and the Department of Information ultimately cancelled its old permit (SIT) on the grounds that it had failed to appear for some time.[36]

While the impression generally of the regional language press is that of magazines dying along with their ageing founders, one new publication turns against the trend. The Javanese-language *Jawa Anyar* weekly, which began publication in Solo in 1993, is the first new regional-language periodical in several decades. Not surprisingly it is an initiative of the innovative and highly successful *Jawa Pos* media group. Its claimed circulation of 35,000 (in mid-1993) was rumoured to be about three times the actual sales, but the 24-page glossy entertainment tabloid is clearly attempting to bring a new production quality to the regional-language press. Observers believe the *Jawa Pos* group is not aspiring to even break-even with *Jawa Anyar*, however, and may more likely be seeking to optimise use of the group's available printing capacity and associated infrastructure, and to establish a long-term presence in the Javanese-language market. Such new investment in a vernacular publication appears to be unique. It is unlikely to revive this flagging sector of the industry substantially, unlike recent developments in the Islamic media which may well signal a revival.

Islamic media

It is somewhat surprising to many foreign observers that, while more than 80% of the Indonesian population is categorised as Muslim, two of the largest daily newspapers are associated with Christian interests. Overall, there has been a sorry history of unsuccessful attempts to establish and sustain explicitly Muslim papers. Since the banning of *Abadi* in 1974 and particularly during the mid-1980s, the Islamic media has been marginalised by more professional, secular or Christian interests.

Even Muslim journalists and editors at a 1991 seminar on the

Islamic press, sponsored by the pro-government Association of Indonesian Islamic Intellectuals (ICMI) and held at the Department of Religion, acknowledged that *Kompas* covered Islamic activities more professionally and in more depth than rival papers like *Pelita* which had an explicit Islamic 'mission'.[37] This is perhaps the ultimate recognition of *Kompas'* success in casting off its image as a 'Catholic' medium and transmuting into a paper which is not obviously 'Christian' at all. Great hopes were expressed by participants at the seminar that the 'Islamic content' of such publications as *Berita Buana* and *Media Indonesia* might be increased, but the mood of the 100-odd participants was pessimistic about the likelihood of a Islamic-oriented daily emerging to rival *Kompas*, although this goal was expressed by several. Speakers observed that it was no longer capital that was lacking, since the appearance of Muslim capitalists like the Bakrie Brothers and the Ika Muda group. The problems lay in identifying and defining the potential readership, and in efficient marketing and distribution.

The Islamic-oriented media have been less able to seize opportunities. Perhaps one aspect of their dilemma is the difficulty in maintaining credibility with their readership while negotiating an accommodation with the State. The fate of *Pelita* illustrates the dilemma of these papers. During the 1977 and 1982 elections, when its usual circulation of 50,000 nearly doubled, it was identified as a voice of the opposition Islamic coalition, the United Development Party (PPP). Banned immediately after the 1982 elections, it reappeared about four months later with a more moderate editorial line and a more commercially pragmatic management. But it was largely abandoned by its readership. In 1985 it was taken over by Golkar figures and in mid-1990 it was given a capital injection of about Rp 4.5 billion by *'pribumi'* capitalists Aburizal Bakrie and Fadel Muhammad who recruited several key personnel from *Kompas*, with ambitions of drawing a large percentage of *Kompas'* Muslim staff.[38] Instead of achieving their goal of emulating the number one daily, by July 1991 *Pelita* was rent asunder by a controversy over the sacking of 52 of their 253 staff in an attempt to trim costs, followed in February 1992 by the resignations of four of the key ex-*Kompas* editorial staff. Circulation, which senior staff claimed at 90,000 in late 1990, may have dropped to under 40,000 by July 1991.[39] It seemed the paper lacked editorial cohesion and was unable to identify and reach its market, losing some of its 'traditional Muslim readers' when taken over by Golkar figures, and others in its unsuccessful attempt to broaden it circulation base.

The ICMI seminar gave credit to modest circulation Islamic magazines, such as *Kiblat [Pointing to Mecca]* (16,000), *Panji Masyarakat [Banner of Society]* (24,000), *Panggilan Adzan [Call to Prayer]* (41,000), *Amanah [Message]* (59,000).[40] Other publications (such as *Media Indonesia*) provided sympathetic coverage of developments in the Islamic world. Nonetheless, compared to the selection of Islamic newspapers in the 1950s and even the 1970s, consciously Islamic communities are largely without a substantial and identifiable voice in the media choir at the beginning of the 1990s.[41] Muslim outrage against the Kompas-Gramedia Group's enormously successful *Monitor* magazine, when it 'offended Islamic sentiments' with its 1990 popularity poll, could be interpreted as an outpouring of frustration, too, at absence of that Muslim voice.

Some attempts have been ambitious if hapless. *Jum'at [Friday]*, an Islamic tabloid weekly, began publication in April 1990 under the editorship of a former Director of Religious Information in the government's Department of Religious Affairs and with a staff of 25 journalists. Despite an optimistic initial print run of about 400,000, a modest cover price of only Rp 200 and distribution network through mosques and religious organisations[42] it quickly vanished without a ripple.

Recent developments, however, have demonstrated the capacity of the Islamic media to move from the margins to the mainstream. In the opening days of January 1993, a commercially ambitious, politically astute, well-connected daily newspaper emerged to face the challenges identified by participants at the 1991 ICMI seminar: *Republika*. Conceived by ICMI through the Abdi Bangsa Foundation chaired by the Minister for Research and Technology B.J. Habibie and owned by the PT Abdi Bangsa company, this daily represents a bold new concept in newspaper production and marketing in Indonesia. With ICMI's backing a SIUPP was obtained speedily, in advance of numerous other less-well-connected applicants. Habibie, whose political fortunes were clearly in ascendance, gained the support of the President himself, who was asked to endorse the concept and even the name, which he reportedly altered from the initial suggestion *Republik* to the final version '*Republika*'.

Republika brought together an impressive clutch of some of the country's major liberal Islamic intellectuals and journalists, into a venture designed to produce a 'quality' paper which was broadly secular in its coverage of events and issues, yet informed ideologically by Islamic values in much the same manner that *Kompas* or *Suara Pembaruan* were by Christianity. The Board overseeing editorial policy incorporated figures such as the often-outspoken Deputy Director of the Central Board of Statistics and frequent columnist for *Tempo*, Sucipto Wirosarjono, the founding head of the highly regarded non-government organisation the Development Studies Institute (LSP) Adi Sasono, political commentator Nurcholish Majid, together with several respected academics: Gajah Mada University political scientist M. Amien Rais, University of Indonesia professor Edi Sedyawati, and Rector (Vice-Chancellor) of the Jakarta State Islamic Institute (IAIN) and expert in Islamic law, Quraish Shihab.

Another indication of the newspaper's influential connection is the fact that on the board of commissioners (*komisaris*) overseeing the holding company PT Abdi Bangsa is Wardiman Joyonegoro, a staunch ICMI supporter and Habibie protege, appointed Minister of Education and Culture in the March 1993 Cabinet.

Editor-in-chief Parni Hadi is a former senior ANTARA correspondent who had spent several years in West Germany (1979-80), during which time he formed a close association with Habibie, a German-trained technocrat. Around Parni Hadi were a collection of highly experienced professional journalists, including Nasir Tamara (formerly with *Tempo, Sinar Harapan, Warta Ekonomi*) and S. Sinansari Ecip (former *Tempo* correspondent and lecturer at Hasanuddin University in Ujung Pandang). The staff is a composite of key ICMI activists and members, together with professionals who are sympathetic but as yet uncommitted to ICMI. Many of the younger editorial staff and reporters, such as Zaim Uchrowi, had formerly worked in *Berita Buana* during the period Sutrisno Bachir was funding it. The establishment of *Republika* proved a life-buoy for several refugees from *Buana* who had left, together with Sutrisno Bachir, over the policy rift in early 1992.

Initial funding for *Republika* appears to have come from major Muslim business people. 'Management guidance' was provided by, among others, Tanri Abeng, a leading executive with Bakrie Brothers and a Board Member of the brewer Multi Bintang Indonesia (formerly Heineken), in the hope that the venture would avoid the management disasters that had sunk so many previous papers.[43] Fifty-one per cent of the company was to be held by ICMI, with 20% by the employees (as specified under the SIUPP regulations). By early February 1993 the paper had 'gone public' floating the final 29% in the form of 2.9 million shares. It was a bold and unique gesture, the first time a newspaper in Indonesia had offered shares to the public. The shares, which could not be re-sold without the permission of the company, could only be purchased by Muslims with a limit of one Rp 5,000 share per family. The initial 50 shares, nominally valued at Rp 1,000 each, were bought by leading government and business figures, including the President, Vice-President, Armed Forces Chief Try Sutrisno and former Pertamina boss Ibnu Sutowo.

The paper's editorial and management staff have obvious strengths. Obvious too is the *cachet* of powerful figures in the New Order Government. Capitalising on these strengths *Republika* has established an Islamic beach-head in the highly competitive secular industry of the 1990s, even if it fell short of its wildly unrealistic projected goal of 500,000 circulation by the end of 1993.[44] By August 1993, when sales had touched 125,000, the end-of-year target had been revised to a more realistic 200,000.[45] Throughout 1993 the paper regularly published long lists of people purchasing shares in *Republika*, including hundreds if not thousands from the Habibie-founded Nusantara Aircraft Industry (*Industri Pesawat Terbang Nusantara*, IPTN). By August, editor Parni Hadi was claiming 1.3 million shares had been sold, just under half the 2.9 million goal. Undeniably the appearance on newstands of *Republika* generated enormous interest amongst the newspaper-reading public, giving every indication that a viable market exists for a quality broadsheet which is professionally produced, liberal-minded yet informed by progressive Islamic values.

The growing strength and influence of ICMI, which also sponsors publications like *Ulumul Qur'an*, has triggered other religious organisations to respond by either founding or reviving their own intellectuals' organisations and launching into print with periodicals catering for their own communities. For example, the Indonesian Hindu Intellectuals' Forum (*Forum Cendekiawan Hindu Indonesia*, FCHI) began to publish its two-monthly magazine *Aditya* in late 1993, even before its publication permit had been approved. That *Aditya* is modelled on *Ulumul Qur'an* is obvious from its contents and lay-out.[46] With the secularisation of the daily press and the identification of markets for religious groups, there will be a blossoming of such specialist periodicals.

English language

Not surprisingly, given the international role played by the English language, there is a tradition of English-language publications in Indonesia and a relatively broad selection from which to choose. The history of English-language newspapers is surprisingly long with the first, the *Java Government Gazette* (1812-14), appearing during the brief English occupation of the colony. One hundred and forty years later the first daily in independent Indonesia was *The Times of Indonesia*, founded in 1952 by Mochtar Lubis, then concurrently editor of *Indonesia Raya* daily. The *Times* began a tradition of determined, if small circulation, English dailies which continues down to today's three: the *Jakarta Post* (32,000/27,000), the *Indonesia Times* (41,000/15,000), and *Indonesian Observer* (3,500/10,000).[47] Within press circles the last two of these are regarded more as 'vanity publishing' ventures of their proprietors rather than self-sustaining commercial projects. Of the three, the *Jakarta Post* stands out as the most reputable and professionally produced. The company which established the *Post* in 1983 is a cooperative venture including *Suara Karya*, the paper of the New Order's electoral organisation, Golkar, together with *Kompas, Suara Pembaruan* and *Tempo*. Nonetheless, although its former Editor-in-Chief has been made an ambassador and although it is widely believed that the current Minister of Information holds shares in the company, the *Post* is not regarded as a government organ.[48] *Tempo's* Eric Samola, who is also President Director of the holding company which owns the *Jakarta Post*, is quoted as saying, 'The *Post's* commitment as an independent newspaper is not only to support the democratic system, but also the culture and all the accompanying values...If the *Post* is seen as being an official organ, then it already faces many constraints, including the issue of credibility, the mainspring of any press medium.'[49] The paper has fostered a sense of political credibility by occasionally publishing sensitive stories which might not have appeared in Indonesian-language papers.

Paralleling the proliferation of economic and business publications in Indonesian in the late 1980s and early 1990s, has been the emergence of similar English-language publications. In 1992 two such small-circulation specialist magazines were established. In March, the 32-page bi-weekly *Economic Bulletin* established in October 1991 was transformed into a fully-fledged commercial colour magazine entitled the *Economic and Business Review Indonesia*, headed by the former Director-General for Press and Graphics, Janner Sinaga. It is believed that the Armed Forces news agency, PAB (*Pusat Pemberitaan Angkatan Bersenjata*) which had cooperated previously in the production of the *Economic Bulletin* continued its involvement in the replacement. It claimed sales of 20,000 by early 1993. A similar publication, launched in December 1992, was the *Indonesia Business Weekly* (IBW), from the same publishers as the highly successful economic daily *Bisnis Indonesia*. Both English-language magazines were hoping to reach break-even point within three years; like the *Jakarta Post* both hoped eventually to find a niche in the larger Southeast Asian regional market, with one eye on the role played by the prestigious *Far Eastern Economic Review* in the region. While such transnational expansion seems somewhat ambitious, IBW at least seemed likely to survive the long haul, having been initially financed to Rp 500 million by such well-connected businesspeople as Sukamdani Gitosarjono, Ciputra, Subronto Laras and Anthony Salim.[50]

There have been other attempts to produce English-language papers, directed primarily at the tourist market, notably in Bali and in Yogyakarta. Not all such publications receive Department of Information blessing. In March 1992, for example, the Indonesian-language *Yogya Post* initiated a weekly four-page English-language supplement *Yogya in a Week*. While this proved a financial fillip to the ailing paper which had been cut back from daily to weekly the previous February, the supplement was deemed to contravene its publishing permit (SIUPP) requirement to publish in Indonesian only. The supplement was prohibited and the paper folded in debt.[51] There are numerous English-language 'special publications', however, produced exclusively for tourist promotional purposes. The tourists of Bali, together with the expanding regional economy of eastern Indonesia, form a potential target too for the *Jawa Pos*'s planned English-language morning daily the *Surabaya Daily News*, due for launching in 1995.

While the total circulation of English-language papers and magazines may be small, they are generally well-received by the business and diplomatic communities. Often their limited circulation and specific readership means that they are permitted a greater latitude when commenting on sensitive domestic political events. For example, while there was virtually no Indonesian-language media coverage of a 14 December 1989 flag-raising demonstration in Jayapura and the subsequent regional protests, a lone report did appear in the *Jakarta Post* eight days later. Giving the government the first word, the paper led with a denial by a senior Indonesian Armed Forces spokesperson of 'foreign media reports' (not published in Indonesia). This official denial was used to introduce the substantive details of the events in Jayapura as reported internationally by Agence France Presse (AFP) news agency. While referring directly to salient parts of that AFP report, the *Post*'s headline 'ABRI denies reports of mass detentions in Irian Jaya' contrasted markedly with the AFP's 'Indonesian official confirms asylum seekers in PNG consulate'. The paper made details of the thus-far unreported incident public, but it covered itself against government retaliation by publishing full official denials. Readers can thus register what information was being carried by the overseas media, compare it with the official line, then choose the more credible interpretation. While the same strategy is frequently used by Indonesian papers, the *Jakarta Post*, which has only one thirtieth the circulation of a major Indonesian-language paper like *Kompas*, is clearly subject to less strict policing of its contents and more able to employ such techniques. It would appear its readership of indigenous Indonesians is growing.

Chinese language

The ethnic Chinese community in Indonesia has never been more than about 2.5% of the general population. Yet since the turn of the century ethnic Chinese journalists have been active in numbers disproportionate to this modest size. The rise of nationalism in China in the first decade of this century stimulated the appearance of several papers in Indonesia serving the ethnic Chinese community. While there were Chinese-language papers these were generally outnumbered by others using a form of Sinicised Malay for those diasporic Chinese who had been largely incorporated into indigenous culture (known as 'peranakan' Chinese). Other papers, such as the successful *Sin Po*, published two editions: one in Malay, the other in Chinese.[52] In 1949, the year the Dutch recognised Indonesian independence, there were 17 Chinese-language daily newspapers, with a circulation of about 85,000, compared to 45 in Indonesian with sales of around 230,000.[53]

As part of the military's efforts to control the press during the period of Guided Democracy, the Supreme Martial Law Administration (*Peperti*) required all publications to obtain a Printing Permit (SIC), in addition to the Publishing Permit (SIT) obligatory since 1958.[54] In 1960, as part of a broader squeeze aimed at the small but economically significant ethnic Chinese minority, the Martial Law Administration banned all newspapers and periodicals using Chinese characters. Only when martial law was lifted in 1963 did Chinese-language newspapers re-appear, albeit for a brief reincarnation.[55]

Long-standing prejudice against the ethnic Chinese minority was justified by the contradictory claims they were pro-Communist (and even represented a 'fifth column' of the Communist Government in China) as well as the accusation that they maintained a strangle-hold over commerce and business in Indonesia, disadvantaging indigenous entrepreneurs. When the Suharto regime gained power in the wake of the 30 September Movement incident in 1965, the military regarded the government of the People's Republic of China as implicated, through its support for the broad left-wing ground swell in Indonesia. Diplomatic relations were severed and the Chinese embassy was razed. Despite the large volume of trade that continued, through third countries such as Singapore and Hongkong, it was not until August 1990 that Indonesia and the People's Republic of China 'normalised' relations.

Nonetheless, it served the interests of the New Order Government to reiterate earlier bans on the Chinese language press, with a 1966 Parliamentary Decision to eliminate foreign publications which did not use Roman characters. A November 1988 Circular from the Director-General for the Development of Press and Graphics reminded press and non-press publishers that any representation of Chinese language or characters was still prohibited, be it in books, on calendars, labels or packaging of food, medicine, clothing, in greeting cards, decorations, logos, other symbols and the like. The justification was that 'the circulation of printed goods in Chinese characters/language could impede the implementation of the creation of national unity and integrity, specifically regarding the development of Indonesian Citizens and Foreign Citizens of Chinese descent who reside in Indonesia (namely, their assimilation into Indonesian society)'.[56] The ban even extended, notably during periods of inter-ethnic tensions, to blacking out Chinese characters inadvertently included, for example, in ads or photographs in imported publications such as the *Far Eastern Economic Review*.

In August 1994 a very modest relaxation of the blanket prohibition occurred when the Coordinating Minister for Political Affairs, Susilo Sudarman, announced that, in response to the growing economic importance of Chinese-speaking foreign tourists to Indonesia, publication of hotel and tourist promotional materials in Chinese characters would now be permissible, provided they were first subject to official scrutiny and were only published by a government-authorised printing firm.[57]

In the realm of the news media industry, however, there remains only one specific legal exception to the prohibition on Chinese characters: the daily paper *Harian Indonesia*, produced by the publisher of the military-aligned *Berita Buana* under the supervision of the State Intelligence Coordinating Agency (BAKIN). A merger of three earlier Chinese newspapers, this outlet has been maintained as an army voice within the Chinese-speaking community. Of the paper in the early 1970s Charles Coppel wrote, 'Its editor-in-chief is an army officer who does not speak or read Chinese. All copy (with very few exceptions) is written first in Indonesian and then translated into Chinese, the translations being carefully checked by Sinologists on the staff... It has been editorial policy gradually to increase the amount of Indonesian language material.'[58] Today about half its contents are in Indonesian, with the remainder in Chinese. The paper is rumoured to tap a rich source of advertising revenue by businesses which see it as a means of reaching a commercially active, highly-targeted readership. Despite a modest circulation of about 55,000 and secure in its market monopoly, it ranks as the twelfth largest newspaper advertising earner (with about 2% of the total earnings).[59] Perhaps to avoid stimulating an increased readership the paper is available only by subscription, not street sales[60] to a readership almost totally over 35 years of age since few younger ethnic Chinese can speak, let alone read, Chinese. *Harian Indonesia* is evident particularly in the commercial Chinese quarters, such as Glodok in Jakarta, but invisible elsewhere.

Given the government's apparent intention to eliminate the use of Chinese language by ethnic Chinese communities within Indonesia it seems unlikely that such sales will do anything but decrease as the older generation of Chinese-speakers declines, replaced by their offspring fully schooled in Indonesian language and unable to read Chinese script. Of all the 'marginal' presses mentioned, the Chinese language paper is the most vulnerable and most likely to disappear (or perhaps transmogrify into a limited circulation economic and trade bulletin for import-exporters) despite the government's strengthening trade connections with China and other Chinese-speaking countries. Even Indonesian-language publications aimed at the ethnic Chinese, like Sudwikatmono's *Sinar*, seem unable to strike a successful chord in what is a scattered and heterogeneous Chinese population. The role of the Chinese-language press, like that of the Chinese ethnic minority itself, seems doomed to remain forever marginalised and under suspicion in Indonesia.

ENDNOTES

1. As published in Departemen Penerangan RI (1986), *Beberapa Aspek Pembinaan Kewartawanan,* Directorat Jenderal Pembinaan Pers dan Grafika, Jakarta, p.54.

2. That is, the Minister of Information's Regulation No. 01/Per/Menpen/1975 concerning Determinations relating to Special Publications.

3. For details on STT, see Junaedhie 1991:256-7, and 'Pedoman Penyelenggaraan Penerbitan khusus dengan STT', Reporter, No. 17, Vol. III, October-November 1991, pp.38-9.

4. According to figures given by him at the ICMI seminar on the Islamic Press, Jakarta, December 1991.

5. Such as Atang Ruswita, Director of the Bandung-based regional press group centred on *Pikiran Rakyat.* See 'Penerbitan STT Diperdagangkan', in *Reporter,* No. 26/V/April-May 1993, p.45.

6. In-house company publications include *Warta Bimantara (Bimantara News}, Warta Bukaka, Warta AP* (of the Asia Permai Group) and *Warta Indosat.* See 'Mengapa menerbitkan Media' *Editor,* 9/6/90, p.100.

7. On the golf magazines, see 'Bacaan Kelas Atas' *Sinar,* 13/12/93, p.13.

8. Junaedhie 1991:16

9. For example, in Ujungpandang in July 1992 the South Sulawesi Regional Office of the Department of Information cracked down on four 'illegal' press and 'special publications' which it claimed could 'disturb national stability in the area'. See 'Penerbitan Ilegal Muncul di Ujungpandang', Pelita, 14/7/92.

10. The Committee to Protect Journalists (1991), *In the Censor's Shadow: Journalism in Suharto's Indonesia,* CPJ, New York, p.13.

11. Much of the following detail is taken from Junaedhie 1991:207-9, while the most comprehensive study of the student press is Amir Effendi Siregar (1983), *Pers Mahasiswa* Indonesia: *Patah Tumbuh Hilang Berganti,* Karya Unipres, Jakarta.

12. See Siregar 1983:39-41.

13. Among those who rose to professional or political prominence through their involvement in the student press are: Sarwono Kusumaatmaja (currently Minister for Environment); Gunawan Mohamad (head of the influential Tempo group of magazines; Fikri Jufri (Editor-in-Chief of *Matra* monthly and Deputy Editor-in-Chief of *Tempo);* Christianto Wibisono (now running the prestigious Indonesian Business Data Centre (PDBI); Nono Anwar Makarim (founder of one of the country's most highly regarded international legal

firms); the late Zulharmans (Editor-in-Chief of the daily *Neraca* and senior office-bearer in the PWI and SPS at the time of his death in March 1993).

14. For a study of *Mahasiswa* Indonesia, see Francois Raillon (1984), Les *etudiants indonesiens et l'Ordre Nouveau: politique et ideologie du Mahasiswa Indonesia (1966-1974)* (Editions de la Maison des Sciences de l'Homme, Paris) translated as *Politik dan Ideologi Mahasiswa Indonesla: Pembentukan dan Konsolidasi Orde Baru 1966-1974* (LP3ES, Jakarta, 1985).

15. Claimed sales figures given in Siregar 1983:101 and sourced to Zulharmans, formerly Deputy Editor-in-Chief of the paper.

16. Claimed peak sales figures are given in Siregar 1983:101 and sourced to interviews with Antony Zeidra Abidin (Chairperson) of *Salemba* and Indro Cahyono (Editor-in-Chief) of *Kampus*.

17. On the NKK policy and the student press in the 1980-90s, see Laksmi W. Pamuntjak (1993), 'The Indonesian Student Movement in the 1980s/1990s: The development of resistance by a "marginalised minority"', BA Honours thesis, Murdoch University, unpublished, particularly pp.9-20 & 53-5. The New Order position on containing the campus press under the NKK policy is outlined in Departmen Penerangan RI [1982], *Kedudukan, Fungsi dan Tugas Pers-Kampus Mahasiswa*, Direktorat Jenderal Pembinaan Pers dan Grafika.

18. 'World Press Freedom Review', *IPI Report* (Monthly magazine of the International Press Institute), Vol. 42, No.12, December 1993 (reported on 'apakabar@clark.net' e-mail network 23/6/94).

19. 'Terbit perdana 200 eksemplar, "Dialogue" langsung "diberangus"' and 'Ide bagus, cara keliru', *Surya*, 19/1/93, p.3.

20. The following statistics are drawn from *Data Oplah dan Peredaran IPPPN Tahun 1991*, Departemen Penerangan RI, Direktorat Jenderal Pembinaan Pers dan Grafika, Proyek Pembinaan Pers 1991/1992, various pages.

21. Christianto Wibisono (1991), 'Transformasi Pers dari Profesi ke Bisnis' (pp.30-4) in Pet Parmono (ed.) (1991), *Peringatan Hari Pers Nasional 1991: Reorientasi Pers Nasional Menjelang Tahun 2000*, Panpus HPN 1991 Bidang Publikasi dan Dokumentasi, Jakarta.

22. The cities were Jakarta, Bandung, Semarang, Surabaya, Medan and Ujungpandang. The regional dailies were *Jawa Pos, Pikiran Rakyat, Suara Merdeka, Surabaya Post* and *Waspada*. See Subakti and Katoppo 1993:87.

23. Octarina 1991 documents the problems of such regionals, with cases studies in Aceh and Bandung.

24. Cuk Suwarsono, *Surabaya Post*, Surabaya, 21/1/93.

25. L.E. Manuhua, pers. comm., Surabaya, 21/1/91.

26. Comments made during discussions with the author at the *Jawa Pos* office, Surabaya, January 1993.

27. Information from Mr Cuk Suwarsono, *(Surabaya Post,* Surabaya, 21/1/93) who undertook the training of the *Semarak* staff.

28. On the 'battle' for the Surabaya market, see "Pertempuran' di Surabaya', *Tempo,* 25 November 1989, p.37. Unless otherwise noted circulation figures in this section are taken from USIS 1992 (various pages) corroborated by *Data Oplah dan Peredaran IPPPN Tahun 1991* (various pages). Most papers enjoyed a significant rise during the January 1991 Gulf War, but slid back to the figures noted.

29. While August Parengkuan, head of the Kompas-Gramedia Group's Public Relations section, denied that they injected any money into *Surya* and emphasised that only editorial and management support was provided, other (unnamed) sources in *Surya* are quoted as saying that *Kompas* invested about Rp.6 billion, of which one third went on promotional expenses and Rp.1.2 billion went to purchase a new printery. See "Pertempuran' di Surabaya', *Tempo,* 25 November 1989, p.37.

30. See '"Pertempuran" di Surabaya', Tempo, 25 November 1989, p.37, and 'Koran Lokal Berebut Pasar', *Prospek,* 24 August 1991, p.62.

31. 'Pasar Besar, Oplah Turun', *Tempo,* 15 February 1992, p.33.

32. Sales figures for 1991, based on Departemen Penerangan RI (1991/1992) Data *Oplah dan Peredaran IPPPN Tahun 1991,* Direktorat Jenderal Pembinaan Pers dan Grafika, Proyek Pembinaan Pers, Jakarta, various pages.

33. On details of *Penyebar* Semangat, see Atmakusumah's entry in *Ensiklopedi Nasional Indonesia,* Volume 12, PT Cipta Adi Pustaka, Jakarta, 1990, pp.133-4. I would like to thank Atmakusumah Astraatmaja for bringing this source and related ones to my attention.

34. The figure of 17,000 is given in Departemen Penerangan RI (1991/1992) Data *Oplah dan Peredaran IPPPN Tahun 1991,* Direktorat Jenderal Pembinaan Pers dan Grafika, Proyek Pembinaan Pers, Jakarta, p.25.

35. On Mangle see Maskun Iskandar's entry in *Ensiklopedi Nasional Indonesia,* Volume 10, PT Cipta Adi Pustaka, Jakarta, 1990, pp.138-9 and Dedi Muhtadi (1993) '"Mangle", Meliuk di Tengah Derasnya Informasi', *Kompas,* 9 February, p.16.

36. On *Sipatahunan* see Tribuana Said's entry in *Ensiklopedi Nasional Indonesia,* Volume 15, PT Cipta Adi Pustaka, Jakarta, 1991, p. 82.

37. This argument was put by several speakers at the 28 November 1991 seminar, addressed by ICMI founder B.J. Habibie, the Minister for Research and Technology. One authority endorsing this view was Warta *Ekonomi's* Amir

Effendi Siregar, who lectures in Journalism at Gadjah Mada University, Yogyakarta.

38. According to official 1991 figures, 39~ of *Kompas* journalists are Muslim. There are no non-Muslim journalists with *Pelita (Data Kewartawanan IPPPN Tahun 1991*, p.10).

39. Details on *Pelita* from 'Pelita: Tidak Hijau Lagi?', Tempo, 15 March 1986, p.77; USIS 1992 (Vol. 1), pp.29-30; 'Setelah Pelita Tambah Minyak', *Tempo*, 24 November 1990, p.102; 'Dana, Irama, dan PHK', *Tempo*, 20 July 1991, p.25; 'Cahaya Remang di Pelita', *Editor*, 27 July 1991, pp.36-7; and 'Pijar-pijar Pelita' *Prospek*, 10 August 1991, p.29. Official statistics (Data *Oplah dan Peredaran IPPPN Tahun 1991*, p.12) still give Pelita's circulation as 170,000.

40. Figures from Data *Oplah dan* Peredaran *IPPPN Tahun 1991*, various pages.

41. On the range of small-scale publications directed towards Islamic teaching institutions (pesantren), see 'Pasar di Antara Pesantren', *Tempo*, 23 May 1987, p.32.

42. On Jum'at, see 'Menggemakan Suara Masjid', Tempo, 28 April 1990, pp.878.

43. On Tanri Abeng, see Ciptawidya Swara (ed.), *TOP Eksekutif Indonesia*, PT Ciptawidya Swara, Jakarta, 1992, pp.871-83.

44. 'Republika Siap untuk *Go Public*', *Republika*, 28 January 1993, p.2.

45. 'Andalan ICMI Bernama *Republika*', *DeTIK*, 1-7 September 1993, p.7.

46. Obvious similarities (between UQ No.5, Vol. IV, 1993 and Aditya No.3, October-November 1993) include Aditya's description of itself as a 'Magazine of Religion and Culture'; *Ulumul* Qur'an is a 'Journal of Science and Culture. Whereas *Ulumul* Qur'an's mission statement on the title page says 'Sebagai arena pemikiran ilmu dan kebudayaan, UQ menerima dan menghargai tinggi tulisan-tulisan dari kalangan manapun' [As an arena for thoughts on science and culture, UQ accepts and values highly articles from all circles], Aditya has simply changed the italicised word 'ilmu'(science) into 'agama' (religion).

47. Of the 1991 sales figures in brackets, the first is the official figure provided to the Department of Information's Directorate-General for the Development of Press and Graphics (Data *Oplah* dan Peredaran *IPPPN 1991)*, while the second is the estimate of the United States Information Service publication A Brief Guide to the Indonesian *Media (1992)*.

48. It is widely believed that Suara Karya holds the largest share interest (35%) with the current Minister of Information, Harmoko also holding 5%. *Kompas* is estimated to have 25%, *Tempo* 15% and Suara Pembaruan 10% (USIS 1992 Vol. 1, p.15). Sabam Siagian, former Editor-in-Chief, became Ambassador to Australia in 1991. He had been a senior editor of the independent-minded Sinar *Harapan* for a critical decade (1973-83) which included the two greatest

crack-downs on the Indonesian press (in 1974 and 1978). Siagian was the first journalist to be appointed ambassador by the New Order government, a practice frequently followed during the 1950s, suggesting that the profession may once again become important politically as a training ground for spokespeople, now promoting a new image for an ageing New Order.

49. Quoted in USIS Vol.1 1992:15-6.

50. 'Majalah dengan Bahasa Bisnis', *Tempo*, 16/1/93, p.94.

51. 'Money-losing "Yogya Post" is stopping publication', *The Jakarta Post*, 12/6/92.

52. Soebagijo 1977:37.

53. Soebagijo 1977:108.

54. See *Junaedhie* 1991:204. For a detailed discussion of this period, see Oey 1971:117-32.

55. Coppel 1983:41.

56. The circular (Surat *Edaran*), No. 02/SE/Ditjen-PPG/K/1988, is reproduced in [Anon.] (1989) *Pers National: Himpunan Peraturan dan Perundangundangan serta Ketentuan-ketentuan yang bertalian dengan Pers Nasional*, Yayasan Pengelola Sarana Pers Nasional, Jakarta, pp.125-8.

57. Patrick Walters (1994) 'Indonesia relaxes ban on Chinese language', the *Australian*, 4 August (as listed on internet apakabar@clark.net).

58. Charles A. Coppel (1983), *Indonesian Chinese in Crisis*, Oxford University Press, Kuala Lumpur, p.162-3.

59. See Table 3.

60. USIS 1992 (V01.1):11.

CHAPTER SIX
Facing the Future

'There are two sources which can bring light to everything on this earth: the first is the sun and the second is the press and mass media...'

> President Suharto
> opening the
> Conference of Non-Block
> Information Ministers, 1984[1]

'SIUPP, the existing press-licensing law, hangs like a dagger over the head of Indonesia's journalists; so long as it remains in force, genuine freedom of the press will not be attainable.'

> Committee to Protect Journalists
> August 1991[2]

Government policy statements and regulations continue to emphasise the role of the press as the guardian of the Pancasila and the 1945 Constitution, whose responsibility it is to promote and embed these within the society. The government appeals to those involved in the press to work 'within the framework of our collective and individual devotion to national development'.[3] But, while such rhetoric has changed little since 1967, the political, social and economic environment in which the press functions has altered significantly as the New Order now approaches the close of its third decade in power. Developments in the press industry reflect many of these broader circumstances which have changed the anatomy of the press markedly.

There is a gradual shift in power from within the State to economic interests outside it. Put crudely such a shift involves a diminution of power within the hands of the military and the State's bureaucrats, and an increase in power and influence amongst those acquiring capital and wealth. Such a transition becomes apparent in the increasing tensions between, on the one hand, State bureaucrats as gatekeepers of the press industry, trying to control entry into it and the content of the material it disseminates, and, on the other, capitalists wanting freedom to invest in the print media and to determine the type of press product they sell in the expanding marketplace, free of government constraint and regulation. In this regard, the latest banning of three weekly publications in June 1994 may be a victory for the hardline bureaucrats, but it will only temporarily slow down, and not reverse, the inexorable trend for an expanding liberal economy to require a diverse, heterogeneous and open media.

The Indonesian print media industry shares similar tensions to those experienced by the media (both electronic and print) in many countries, including Australia, where attempts at government regulation (on such matters as cross-media ownership and the level of permissible foreign ownership) are continually under challenge from the pressures of entrepreneurs constantly seeking profit maximisation. The nature of government regulation may differ between Indonesia and Australia but there are numerous similarities obscured by the more frequently highlighted contrasts.

Bearing in mind the pressures to deregulate the print media, this chapter outlines some possible future trends for the industry and comments on what such changes may indicate about Indonesian society and politics more generally.

Economic fluctuations

If one single event symbolises the recent expansion and enormous growth potential for the print media in Indonesia it was the January 1991 Gulf War. The War brought Indonesia's loyalties to both the Muslim nation of Iraq and to the United States of America into sharp contrast. Perhaps more than any other outside power the US supported Suharto's rise to power and, albeit more covertly, the extermination of the Indonesian Communist Party. But while Indonesia is a secular, not a Muslim, State its borders encompass the largest Muslim population of any country in the world. It has maintained good diplomatic relations with the countries of the Middle East and is an active member of the international Islamic community of nations, while depending heavily on economic and political relations with the USA. Throughout Indonesia a sense of Muslim identity and pan-Islamic pride had been strengthening during the 1980s, particularly among young people and students. For many, Islam represented a powerful mobilising faith to be used symbolically against a secular State seemingly edging further towards 'free-fight

Facing the Future

capitalism' and consumerism. While its methodology was hardly scientific, it is illustrative that, in the infamous *Monitor* popularity poll in October 1990, that personification of assertive Islam, Iraq's President Saddam Hussein, ranked seventh, even above the Prophet Mohammad's eleventh place.

As tensions mounted after the invasion of Kuwait popular attention in Indonesia focused fixedly upon the Middle East, with the public thirst for information after the United Nations' counter-attack evident as large crowds gathered outside newspaper offices awaiting details hot off the presses. National press circulation figures, which had been growing steadily throughout the previous decade, skyrocketed. Sold out were *Kompas*' increased print run of 700,000 and *Suara Pembaruan*'s 406,000, leaving the street vendors short of stock. Papers with cover prices of Rp 250 were being hawked on the roadsides for Rp 1,000.[4] Despite difficulties competing with the national giants with their superior technology, even regional papers' sales generally increased by about 10%. Surabaya's daily *Jawa Pos* in the Tempo-Grafiti group, which sent two journalists to the war front, claimed a massive surge in circulation to 550,000![5]

In practice, however, a growth in newspaper sales without an increase in advertising revenue does not equate with a growth in profitability. For many papers, the return on the cover price, even with the increased circulation, was not enough to balance an overall decline in the advertising budget. Subsequently some publications, which had over-stretched themselves during the Gulf War boom, had to cut-back production. No paper was able to sustain this tremendous upsurge generated by interest in the Gulf War and sales generally fell back to pre-War levels. The rapid expansion was followed by a painful contraction.

After commercial television stations began regular satellite broadcasts in August 1989 (when viewers had to pay for a signal decoder attached to their sets to receive the coded transmissions) and particularly since broadcasts went 'free to air' removing the need for a de-coder in mid-1990, the print media's portion of the national advertising budget drastically declined. In 1988 there was no advertising on television, while newspapers had nearly 52% and magazines about 19% of total advertising expenditures. In 1989 TV took about 6% of total advertising expenditure, rising to 8% in 1990, roughly 25.4% in 1991, and a predicted 51.1% by 1994. By 1994, newspapers and magazines were predicted to have declined in percentage terms to 30.8% and 6.9% respectively. Fortunately for the print media, in monetary terms the whole advertising pie increased markedly over this period, more than trebling from Rp 314 billion in 1988 to Rp 1,027 billion in 1992, and to a predicted Rp 1,600 billion by 1994. This has resulted in an increase in the spending on advertising in newspapers overall (from Rp 163 billion in 1988 to Rp 452 billion in 1993) and magazines (from Rp 60 billion in 1988 to Rp 103 billion for 1993).[6] Clearly however, the print media is losing ground to its electronic rival and the pressure is showing as marginal publications fold, victims of this new market competition. Industry observers argue that while TV initially drew advertising away from radio, and weaker circulation magazines, increasingly middle-ranking daily papers began to suffer.[7] However, it appears that, as the market adjusts to the presence of television, advertising revenue is likely to remain with those strong print media companies which produce the leading publications in their particular markets.

Recent entrants into the market felt the squeeze most acutely. Surya Paloh of the Surya Persindo-*Media Indonesia* group, one of the most expansionist of the new press entrepreneurs, complained in February 1992 that 'we did not even reach half of our projected advertising targets [for 1991]'.[8] New forms of advertising were sought in a move away from dependence upon large accounts with national and international companies. D.H. Assegaff, head of the Dr Sutomo Press Institute and Editor-in-Chief of *Warta Ekonomi*, argued that a partial solution to declining retail press advertising budgets was an increase in small classified (or 'mini') ads, that had never been substantial in Indonesia.[9]

In addition to advertising cut-backs, there was another major economic constraint upon business expansion in the press: the impact of the government's 'Tight Money Policy'. Many of the new entrepreneurs who invested so heavily in the late 1980s found it difficult to maintain the high level of funding required. It was not easy to achieve 'break-even point' faced with the greater cost of money, a tightening credit squeeze and a malaise in the industry from the loss to television of projected advertising revenue. Surya Paloh, for example, announced in February 1992 that he was cutting the Surya Persindo-*Media Indonesia* Group's staff numbers by one quarter as part of a drastic cost rationalisation after rumoured losses of more than Rp.8 billion.[10] The group baled out of several regional ventures yet the *Media Indonesia* giant is still more stable than many smaller publishers.

On the basis of his analysis of the approximately 260 SIUPP in operation in early 1992 the respected media analyst Christianto

Wibisono has claimed that about 100 permits are held by ten major mass media conglomerates (by implication in relatively strong financial shape), with the remaining 160 in dire straits, requiring, in his estimate, an average capital injection of Rp 1 billion.[11] Edward Depari, Director of Research and Development with the largest private commercial television station, RCTI, concurs that 'Television will suck away the largest allocation of advertising which had been the lifeblood of newspapers, so that in time small papers will die a slow death'.[12]

The ramification that such struggling enterprises will be swallowed up is supported by the work of Daniel Dhakidae who observed in 1991 that, as total sales increase, there is a corresponding decrease in the number of publications.[13] However, since Dhakidae's research there has been a modest increase in the number of publishing permits (from a low of 252 in 1986 to 276 in 1992) suggesting that his predicted contraction requires some qualification. It seems that as bankrupt smaller publications cash out of the industry a core of large established companies (like *Jawa Pos*) and secure fresh enterprises (like *Republika*) are able successfully to launch new publications to tap specialised markets, more than taking up the slack left by the departures. But, as press conglomerates expand to absorb smaller competitors, Dhakidae's basic premise seems sound: that in future there is likely to be a greater economic concentration in the hands of a diminishing number of proprietors.

Furthermore, as a consequence such proprietors, while rivals in the press market, are likely to have a significant coalescence of interests, both economic and political, both amongst themselves and with the government in seeking an open de-regulated economy (albeit with limitations on new entries into the press sector) and a stable political environment. The threat of losing a SIUPP for antagonising the government already makes investment in the press industry extremely hazardous. Yet with enormous financial risks involved in any disruption, press proprietors are likely to be highly wary of the destabilising uncertainty of political and economic change.

Secularisation

If we compare the types of papers in the marketplace in the early 1990s with the groupings of the 1970s (noted in Chapter 2) there is a marked change from the early years of the New Order. While political alignment may have been the distinguishing feature two decades ago, commercial orientation and the targeted socio-economic market sector are far more significant now.

Six overlapping categories could be identified. The first would be the large-scale newspaper empires which have sprouted from established (formerly politically-aligned) flagships, chiefly *Kompas* and *Suara Pembaruan*. These are now concerned more with the profitable production of the newspaper as commodity rather than bearer of an explicit political posture or voice of a particular community or religious group. They are regarded as 'quality' broadsheets for the middle- and upper-middle class reader. Secondly there has emerged a new category of market-driven 'professionalised' ostensibly 'a-political' commercial ventures, such as *Jawa Pos* and *Media Indonesia*, which were conceived as investments capitalising on the economic deregulation of the 1980s and the increasing 'need to know' of the business sector and the emerging middle class. Many of the new-style 'business' and 'economic' papers that emerged after 1985, such as *Bisnis Indonesia [Indonesian Business]* and *Neraca [Balance]*, could be included in this category.[14]

Thirdly there are the occasional surviving nationalist 'papers of political struggle' *(pers perjuangan)*, such as *Merdeka* (whose circulation appears to have plummeted from a peak of 100,000 to around 30,000 by 1990[15]). In the fourth category are the explicitly pro-government or pro-Army papers, such as *Suara Karya, Angkatan Bersenjata, Berita Yudha* and now even *Pelita*. Had it not been for strong government (or Golkar) support these papers, lacking an autonomous commercial footing, would slide into the fifth group, namely the poorly capitalised small-scale, small-circulation papers, struggling to maintain any market presence. Most of the regional papers not associated with the press empires of the first category could be placed in this group. Finally, the sensationalist entertainment press, such as *Pos Kota*, continues to expand by targeting the lower end of the market.

The trend towards increasing commercialisation and capital concentration within the industry may also be linked to a decline in the pull and influence of the primordial loyalties of ethnicity, religion, and party political affiliation. *Kompas* exemplifies this shift, having discarded its identification as a Javanese/Chinese, Catholic, party paper, and has largely succeeded in redefining itself as a truly 'national', secular, non-party daily. Similarly *Suara Pembaruan*, despite its origins in the Protestant-affiliated *Sinar Harapan*, now emphasises the image of the secularised 'professional' rather appealing to any religious affiliation. Such changes in target market are reflected in the changing composition of the workforce within such papers, which are now increasingly employing Muslim staff.[16] The phenomenon of redefinition of identity is occurring more broadly in the community as the importance of the 'aliran' or socio-religious affiliation declines.[17]

It is too early to determine whether, in the long term, the appearance of the Islamic *Republika* in January 1993 will successfully challenge the dominance of secular papers. If so, it may force us to add a final seventh category to the schema outlined above. The editorial leadership of *Republika* however, seems determined to avoid lapsing into the rut of the 'old style' Muslim papers which spoke only to the devout. Instead, *Republika* presents a more cosmopolitan and sophisticated image, redefining what it means to be a Muslim newspaper in contemporary Indonesia.

Market stratagems

A range of strategies has been used in the competition for increased circulation. Partly to compete with challenges posed by international and national satellite television news, there has been a rapid adoption by the print media of high technologies and an increase in the 'standards' of production (with computerisation, more use of colour photos, more striking layout and a range of international and provincial correspondents). Survivors have achieved a greater efficiency in administration and distribution, often causing bitter local competition.[18] Companies are increasingly active and innovative in self-promotion, using a range of inducements from free promotional copies and lucrative readers' competitions to the sponsorship of sports teams, public events, academic seminars and even academic institutes. Competitive pressures are also emboldening coverage of key newsworthy events, which might be regarded as politically sensitive. Controversial news is a commodity which drives up sales, even if it exposes a paper to the risk of closure.

A striking initial example of this was the extensive, often graphic, coverage of the 12 November 1991 Dili massacre outside the Santa Cruz cemetery, demonstrating a degree of press freedom unknown since the 1974 mass bans, and a stark departure from the muted reporting of previous comparable incidents in Lampung, Aceh, or Tanjung Priok.[19] It signalled the beginning of a period of increasingly explicit and investigative political reporting which peaked with the June 1994 bans.

Coverage of the Dili massacre began hesitantly. While news of the early morning massacre reached Jakarta's press rooms within hours, no Jakarta newspaper that afternoon mentioned the event. Editors were waiting impatiently for an official government statement from the Armed Forces Information Office (*Puspen ABRI*) which screens controversial stories. Newspapers withheld available information from eye-witnesses or international wire services, exercising self-censorship in the absence of a green light from the government. The following morning a number of newspapers ran accounts self-consciously sourcing every piece of information to the military's press release and government spokespeople. *Kompas*' front page story, reassuringly headined 'The Situation in the Town of Dili has been Overcome', recounted the government's call in the form of a press release for the community to remain calm and avoid being inflamed by 'irresponsible agents'.

Editors adopted the established practice of reproducing the official line while indicating tactfully that credible individuals or groups doubt this position. The *Jakarta Post*, for instance, reported the Armed Forces press release in its story headlined 'Security Forces in East Timor Clash with Demonstrators', but it noted too the highly respected non-government Legal Aid Foundation's call for an independent inquiry into the incident.

Gradually added were reports of the international (and particularly United Nations') reactions together with government counter-claims that foreign press reports were 'exaggerated'. Within days, saturation reporting filled the pages of most national papers, with colour photographs, 'on the spot' reports, commentators' evaluations, editorial comment, criticisms from opposition lobby groups, always accompanied by official government and military explanations. By the end of the first week after the massacre the official chronology and explanation had appeared in all the papers. But the story had become too big to control easily and the sheer volume of material enabled numerous challenging and critical reports to surface. The press, as an industry, was becoming so large and so productive that it was getting more difficult to monitor and intimidate.

Despite a long history of government repression, the Jakarta press corps had managed to get out an enormous amount of detail on the massacre, without suffering any bans. Journalists privately welcomed this as initiating a new phase of openness and press freedom. For them, it augured well for the future of the press, as commercial pressures for scoops and public demand for detailed reporting came increasingly to outweigh the heavy 'security' hand of the authorities.

It might reasonably be assumed that the widespread domestic

press coverage also played its part (together with international diplomatic overtures) in pressuring the government to establish a National Investigative Commision to hold a public inquiry into the incident. In the past, elite political rivalry had occasionally opened windows of opportunity for bolder press coverage, but such fulsome coverage of the Dili massacre came to be interpreted increasingly as demonstrating publishers' responses to a public demand for information, expressed in booming sales.

The graphic coverage of the Dili massacre came in the wake of various calls by prominent conservative political figures during 1990 for greater political 'openness' and economic deregulation to be extended to the media generally. Divisions within the power elite were evident when the Co-ordinating Minister for Security and Political Affairs, the perennial Admiral Sudomo, who had headed the all-powerful KOPKAMTIB Security Command for more than eight years till 1981, expressed the belief that there was no longer a need for newspapers to be banned. In a quick but insincere retort, Minister of Information, Harmoko, agreed, adding with sleight of hand that it may be necessary nonetheless to withdrawn a paper's SIUPP permit, as he had done in several cases since becoming Minister in 1983![20] The press, then, is a barometer of broader political debate regarding 'openness', reporting it and, in so doing, demonstrating the nature of permissible discourse, ever conscious of the penalties.

Press companies would be naive to ignore the continued possibility of bans even despite the President's periodic disingenuous endorsements of 'openness'. So they employ various ploys to minimise risks. Some networks cultivate powerful political 'protectors' or have integrated military or Golkar publications into the empire, such as *Suara Pembaruan*'s relationship to *Jayakarta* (partly owned by the Jakarta Military Command) or the *Jawa Pos*' association with the pro-Golkar paper *Bhirawa*. Some proprietors have strongly entrenched institutional links with government or semi-government organisations, such as Yakob Utama's membership of such bodies as the Newspaper Publishers Association (SPS), the Indonesian Journalists Association (PWI) and the semi-government Press Council. In many cases, the the press empires have been consciously structured so that sub-sections are dispensable. The Kompas-Gramedia group could jettison even the enormously profitable *Monitor*, not to mention run-of-the-mill periodicals like *Senang*, to keep the rest of the empire afloat. Even without the flagship *Kompas* daily, insiders have claimed the empire would remain resiliently profitable.

The fact that three of the four major conglomerates detailed in Chapter 4 had suffered government bans and resultant financial disasters illustrates the enormous economic impact of State power over the media industry. Undeniably, the fortunes of press entrepreneurs are clearly dependent upon government media policies, but astute operators in the industry have guided the successful expansion of the complex interlocking empires such as the Tempo-Grafiti, *Jawa Pos* or the Kompas-Gramedia groups, despite the occasional ban of individual publications, like *Tempo* or *Monitor*.

A press empire can employ smaller subsidiary papers to test the political waters on controversial issues. The modest-circulation *Jayakarta* was one of the frankest papers in its coverage of the Dili massacre and its consequences, while the larger flagship *Suara Pembaruan*, with a much more substantial financial stake at risk, took a more moderate line.[21] As one editor familiar with the relationship between the two described it, *Jayakarta* 'is like a kind of destroyer, which operates ahead of the cruiser or the aircraft carrier. It is much more manoeuvrable, and it can draw the fire or sweep for mines' protecting the more valuable *Suara Pembaruan*.[22]

Conversely, the smaller subsidiary papers may enjoy tactical support and protection from their larger associates. For example, in May 1992 when officials from the regional government 'proofread' and 'authorised' election reports going to press in Palembang's *Sriwijaya Post*, *Kompas*, with which the *Post* had a cooperative agreement, gave the incident front page coverage and published a pointed editorial critical of this breach of freedom of the press. The Governor was called to account by the Minister for Internal Affairs, Rudini, and formal apologies given to the *Post*'s staff.[23] In responding in this supportive manner, *Kompas* was far from unique since the case aroused considerable support for the *Post* from large papers, but the Palembang paper may have counted on *Kompas*' paternal support at least.

While sophisticated communication and press production technologies now give the Jakarta giant papers the capability of simultaneously producing identical editions in virtually any town throughout the archipelago, shrewd operators in the industry like Dahlan Iskan predict that the future will see the decline of the 'national' newspaper and the rise of truly 'regional' or sub-national dailies. He argues that the Indonesian industry will increasing resemble that of Australia where each state capital city has its 'market leader'. Throughout Indonesia strong provincial dailies will come to dominate the local market by providing detailed local news (as only a newspaper based in that city can), using communications technologies to provide broad coverage also of national and international events. Such a combination would enable well-managed, well-funded regional papers to match Jakarta-based leviathans.[24] It seems consistent too with the central government's recent emphasis on the development of regional economies, notably that of Eastern Indonesia, the *Jawa Pos'* backyard. Iskan believes the *Jawa Pos* group's current strategy of strengthening a multitude of local papers will be more successful than primarily promoting the flagship daily and only secondarily offering assistance to local papers.

Taking Iskan's strategy one step further exposes one of the great mysteries of the Indonesian press world: the absence of the truly local suburban or 'community' newspaper. Given that freely distributed suburban newspapers in an Australian city like Perth employ more staff than that city's major daily paper and command a healthy advertising budget from small businesses, it is surprising that such community papers have not yet emerged in Indonesia. While, to some extent, existing small-town Indonesian provincial papers (where they appear) may fulfil this role, there is little in the major urban areas comparable to the free suburban paper; nothing therefore to serve the needs and tap the advertising budget of local medium and small businesses. It would seem likely that, with the growth of the Indonesian middle-class, and the physical spread of Indonesian cities, particularly in real estate development housing complexes, that such 'local' free papers will begin to appear. These would be able to take advantage of small-scale high-technology production techniques, increasing supplies of skilled editorial and technical staff, cheap distribution possibilities and the proliferation of increasingly self-contained real estate 'suburbs'.

Globalisation

The national trend away from *'pers perjuangan'* [press of political struggle] towards greater technological 'modernisation' and 'professionalism' could be interpreted as going hand-in-hand with a greater assimilation into the networks and operating style of international (Anglo-American) media. These pressures may well also be activated through such organisations as the Press Foundation of Asia, the Confederation of ASEAN Journalists together with various other international training programs such as journalist scholarships offered by the East-West Centre in Hawaii or the Niemann

Fellowships to Harvard, and perhaps also through such professional institutions as the Dr Sutomo Academy of Journalism under the auspices of the Dr Sutomo Press Foundation.[25]

While such 'trans-national' assimilation might mute the more specific nationalist ethos of the 'pers perjuangan', there is evidence of counter-pressures, albeit not worth over-emphasising. Several of the major journalism training institutions have on their teaching staff editors from newspapers long banned by the government for their critical coverage, such as Aristides Katoppo (of *Sinar Harapan*) at the University of Indonesia, Atmakusumah Astraatmaja (of *Indonesia Raya*) at the Dr Sutomo Academy, and Ashadi Siregar (of the student paper *Sendi*, banned in 1972) at Gadjah Mada University. Academe, it seems, has provided something of a haven for those previously excluded by the government from working in the profession.

The tremendous pressures to adopt the ethos and practices of the Anglo-American international press industry are growing however. The political, economic and linguistic *cordon sanitaire* which has protected the national Indonesian print media industry from outside competition may be under threat from domestic economic deregulation and international pressure against 'protectionism'. The 1966 Basic Press Law (No.11, Article 13) provides what was assumed to be an impenetrable barrier against foreign involvement in the press, stating 'The capital of press companies has to be entirely national capital, and all founders and managers have to be Indonesian citizens' (Paragraph 2). Furthermore it continues, 'Press companies are prohibited from giving or receiving services, help or contributions to or from foreign interests, except with the agreement of the Government after hearing the opinion of the Press Council' (Paragraph 3).

Despite such prohibitions, speculation began in the early years of the 1990s that these provisions may be weakened, exposing the domestic industry to competition from international press companies.[26] Such foreign concerns could then, conceivably, use their world-wide resources to produce Indonesian language newspapers with an international *cachet*. How would the market respond to an Indonesian-language 'trans-national' edition of the *International Herald Tribune*, *The New York Times*, or *Newsweek*? Would the 'prestige' of such publications erode the Indonesian market and lure readers away, at least from *Kompas* and *Suara Pembaruan* at the top end? When faced with such international competition, other sectors of the Indonesian media have fared poorly. American pressure has long ensured an open Indonesian market for imported Hollywood movies, which have swamped Indonesian film producers. Satellite television from CNN, BBC, ABC, Malaysia's TV3, and a raft of other international commercial broadcasters has long permeated Indonesia's national borders, proving stiff competition for domestic broadcasters, both government and private.

Indonesian press investors responded to such early speculation by calling for the local industry to gird itself against possible competition. Capital strength, deregulation and technological sophistication are the answers, according to Sutrisno Bachir.[27] Foster critical analytical skills in the society, so it is able to distill and interprete information from a range of sources, he argued. Next, relax the SIUPP provisions to allow the market to determine the number of viable publications, together with the level of investment and financial returns. Ensure a clear division of responsibility between investors and their editorial staff, to avoid potential conflicts of interest, and return integrity to the professional organisations like the PWI. Finally, echoing one of the most insistent themes voiced by investors and workers within the industry, Bachir called for legal security within the industry, by asserting the rule of law and guaranteeing those who contravene it the right to a trial rather than arbitrary penalty by ministerial whim.

In mid-1994, what had begun several years earlier as idle speculation within the industry about foreign investment, became an embarrasing public display of government incompetence and cabinet confusion over economic policy. On 2 June, as part of the ongoing policy of economic de-regulation, key economic ministers announced 'Government Regulation No. 20', which opened up various sensitive sectors of the economy to foreign investment and majority foreign ownership. Most controversially, among the previously off-limits sectors to be opened was the mass media.

Immediately Information Minister Harmoko, who had not been a party to the deliberations and was clearly caught off-guard, vehemently dissociated himself from the Government Regulation, asserting that it contradicted superior Indonesian legislation, notably the 1966 Basic Press Law, explicitly prohibiting any kind of foreign investment or intervention in the press. Obviously annoyed at his exclusion from such crucial policy negotiations which demonstrably fell within his portfolio, an emotional Harmoko instructed journalists to quote his public rebuke of his ministerial colleagues. For several days, the press reported extensively on the split and apparent inconsistencies between the various Acts and Regulations governing foreign investment in the media.[28]

In an attempt to assert his authority and terminate debate Harmoko finally declared angrily that, irrespective of the letter of the Government Regulation, he had the full support of the President in keeping foreign interests out of the press. Despite having earlier signed the Government Regulation, the President endorsed Harmoko's excision of the press from the new policy. The back-flip suggested to some observers that the President was losing touch with the increasingly complex web of government policy. Others suggested he was also having difficulty balancing competing ministers within the Cabinet. It was a further indication of the President's willingness to side with Harmoko (and Habibie) rather than more liberal rationalist ministers determining overall economic policy. As Indonesia was increasingly integrating with the world economy and international information order, Suharto and the press' gate-keepers were still stubbornly attempting to control information flows. Although the public debate on foreign investment in the media was silenced, these general conclusions about the President and his Minister were reinforced within weeks by the triple bans of *Tempo*, *Editor* and *DeTIK*.

Industry speculation continued that one of the driving pressures pushing for foreign investment came from the electronic media, owned by members or associates of the Presidential family. The enormous capital costs of establishing and maintaining television networks and associated satellite technology were draining domestic investment. During Rupert Murdoch's whirlwind visit to Jakarta in March, RCTI head Peter Gontha had already signed a cooperative agreement with the magnate.[29] Sceptics within the print media industry argue that, while Harmoko will ensure that the press remains off-limits to foreign funds, well-connected conglomerates with interests in the electronic media will deftly evade restrictions on foreign investment. Outside funds could easily be disguised by a series of transfers between media and non-media branches within these giant conglomerates. With influential political protectors, such holding companies would not require government implementation of Regulation No.20 explicitly in regard to the mass media.

While the government's position on future foreign investment in the Indonesian media is open to question, some publishing ventures are exploring the benefits trans-national distribution and investment may have for them, as part of the broader internationalisation of capital. Staff from the *Jakarta Post* have indicated that it aspires to a distribution throughout Southeast Asia, eyeing jealously the role played by international English language papers and magazines like the *International Herald Tribune* and the *Far Eastern Economic Review*. While the logistics would be daunting, the paper's strategists recognise both the limited potential market for an English paper in Indonesia and conversely the vast English-speaking readership in neighbouring Singapore, Malaysia and the Philippines. The energetic head of the *Jawa Pos* empire, Dahlan Iskan, has pursued his belief in the future of regional papers by exploring the possibility of investing in the regional press in Australia. Factors to consider include Australia's general attraction as a secure site for foreign capital and specifically its lax regulations concerning foreign investment in the media, combined with the technological superiority and financial strength of the *Jawa Pos* empire. Such a suggestion might have been viewed with some amazement, even in the recent past. It was only in 1983 that senior staff from the *West Australian* daily newspaper were brought in as consultants to the fledgling *Jakarta Post*. Now it seems a growing possibility that the flow of funds and experience may be the other way.

In attempting in the 1990s to cordon off the domestic media from events in the neighbouring region and throughout the world, both with regard to the flow of capital as well as the transfer of news and information, the New Order faces a more enigmatic national and international media-scape than it did in the 1960s. Political instability, public protest and regime change in neighbouring countries have always been sensitive issues for governments in the Southeast Asian region, and highlight both domestic and bilateral tensions, and the increasing inter-relatedness of the regional political environment. Each decade throws up examples of the discomfort caused by media reports reverberating across national boundaries. Three incidents highlight the problems and illustrate something of the impact of improved technologies and financial capacities of the Indonesian press.

When student demonstrations in Thailand brought an end to the Thanom-Prapas military regime in October 1973, the Indonesian press was then enjoying one of its most outspoken periods of criticism of its government. Inter-elite rivalries between senior military officers were fragmenting power, and enabling assertive editors to exploit this political 'room to move'. The press, notably critical papers like *Indonesia Raya*, published detailed reports of the public upsurge bringing political change in Thailand,[30] which some commentators believe emboldened Indonesian student protests leading to the 'Malari' disturbances of January 1974. Ultimately, the widespread press bans which followed 'Malari' remain the most far-reaching since 1966, indicating the consequences then for a vociferous press.

When the 'people's power revolution' in Manila was ousting the Marcos regime in 1986, once more the Indonesian press gave events considerable prominence. While financial contraints had prevented even major Indonesian papers sending correspondents to Bangkok in 1973, this time numerous Indonesian journalists reported directly from Manila, ensuring the uprising had a profile which caused some unease within the Indonesian Government, not least among those charged with ensuring the re-election of the government organisation Golkar in the forthcoming April 1987 general elections. The Philippines 'revolution' coincided with intensifying competition between Indonesian press companies vying for readership, and eager to provide the most graphic and comprehensive account of this major international affair. Yet, conscious of the government's apprehensions, Indonesian papers exercised 'self-restraint' and made no explicit comparisons between Indonesia and the Philippines, although correlations were widely noted by the public.

The resemblance was underlined, however, in a front page article in *The Sydney Morning Herald* by David Jenkins, one of Australia's most experienced and best informed journalists specialising in Indonesian affairs. Entitled 'After Marcos, now for the Soeharto billions',[31] the article fomented one of the bitterest diplomatic tensions between Indonesia and Australia. Australian journalists were banned from Indonesia and a plane-load of Australian holiday-makers was refused tourist visas which, at that time, were routinely issued on arrival.

Pressure was brought to bear upon the Indonesian press to represent the Jenkins article as a slur against all Indonesians rather than a factual critique of a Marcos-like President. The article contained material already widely published elsewhere abroad and broadly accepted as true even by moderate critics of the government. Photocopies of it were hot property in opposition circles, but papers were advised strongly not to report its specific claims. While there were no dissenting press voices defending Jenkins publicly, for many critical journalists and members of the public, the Australian journalist became something of a hero and professional champion. The incident highlighted for many journalists just how much about the President and his family was widely known yet could not be stated explicitly in the Indonesian press. At the time, the government crackdown on the contents of the Jenkins article was largely successful in stifling discussion. In today's changing political and economic climate much of the detail is now widely reportable in the press, so long as the financial successes of the first family are presented positively, as enhancing Indonesia's economic development, rather than as rapacious nepotism.

The Indonesian Government still attempts occasionally to plug the State borders rendered so porous by satellite transmissions. While in so-doing it may achieve diplomatic success, it can rarely control the images accessible to its populace. The widepread broadcasting in Europe, Australia and the USA, of video film taken by British journalist, Max Stahl, during the November 1991 Santa Cruz massacre vividly condemned the Indonesian military in international public opinion. However, when Malaysia's state-owned television station re-broadcast the controversial film in a September 1992 documentary on East Timor, which was picked up by viewers across the Straits of Malacca, the Indonesian Government formally protested, with Information Minister Harmoko demanding an explanation. The Malaysian Deputy Information Minister, Railey bin Haji Jefri, swiftly apologised and assured Indonesia that such oversights would not recur.[32]

While diplomatic leverage might succeed with near neighbours, there is little the government can do to filter select messages out of the bombardment of transnational information flows, whether in print or in the electronic media. Increasingly, its attempts at strict control and 'self-regulation' by domestic media organisations will become ineffectual in the face of international competition as the government struggles to come to terms with a rapidly evolving, dizzyingly complex, and economically powerful world media scene.

Control and self-regulation

In the early 1990s, as the continuing process of economic deregulation began to be accompanied by pronouncements of political openness, the press adopted an increasingly forthright tone in its coverage of domestic political issues. Formerly off-limits topics, such as the emerging tensions between civilian and military factions within the government alliance and antagonisms between key civilian ministers, were exposed and analysed in detail by the emboldened press. Eros Jarot, editor of the fastest-growing if ill-fated *DeTIK* weekly, was frank, almost cocky about the frequent, but largely ignored, warnings given to his roguish tabloid. Most like-minded editors believed that, by constantly pushing back the acceptable limits upon political coverage, the press was pursuing a rational strategy to contribute to political openness while maximising their market share, most noticably by tapping a growing (and increasingly inquisitive and politically assertive) middle-class.

Their observations, too, were that the nature of power in the New Order had changed significantly since the mass bans of the 1970s. Power had become less centred on the President, more diffuse and fragmented, reducing the likelihood, they argued, of the State acting in unanimity against the press. There were now strong counter forces in the State - economic, political, even liberal elements in the military, signs of a more independent judiciary - whose interests would not be served by arbitrary ministerial bans. An open, boisterous media permitted such emerging forces a voice. All such competing social forces would have greater difficulty in putting their views across if the media was reined in again.

There was apprehension too about the detrimental effect of arbitrary ministerial authority upon Indonesia's economic reputation as a secure site for foreign investment, assiduously being cultivated. The rule of law, public accountability, especially for public funds dispensed by the government and its agencies, and the transparency and equitable operation of the investment market were becoming greater priorities than long-standing preoccupations with national 'security' and the suppression of peaceful opposition and non-violent dissent. Unless the government was prepared to set an example and use the courts to adjudicate in its claims against press companies how, its critics questioned, could foreign investors be sure the government would abide by the law when dealing with disputes within any other sector of the economy?

While the Indonesian Constitution guarantees freedom of expression, and the Press Act declares unequivocally that the press is not subject to 'censorship or ban' and that 'freedom of the press is guaranteed in accordance with the fundamental rights of citizens', the publication permits and the ministerial authority to revoke these, starkly undermine these constitutional rights. This self-contradictory legal system and the lack of due legal process in media cases may trigger concerns amongst the business community more generally for clear legal guidelines in the event of conflict with the government or its departments. A demonstrable commitment to the rule of law would be expected to encourage both foreign and domestic long-term investment in all sectors of the economy.

Such public concerns may translate into a strengthened judiciary, more independent of the executive. There have been several indications of this increasing independence in the wake of the June 1994 triple press bans. Protesters arrested during the anti-bans demonstrations in July received minimal fines of only Rp. 2,000 (approximately $AUD 1.30). That month, in another surprise verdict, the Supreme Court ruled in favour of $1 million compensation for 34 farmers evicted from the controversial central Java Kedung Ombo damsite, thus overturning unfavourable verdicts in the Semarang District Court and the Central Java High Court.[33] Despite government attempts to have the case reviewed to avoid payment, Chief Justice, Purwoto Gandasubrata declared that the government was obliged to pay the compensation immediately. The government feared a rash of such compensation claims. In another step towards redefining the legal process, at the end of July, a meeting of 350 senior legal experts convened in Jakarta to revise the legal system largely inherited from the Dutch colonial period (without substantial change in the case of civil and criminal codes). The indigenisation of the legal system has been identified as a government priority.

While the power of the State to regulate the press industry, through legislation and extra-judicial means, has not diminished since the founding of the New Order, amidst the enormous commercial explosion which has taken place over the past decade, one striking feature is the increasing tendency for the state-sponsored synapses with the press industry, such as the Press Council, the Journalists' Association and the Publishers Association, to appear to 'self-regulate', enforcing conformity with government policies upon renegade journalists and publications. Of the 1970s, Dhakidae observed 'The quelling of opinionated journalism ... was, curiously enough, carried out more by the press itself than by the state',[34] a trend accelerated throughout the 1980s. However, while on a day-to-day basis it is industry 'restraint' borne of decades of arbitrary penalty, which keeps mavericks in line, in the ultimate analysis 'The real power over Indonesian journalism rests with this state repressive apparatus'.[35] As editor, Gunawan Mohamad claimed after *Tempo* was banned in June 1994, trying to run an Indonesian news magazine was like being a 'pilot in a hijacked plane'. Referring to government interference in editorial content, he added that, even if the government was prepared to issue *Tempo* a fresh publishing licence, he would only end up with 'a new plane complete with new hijackers'.

As anthropologist Ariel Heryanto has noted:
'There are more than enough lessons in the immediate past to show

that if the government deems it necessary, it has the power to ban any publication, or even publisher, at any time and without trial. Prior experience, and perhaps some perceptiveness to occasional occurrence of subtle and largely silent changes in the political dynamics of the top state leadership, have taught [those in the press] which areas are strictly proscribed, which are conditionally publishable, which are permissible, and which are imperative...[Readers of the press] should keep in mind at least the fact that these constraints exist.'[36]

Despite the financial changes in the industry in the 1990s, an understanding of the content of the nation's press still requires a honed ability to read the unsaid rather than the explicit.

Capitalism and Democratisation

Even allowing for the financial squeeze in the press industry in Indonesia in the early 1990s, the overall growth during the past decade, with the skyrocketing of print media circulation since the 1980s indicates an expanding reading public. With their concerted push into the regional press, empires such as Kompas-Gramedia, Tempo-Grafiti/Jawa Pos and Surya Persindo-Media Indonesia have identified and tapped the emergence of a substantial readership outside Jakarta. On the one hand the survival of 'regional' papers (albeit as subsidiaries within press empires) is premised, partially at least, on the pull of regional loyalties. On the other hand the greater success of 'national' publications points to a contrasting trend away from defining mass readership in terms of religious or ethnic submarkets. Instead their market divides into a complex cross-hatching of socio-economic and 'interest' groups, exemplified by the success of an enormous variety of specialist periodicals. Given the increased targeting of publications at lower-middle and lower class readers (notably by the *Jawa Pos* group), personal expenditure on newspapers may be spreading beyond the 'middle classes' (however defined). Furthermore, as the industry faces a tough decade economically, and with the pressure for financial 'de-regulation' and political 'democratisation', it will increasingly be capital, not political connections, which will ensure the durability of newspaper conglomerates and the future face of the Indonesian press.

One of the lessons of Bimantara's association with the Surya Persindo empire and Surya Paloh's challenge of the Minister of Information's right to ban papers may be that the clammer for greater 'freedom of the press' and 'the rule of law' may not be spearheaded so much by a middle-class demand for 'liberal democratic rights' for 'free speech' and a 'free press'. Instead, it may be that it is more attributable to pressures from within capitalist elements of the ruling compact, precipitating if not its own downfall, then at least significant amelioration of its more repressive aspects. While the interests of the State, politico-bureaucrats and political powerholders are best served by a strongly controlled and docile press, capitalist entrepreneurs like Surya Persindo and conglomerates like Bimantara, which are new to the press industry, would benefit from increasing liberalisation of both press constraints and entry into this restricted sector of the economy. Surya Paloh's call for a Judicial Review of ministerial authority over press regulation, which has opened the possibility for aggrieved companies to query arbitrary ministerial discretion, may encourage the State to use judicial process more in controlling the media. By strengthening the legal basis and durability of press permits, this would then make investment in the print media more secure, beyond threat from an individual Minister.

Ironically, the public trial of Arswendo Atmowiloto, the hapless editor of *Monitor*, was cause for some relief within press circles. Although *Monitor*'s indiscretion provided ammunition for bureaucrats like the Minister of Information to assert that the press still required firm regulation, the trial of the magazine's editor demonstrated the State's preparedness to use judicial rather than arbitary power to deal with possible breaches of press legislation.[37] The industry's call for an open trial for a renegade editor or paper is a claim for transparent rights before the law for a newspaper just as for any other commercial venture. Investors, both foreign and local, become wary on seeing a press business, or any other enterprise, closed by ministerial decree, without recourse to legal defence; an action that is, in the words of *Tempo* editor Fikri Jufri 'not good public relations for Indonesia'.[38]

Despite the continued arbitrary exercise of ministerial (and presidential) power over the press, it might be argued that accountability and transparency, deemed so necessary for the successful operation of an open market economy and particularly for the smooth operation of a stock exchange and international financial markets, may be becoming more central to the operations of press control, just as it has become crucial to the government's policies for broader economic development in the 1990s.

Atmowiloto's trial, Surya Paloh's appeal for a judicial review, the

Parliamentary Commission's public questioning of Minister Harmoko over the June 1994 bans, military spokespeople's encouragement for aggrieved press companies to challenge the revocation of their SIUPP in the Administrative Court: these are all signs, sanctified by wide public debate in the media, of the increasing legitimacy and authority of legal procedure in the New Order. As the popular movement for democratisation progresses, the calls for accountability, which are as relevant to and as supported by the media companies as they are by any other financial sector, may operate ultimately to undermine those factions within the regime which would seek to maintain blanket control of the political process and of the media.

ENDNOTES

1. The original quotation is repeated in the Minister of Information's opening speech at the First National Press Day Celebration, 9 February 1985, Jakarta, see Departemen Penerangan RI (1986), *Beberapa Aspek Pembinaan Kewartawanan*, Directorat Jenderal Pembinaan Pers dan Grafika, Jakarta, p.91.

2. The Committee to Protect Journalists (1991), *In the Censor's Shadow: Journalism in Suharto's Indonesia*, CPJ, New York, p.20.

3. As examples of such appeals, see the sections on Information and Mass Media in the Broad Outlines of State Policy *(Garis Besar Haluan Negara*, GBHN) and the Introduction by Director General of Press and Graphics, Janner Sinaga, to Anon. 1989:4 & 137-8.

4. See 'Teluk Meledak, koran meledak', *Prospek*, 2 February 1991, pp.44-9.

5. See 'Di sana hujan bom, di sini hujan emas', *Tempo*, 2 February, 1991, p.100. Figures are rubbery, since 'Demam Scud dan Patriot', *Editor*, 2 February 1991, pp.93-4, gives the increase in *Jawa Pos* circulation as a nonetheless considerable 80%.

6. Figures drawn from Table 4.

7. Interview with Aristides Katoppo, of the *Sinar Harapan* group, Jakarta, December 1991.

8. 'Bisnis Pers: Kelesuan dan Bentrokan', *Tempo*, 29 February 1992, p.71-2 (quotation p.72).

9. Djafar H. Assegaff (1992), 'Catatan Akhir Tahun: Industri Media Massa 92', *Reporter*, No. 24, Year IV, December 1992/January 1993, p.3.

10. 'Bisnis Pers: Kelesuan dan Bentrokan', *Tempo*, 29/2/92, p.71.

11. Christianto Wibisono (1992), 'Piramida Pers Indonesia', *Tempo*, 15 February, pp.104-5.

12. 'Edward Depari: Kebijakan Menghindari Maling', *Republika*, 3/2/93, p.10.

13. Dhakidae 1991:66-7.

14. The English-language business magazines *Economic and Business Review Indonesia* and *Indonesia Business Weekly* would also fit into this category.

15. USIS 1992 (Vol. 1), p.27.

16. Dhakidae 1991:350 provides a graph indicating that the number of Muslim employees equalled Catholics in the total Kompas Gramedia Group by the

mid-1980s. Official 1991 statistics indicate that of the 127 journalists in *Kompas* daily however only 39% are Muslim, 12% are Protestant and 48% are Catholic. In *Suara Pembaruan*, of the total of 106 journalists 28% are Muslim, 60% are Protestant and 10% are Catholic.

17. The term 'aliran', popularised by Clifford Geertz in the 1960s, refers to the Javanese 'world outlook' encompassing 'religious beliefs, ethical preferences, and political ideologies' which divided the Javanese into ~three main cultural types which reflect the moral organization of Javanese culture' (see Clifford Geertz (1976), *The Religion of Java*, University of Chicago Press, Chicago (lst ed. 1960s, pp.4-6.) While sociological discourse still refers to Geertz's classic tripartite social sub-division of Islamic traders *(santri)*, syncretic peasants *(abangan)* and aristocratic bureaucrats *(priyayi)*, its originally blurred borders have now become so porous as to make the differentiation somewhat arbitrary.

18. 'Main Kotor di Bursa Media', *Prospek*, 23 February 1991, p.11.

19. David Hill & Krishna Sen (1991), 'How Jakarta saw the massacre', *Inside Indonesia*, No. 29, December 1991, pp.6-8.

20. Michael R.J. Vatikiotis (1993), *Indonesian Politics Under Suharto: Order, Development and Pressure for Change*, Routledge, London & New York, pp.107-8 examines this incident and the broader political climate

21. For example, *Jayakarta* (14 November 1991) quoted extensively from Armed Forces chief, General Try Sutrisno that 'those who misbehave must be shot' and that the Armed Forces 'is determined to eliminate anyone who disturbs stability'. In addition *Jayakarta* was one of two papers to feature graphic front page colour photographs of the peaceful demonstration by East Timorese students held outside Jakarta's United Nations offices and the Japanese and Australian Embassies held on Tuesday 19th, reporting that seventy were held for interrogation.

22. Confidential interview, December 1991.

23. Coverage included 'Tidak ada maksud untuk melakukan sensor berita', *Kompas*, 29 May 1992, pp.1 & 5; 'Mendagri Rudini Panggil Gubernur Sumsel', *Kompas*, 30 May 1992, pp.1 & 13; and editorial 'Dalam Zaman Keterbukaan Sekarang, Sensor Pers Merupakan Keanehan Besar', *Kompas*, 30 May 1992, p.4.

24. Dahlan Iskan made these comments at the Murdoch Asia Research Centre conference, Indonesia: Paradigms for the Future, Fremantle, July 1993.

25. The Dr Sutomo Press Institute *(Lembaga Pers Dr Sutomo)*, based on an idea emerging from the Press Council's 1987 Plenary Session to establish a training institute for professional journalists, was opened by the Minister of Information, Harmoko, in July 1988 (see 'Mencetak Kuli Tinta yang Profesional', *Tempo*, 30 July 1988, pp.76-7). It ran short professional courses. This program was expanded into the Dr Sutomo Academy of Journalism in April 1989, with the goal of providing yearlong 'MBA-style' courses in

journalism. Staff have included a former head of the Supreme Court (now deceased), academics, leading journalists and editors, and an American Cornell University graduate as curriculum designer (see 'AJS, buat Reporter M.B.A.', *Tempo*, 5 May 1990, p.33).

26. These issues have been raised particularly in Adhie M. Massardi (1992), 'Jika Pers Asing Berbahasa Indonesia', *Suara Pembaruan*, 8/2/92.

27. Soetrisno Bachir (1992), 'Bisnis Pers di Tengah Arus Globalisasi', *Kompas*, 10/2/92.

28. On Government Regulation No.20 and the media coverage, see for example, *DeTIK*, 8-14 June 1994, pp.4-12; *Tempo*, 11 June 1994, pp.28-30; *Kompas*, various articles, 3-4 June 1994.

29. See 'Harmoko Mengecam, Di Mana Gontha', Tempo, 11 June 1994, pp.29-30.

30. For example, 'Revolusi di Negeri Pagoda' (4 parts), *Indonesia Raya*, 1-5 November 1973.

31. *Sydney Morning Herald*, 10/4/86.

32. 'Everybody needs good neighbours', *The Sunday Age*, (Melbourne), 27/9/92.

33. See Patrick Walters (1994), 'Jakarta's double-Dutch legal system ready for overhaul', *The Australian*, 27 July 1994, p.13.

34. Dhakidae 1991:214.

35. Dhakidae 1991:546.

36. Ariel Heryanto (1990), 'Introduction: State Ideology and Civil Discourse' (pp.289-300) in Arief Budiman (ed.) (1990), *State and Civil Society in Indonesia*, Monash Centre for Southeast Asian Studies, Clayton. Quotation from pp. 293-4.

37. See Karto Wijoyo (1990), 'Letter from Jakarta', Inside Indonesia, No. 25, December 1990, pp.2-5. I would like to thank David Bourchier particularly for suggesting some of these lines of inquiry.

38. Quoted in Michael Day (1994), 'Press bans will harm Indonesia, says editor', the *West Australian*, 5/7/94, p. 10.

TABLE 1:
NUMBER OF PUBLICATIONS IN CIRCULATION IN INDONESIA (by year)

Year	Number	Year	Number
1949	75	1971	292
1950	319	1972	490
1951	317	1973	473
1952	318	1974	459
1953	335	1975	283
1954	399	1976	282
1955	457	1977	273
1956	416	1978	273
1957	401	1979	271
1958	368	1980	255
1959	324	1981	276
1960	456	1982	273
1961	223	1983	267
1962	286	1984	263
1963	476	1985	264
1964	609	1986	252
1965	477	1987	260
1966	406	1988	263
1967	274	1989	271
1968	297	1990	275
1969	259	1991	270
1970	316	1992	276

Note: Includes all kinds of newspapers (both daily and weekly) and magazines.

Source: 1949-1987: Dhakidae 1991:551
1988-1992: Subakti & Katoppo 1993:57

TABLE 2:
MAJOR CURRENT NEW ORDER PAPERS

The following table lists only selected newspapers, with an emphasis on dailies. Information is drawn primarily from USIS 1992, with circulation figures drawn from IPPPN 1992 asterisked (*), and estimates provided from other (mainly oral) sources marked with a hash(#). Details are laid out alphabetically by title, according to the following template:

NAME   ESTABLISHMENT DATE
OWNERSHIP   ESTIMATED CIRCULATION
COMMENTS:

ANGKATAN BERSENJATA   1965
YAYASAN MANGGALA PRESS JAYA   17,500*
Comments: Army paper, with half its circulation distributed through Department of Information and the Army. Struggling.

BERITA BUANA   1971 (predecessor 1965)
PT BERITA BUANA PRESS   30,000
(1990-92 collaboration with Sutrisno Bachir's Ika Muda Group)
Comments: Pro-government Islamic. Sales rose significantly during Ika Muda's control (to about 160,000*) but plummeted again after split between 'old' and 'new' management. Struggling.

BERITA YUDHA   1965
YAYASAN PARIKESIT   25,000
Comments: Pro-Golkar, Army-related paper, with nearly half its circulation distributed through Department of Information contract. Struggling.

BISNIS INDONESIA   1985
JURNALINDO AKSARA GRAFIKA   40,000*
Comments: Strongest business paper, backed by three major business groups: Sahid, Indocement and Jaya. Strong presence in this specialist market.

DeTIK 1977
YAYASAN PANCASILA MULYA
215,000 (claimed in Feb. 1994)
Comments: When revamped by Surya Persindo group in late 1992, this tabloid quickly established itself as a radical alternative to established newsweekly magazines. Known for its frank detailed interviews with opposition political figures and critics. Banned June 1994. Innovative. Captured the public imagination.

HARIAN INDONESIA 1966
YAYASAN INDONESIA PRESS 65,000*
Comments: Only Chinese-language paper, co-published by Berita *Buana* and BAKIN intelligence agency. Specific market.

HARIAN TERBIT 1972
PT SURYA KOTA JAYA 46,000*
Comments: Afternoon sister publication to the sensationalist *Pos Kota*, originally called *Pos Sore*, founded by the current Minister of Information. Racy style, lower-class readership. Stable circulation.

THE INDONESIAN OBSERVER 1966
THE INDONESIAN OBSERVER LTD 3,634*
Comments: English-language sister publication of the Indonesian-language daily Merdeka, headed by B.M. Diah. Critical, nationalist in tone, includes pseudonymous column by 'Petition of 50' Opposition politician Slamet Bratanata. Struggling.

INDONESIA TIMES 1974
PT MARGA PERS MANDIRI >10,000#
Comments: Pro-government English-language; replaced *Jakarta Times*, banned in 1974. Struggling.

JAKARTA POST 1983
PT BINA MEDIA TENGGARA 31,610*
Comments: The publishers' holding company brings together *Kompas, Suara Pembaruan, Suara Karya*, and *Tempo*. Shares are reportedly held also by the Minister of Information, Harmoko. Leading English-language daily.

JAWA POS 1949
PT JAWA POS 350,000*
Comments: Taken over by Tempo group in 1982 with a circulation of

7,200 and expanded by editor Dahlan Iskan into one of the country's largest and most financially successful newspaper empires, dominating the press industry in East Java and Eastern Indonesia. Surabaya's up-market broadsheet daily that successfully broke Jakarta's exclusive control of the industry.

JAYAKARTA 1985
PT CITRA JAYA PRESS 70,000*
Comments: Army-related, affiliated with the Jakarta Military Command, joined the Sinar Kasih group in 1989. Entrepreneur Ponco Sutowo was initially involved although his involvement has now ceased apparently. Struggling.

KEDAULATAN RAKYAT 1945
PT BADAN PENERBIT KEDAULATAN RAKYAT 102,000*
Comments: Nationalist, resilient regional Yogyakarta daily, with modest family of associated publications. In 1991, President's stepbrother became 'adviser'. Holding ground against newer competitors.

KOMPAS 1965
PT KOMPAS MEDIA NUSANTARA 522,872*
Comments: Founded by Catholics, this is an independent, high-quality broadsheet, widely acknowledged as the country's 'paper of record'. Second largest selling newspaper in Southeast Asia and flagship of the nation's largest print media empire, the Kompas-Gramedia Group.

MEDIA INDONESIA 1969
PT CITRA MEDIA NUSA PURNAMA 150,000
(PT SURYA PERSINDO as co-publisher)
Comments: Taken over in 1989 by the Surya Persindo Group headed by Surya Paloh, and associated with the Bimantara conglomerate of the President's son Bambang Trihatmojo. Replaced Paloh's *Prioritas*, banned in 1987 (IPPPN 1992 circulation hit 302,700). Contracting and consolidating its circulation.

MERDEKA 1945
PT MERDEKA PRESS 16,140*
Comments: Oldest daily, with nationalist, occasionally strident anti-foreign, editorial line. Owner-founder B.M. Diah has small family of publications, but now his major business ventures are non-press

enterprises. Circulation declining sharply.

HARIAN NERACA 1985
PT PERSINDOTAMA ANTARNUSA 39,380*
Comments: Economic daily, independent, small circulation. Struggling.

PELITA 1974
PT PELITA PERSATUAN 40,000
Comments: Pro-Golkar Islamic daily. Replaced Abadi which was banned in 1974. Initially critical of the government, being banned during 1982 elections, but was taken over by Golkar figures in 1985. In 1990 Muslim entrepreneurs Aburizal Bakrie (of Bakrie Brothers) and Fadel Muhammad (from Bukaka Group) invested heavily in it, boosting sales briefly to 170,000* before the decline. Struggling.

PIKIRAN RAKYAT 1956 (restructured 1966)
PT PIKIRAN RAKYAT BANDUNG 180,600*
Comments: Independent. Strong provincial daily based in Bandung with a modest family of associated publications. A regional market leader.

POS KOTA 1970
YAYASAN ANTARKOTA 500,000*
Comments: Sensationalist down-market daily, established by current Minister of Information, Harmoko, specialising in titilation and gruesome crime stories. Ninety per cent of readership is in Jakarta. Down-market leader.

REPUBLIKA 1993
PT ABDI BANGSA 125,000 (Aug. 1993 est.)
Comments: Pro-government Muslim paper associated with Minister of Research and Technology B.J. Habibie and the Association of Islamic Intellectuals, ICMI. Innovative sophisticated redefinition of the 'Islamic' paper.

SINAR PAGI 1971
YAYASAN PERS ELH JAKARTA 74,617*
Comments: Sensationalist down-market daily, losing circulation to *Pos Kota*. Struggling.

SUARA KARYA 1971
PT SUARA RAKYAT MEMBANGUN 158,917*
Comments: Founded as the official Golkar paper, in 1991 it claimed to be wanting political independence. Still mainly distributed through government offices to members of the Civil Servants Association (Korpri) with little public readership. Declining.

SUARA MERDEKA 1950
PT SUARA MERDEKA PRESS 170,700*
Comments: Leading Semarang daily, which heads modest regional family of publications. Now run by son-in-law of founding editor, H. Hetami. Holding ground against newer competitors.

SUARA PEMBARUAN 1987 (predecessor 1961)
PT MEDIA INTERAKSI UTAMA 338,802*
Comments: Replaced the Protestant-linked *Sinar Harapan*, banned in 1986, as head of the Sinar Kasih Group. *Sinar Harapan*'s fierce independence has been eroded somewhat by the insertion of some more moderate administrators in the new daily. Gradually regaining Sinar Harapan's market share.

SURABAYA POST 1953
CV SURABAYA POST 100,800*
Comments: Modern professional independent broadsheet, which has survived the death of its founder, Abdul Azis. Resilient but losing ground to Jawa Pos.

SURYA 1986
PT ANTAR SURYA JAYA 127,983*
Comments: Initially launched as weekly by *Pos Kota*, but in 1989 Kompas began a collaboration to re-package it as a politically independent daily. Struggling against *Jawa Pos* market leader.

TABLE 3:
ADVERTISING EXPENDITURES: LEADING PRINT EARNERS (1988 - 1993)

Media, City	Mill-Rp	%	Mill-Rp	%	Mill-Rp	%	Mill-Rp	%	Mill-Rp	%	Mill-Rp	%
Any Newspaper	130,239	100.0	187,270	100.0	255,634	100.0	265,950	100.0	280,934	100.0	266,955	100.0
Kompas, Jakarta	39,142	30.1	50,258	26.8	74,358	29.1	68,586	25.8	76,387	27.2	85,916	32.2
S.Pembatuan, Jkt	15,405	11.8	28,510	15.2	40,390	15.8	30,243	11.4	29,420	10.5	27,550	10.3
Bisnis Ind, Jakarta	3,306	2.5	6,079	3.2	14,019	5.5	15,322	5.8	20,900	7.4	25,255	9.5
Jawa Pos, Surabaya	7,927	6.1	13,846	7.4	21,856	8.5	20,231	7.6	18,994	6.8	13,153	4.9
S.Merdeka, Smg	8,679	6.7	13,274	7.1	13,953	5.5	17,852	6.7	13,140	4.7	9,733	3.6
Media Indonesia,Jkt	0	0.0	0	0.0	0	0.0	17,927	6.7	12,920	4.6	9,367	3.4
Pk. Rakyat, Bandung	8,352	6.4	11,275	6.0	14,247	5.6	12,268	4.6	11,831	4.2	8,144	3.1
Bali Post, Denpasar	4,404	3.4	6,731	3.6	7,826	3.1	8,594	3.2	8,371	3.0	7,411	2.8
Poskota, Jakarta	5,951	4.6	8,035	4.3	9,267	3.6	8,143	3.1	7,093	2.5	5,400	2.0
Analisa, Medan	4,197	3.2	5,387	2.9	7,005	2.7	7,509	2.8	6,460	2.3	5,310	2.0
Jkt.Post, Jakarta	924	0.7	1,923	1.0	3,007	1.2	3,282	1.2	6,457	2.3	9,706	3.6
H.Indonesia, Jakarta	3,420	2.6	5,291	2.8	7,528	2.9	5,660	2.1	5,754	2.0	5,447	2.0
K.Rakayat, Yogya	2,047	1.6	2,899	1.5	4,111	1.6	4,542	1.7	5,389	1.9	5,954	2.2
B.Post, Banjarmasin	1,810	1.4	2,284	1.2	2,410	0.9	4,693	1.8	5,330	1.9	7,154	2.7
S.Karya, Jakarta	2,331	1.8	4,214	2.3	5,427	2.1	5,343	2.0	4,507	1.6	2,641	1.0
Surya, Surabaya	n/a	n/a	0	0.0	0	0.0	0	0.0	4,460	1.6	4,272	1.6
Waspada, Medan	1,287	1.0	3,989	2.1	5,146	2.0	4,705	1.8	4,064	1.4	3,460	1.3
Sby.Post, Surabaya	2,908	2.2	2,707	1.4	2,215	0.9	2,771	1.0	3,895	1.4	5,360	2.0
B.Buana, Jakarta	1,988	1.5	2,481	1.3	3,319	1.3	3,845	1.4	2,803	1.0	2,094	0.8

Fajar, Uj. Pandang	n/a	n/a	0	0.0	0	0.0	0	0.0	2,724	1.0	2,588	1.0
Manuntung, Samarinda	n/a	n/a	0	0.0	0	0.0	0	0.0	2,503	0.9	2,378	0.9
Akcaya, Pontianak	n/a	n/a	0	0.0	0	0.0	0	0.0	2,284	0.8	2,170	0.8
Pd.Rakyat, U.Pdg	1,538	1.2	1,885	1.0	2,022	0.8	3,242	1.2	2,230	0.8	2,806	1.1
S.I.Baru, Medan	2,586	2.0	3,571	1.9	3,726	1.5	3,825	1.4	2,163	0.8	2,997	1.1
Any Magazine	48,053	100.0	62,838	100.0	82,010	100.0	82,733	100.0	86,222	100.0	80,741	100.0
Tempo, Jakarta	11,641	24.2	14,837	23.6	21,887	26.7	21,606	26.1	20,879	24.2	18,155	22.5
Femina, Jakarta	5,284	11.0	7,336	11.7	10,100	12.3	10,360	12.5	11,856	13.8	13,194	16.3
Kartini, Jakarta	7,947	16.5	9,648	15.4	10,279	12.5	8,634	10.4	7,732	9.0	7,221	8.9
Gadis, Jakarta	1,727	3.6	2,366	3.8	2,530	3.1	2,692	3.3	3,624	4.2	4,725	5.9
Editor, Jakarta	1,381	2.9	2,885	4.6	3,252	4.0	4,671	5.6	3,332	3.9	2,494	3.1
Prospek, Jakarta	0	0.0	0	0.0	0	0.0	2,872	3.5	2,765	3.2	2,662	3.3
Mode, Jakarta	1,218	2.5	1,886	3.0	2,561	3.1	3,790	4.6	2,696	3.1	2,403	3.0
Matra, Jakarta	820	1.7	1,037	1.7	1,266	1.5	2,219	2.7	2,522	2.9	3,531	4.4
Nova, Jakarta	283	0.6	0	0.0	0	0.0	2,498	3.0	2,360	2.7	2,230	2.8
Bola, Jakarta	936	1.9	1,528	2.4	1,884	2.3	2,361	2.9	2,283	2.6	2,247	2.8
Sarinah, Jakarta	4,800	10.0	5,176	8.2	5,761	7.0	3,814	4.6	2,257	2.6	2,427	3.0
Warta Ekonomi	n/a	n/a	0	0.0	0	0.0	824	1.0	2,205	2.6	2,065	2.6
Swa, Jakarta	360	0.7	633	1.0	1,806	2.2	2,001	2.4	1,895	2.2	1,802	2.2
Eksekutif, Jakarta	974	2.0	1,296	2.1	1,895	2.3	1,604	1.9	1,770	2.1	1,477	1.8
Infobank, Jakarta	474	1.0	341	0.5	737	0.9	1,766	2.1	1,744	2.0	1,720	2.1
Pertiwi, Jakarta	1,667	3.5	1,507	2.4	1,639	2.0	1,264	1.5	1,636	1.9	1,453	1.8

* = projected figures

Source: Subakti & Katoppo 1992:53 and 1993:51

TABLE 4:
ADVERTISING EXPENDITURES BY MEDIA CATEGORY 1988 - 1994 (in billions of rupiah)

Media	1988 #	1988 %	1989 #	1989 %	1990 #	1990 %	1991 #	1991 %	1992 #	1992 %	1993 #	1993 %	1994 #	1994 %
TOTAL	314	100.0	481	100.0	639	100.0	835	100.0	1,027	100.0	1345	100.0	1600	100.0
Newspaper	163	51.9	243	50.5	320	50.1	360	43.1	377	36.7	452	33.6	493	30.8
Magazine	60	19.1	72	15.0	94	14.7	91	10.9	95	9.3	103	7.7	110	6.9
Radio	38	12.1	73	15.2	105	16.4	105	12.6	100	9.7	113	8.4	122	7.6
Cinema	6	1.9	7	1.5	8	1.3	9	1.1	10	1.0	10	0.7	11	0.7
Television	0	0.0	29	6.0	51	8.0	212	25.4	390	38.0	614	45.7	817	51.1
Outdoor	47	15.0	57	11.9	61	9.5	58	6.9	55	5.4	53	3.9	47	2.9

Sources: Subakti & Katoppo 1992:47 and 1993:45
Katoppo 1994

* = 1994 Projected figures

A Note on Further Reading

There have been numerous academic studies of aspects of the Indonesian press written in Indonesia, many in the form of university dissertations, others published as books. The following notes, however, assume that the reader is seeking guidance on English language material to augment and to extend the information contained in this study. It aims to point the interested reader to major, accessible studies on the Indonesian press.

The most incisive recent study focusing on the press in the New Order period is in the form of a Cornell University doctoral dissertation. Daniel Dhakidae (1991), *The State, The Rise of Capital, and the Fall of Political Journalism: Political Economy of Indonesian News Industry* (made available by University Microfilms International, Ann Arbor, Michigan, in 1992) is a seminal work which should form the basis of any further work on this topic. Other dissertations providing a rich source of information, and accessible through University Microfilms include Robert H. Crawford (1967), *The Daily Indonesian-language Press of Jakarta: An Analysis of Two Recent Critical Periods*, (Syracuse University) and Edward C. Smith (1969), *A History of Newspaper Suppression in Indonesia 1949-1965* (University of Iowa, now published in Indonesian translation as *Pembreidelan Pers di Indonesia*, Grafitipers, Jakarta, 1983).

Oey Hong Lee (1971), *Indonesian Government and Press During Guided Democracy* (Centre for Southeast Asian Studies, University of Hull / Inter Documentation Co AG Zug) provides an extremely detailed study of the Sukarno period, strengthened by the author's personal knowledge of the period as an Indonesian journalist and academic. Another personal view which, though concerning the mid-1970s, remains highly instructive of the pressures on editors today, is Nono Anwar Makarim (1978), 'The Indonesian Press: An Editor's Perspective', (in Karl D. Jackson & Lucien W. Pye (1978), *Political Power and Communication in Indonesia*, University of California Press, Berkeley). For the results of a recent group research project by Indonesian scholars, see Don Michael Flournoy (ed.) (1992), *Content Analysis of Indonesian Newspapers* (Gadjah Mada University Press, Yogyakarta), which, while valuable, is rather dense.

Several recent unpublished Australian dissertations (available from the universities' libraries) complement these earlier studies from the late 1960s and early 1970s, including Kerry Groves (1983), *Harian Rakjat, Daily Newspaper of the Communist Party of Indonesia - its History and Role'*, (MA, ANU); Siti Solikhati (1992), 'Press Pancasila in Indonesia: An Analysis of Three Indonesian Dailies, *Kompas, Pelita* and *The Jakarta Post* between 1987-1991' (MA, Canberra); Roswita Nimpuno Khaiyath (1993), 'Indonesian Women's Magazines: A New Order Phenomenon' (MA, Monash); and Andrew J. Rosser (1992), 'Political Openness and Social Forces in New Order Indonesia: The *Monitor* Affair' (BA Hons, Flinders).

The most comprehensive reference listing of newspapers and magazines in Indonesia is the United States Information Service publication *A Brief Guide to the Indonesian Media* (Jakarta, 1992). For statistical information and background details on editorial staff and company ownership, I have drawn heavily on this unpublished two-volume compilation, 'intended as a quick and unofficial reference'. It provides extensive details with addresses, staff listings, and a potted history of the publications, but is theoretically not for external distribution. Nonetheless copies of this or previous editions have been supplied to several Australian and overseas libraries and it was routinely distributed to various Jakarta press attaches, giving it reasonably wide currency. Abdul Razak (1985), *Press Laws and Systems in Asean States* (Confederation of Asean Journalists Publications, Jakarta) provides useful English translations of relevant press legislation. A now-dated but still useful bibliography appears in Mastini Hardjo Prakoso (1978), *Mass Communication in Indonesia: An annotated bibliography* (Asian Mass Communication Research and Information Centre, Singapore).

The recent critical study *In the Censor's Shadow: Journalism in Suharto's Indonesia* (Committee to Protect Journalists, New York, 1991) is detailed and succinct. Similarly Roger K. Paget's two *Indonesia* journal articles (October 1967) on the 1965-7 period are both packed with detail. Paul Tickell (ed.) (1987), *The Indonesian Press: Its Past, its People, its Problems* (CSEAS Monash, Clayton) includes articles by Australians and Indonesians giving a variety of perspectives on developments since the turn of the century. A former *Sydney Morning Herald* correspondent in Jakarta gives his personal perspective of the press in the early 1980s in Peter Rodgers (1982), *The Domestic and Foreign Press in Indonesia: 'Free but Responsible'* (CSAAR, Griffith University, Nathan).

A Note on Further Reading

For statistical information regarding advertising and the media, most helpful are the annual publications of the Indonesian Advertising Companies Association (PPPI) edited by Baty Subakti & Ernst Katoppo entitled *Media Scene Indonesia: The Official Guide to Advertising Media in Indonesia.* Background details are available in Michael H. Anderson (1984), *Madison Avenue in Asia: Politics and Transnational Advertising*, Fairleigh Dickenson University Press, London/Toronto.

Finally, note should be made of the extremely valuable electronic information network run by John MacDougall, available on e-mail as 'apakabar@clark.net'. This network provides an extraordinary range of up-to-the-minute detail on Indonesian politics, culture and society, including English and Indonesian language summaries of press reports and events pertaining to the mass media. Increasingly it will be to such sources that researchers will turn.

Biographical Note

David T. Hill (b. 1954) completed his Bachelor of Arts (Asian Studies) degree at the Australian National University, Canberra, in 1977 with a Honours thesis on Indonesian popular literature. He spent two years living in Jakarta (1980-82) researching his ANU doctoral dissertation 'Mochtar Lubis: Author, Editor, Political Actor' (1988). Having formerly taught in the Department of Indonesian and Malay, Monash University, Dr Hill now lectures in Southeast Asian Studies at Murdoch University, Perth, Western Australia, where he is concurrently Research Fellow in the Asia Research Centre on Social, Political and Economic Change. He has edited and introduced the memoirs of Ruth Havelaar, the wife of a former political prisoner, entitled *Quartering: A Story of a Marriage in Indonesia during the Eighties* (Centre of Southeast Asian Studies, Monash University, 1991). His present research interests cover Indonesian media, literature and culture. In addition, Dr Hill is Project Director of the Australian Consortium for 'In-Country' Indonesian Studies (ACICIS).

Index

A
Abadi (Eternal) 30, 36, 37, 86
advertising
  broadsheets 25
  budget, media's portion 141, 142
  expenditures 87, 96, 141, 142
  industry 65, 75–77, 81
  revenue 28, 77, 81, 85, 87, 90, 95–96, 100, 141, 142
  space, restrictions 48, 87, 112
  tariffs 76, 77
  television see television advertising
Alliance of Independent Journalists 72
Angkatan Bersenjata (Armed Forces) 36
Anglo–American international press industry 149, 150
Antara National News Agency 27, 29, 64
  decimated 1965 34–35
  government control 29
  leftists expelled 34
  anti–Communist 34, 35, 83, 86, 114
  anti–Dutch sentiment 28
  anti–government student protests 38–39
  anti–Sukarno 34, 35, 83, 115
Anwar, Rosihan 27, 53, 68
appeal against government regulation 51
armed forces 28, 30
  coup (1965) 30
  demonstrators, beaten 44
  Information Office 146
  KOPKAMTIB (security authority) 35, 38, 39, 147
  occupation of student campuses 39
  opposition to publication bans 43
  papers 36
  permits to print, issuing authority 35, 131
  power shift 139
  press control 131
  Press Council members 65, 66
  sponsor 121
  support for open press 44
Asia Raya (Glorious Asia) (first paper) 26, 27
Atmowiloto, Arswendo 40, 41, 52, 159
Australian
  journalists, banned 154
  papers 91, 148, 149, 153
  regulation 140
Avisa Relation oder Zeitung 25

B
Bachir, Sutrisno 97, 98
Bafagih, Asa 27
Bahau'ddin, Enggak 37
bans
  Australian journalists 154–55
  Chinese–language press 132
  Dutch language 27
  foreign interference in press industry 81
  Indonesian Socialist Party 29–30
  national television advertising 76
  bans on publications 30, 34, 47, 82, 84, 86, 88, 90, 125
  1970s 37–39
  1980s 39–41
  1990s 41–44, 147, 148
  Dutch Governor–General's power 26
  Dutch–language paper 28
  Jakarta dailies 39
  no recourse to defence or trial 49
  Pedoman 30, 86
  Press Act 156
  special publications 113, 114

student newspapers 39, 116
temporary 44–47
triple June 1994 41–44, 69, 82, 97, 100, 140, 160
Basic Press Law (1966) 150, 151
Bataviasche Nouvelles en Politique Raisonnementes 25
Berita Buana 97–98, 125, 132
Berita Yudah (Military News) 36, 36
Bhirawa 91, 147
Bimantara Group
   relationship with Surya Persindo company 101–103
blacklists
   offending journalists 38, 472
Body for Equalising the Distribution of Advertisements (BPPP) 76, 77
Body for the Support of Sukarnoism (BSP) 34
Bromartani 25

C
campus press *see* student press
Capitalism 141, 158–169
capital investment in media 81, 82, 104, 150
   company collaborations 54
Catholic communities 82
Catholic journals 35
Catholic Party 83
censorship 35, 156
   during Japanese Occupation of Dutch East indies 26
   pre–publication 26, 61
   self–imposed, by journalists 46, 47
Chinese characters, prohibition 132
Chinese community 26, 100
   population 131
Chinese–language 131–133
   daily 97
Chinese Malay newspapers 26
Christian communities 83
Christian Indonesian Democracy Party (PDI) 84
Christian papers 36
circulation 95, 113, 121, 122, 141
   1950s 28
   1980s 53

1994 42
competition for increased 145–49
DeTIK 96, 97
Dutch–language dailies 28
East Java 118
English–language publications 129, 130
Harian Indonesia 133
Harian Rakyat 29, 30
Javanese weeklies 123
Kompas 83, 84
magazines 90
Media Indonesia 94, 95
national 118
newspapers 30, 36, 86, 87, 90
regional papers 141
Republica 128
special publications 112
Sudanese magazine 123
Thai Rath 83
classification of major newspapers 36
closure of publications 41–44
   see also bans on publications
   1965 34
   DeTIK 48
   Dutch newspapers 28
   Editor 48
   martial law 30
Code of Ethics of Press Companies 104
colonial laws and regulations 26
community nespapers 149
Communist journalists, arrests 35
criticism
   constraints 47, 117, 118
   First Family 39, 46, 102
   government 38, 46, 49, 153
   marketplace support 97
   political coverage 101, 102
   public, of government policies 37
   student papers 115, 117, 118

D
Daih, B.M. 27, 39, 68, 104
Daih, Norman 39
De Unie (printery) 27
democracy 28, 114
democratisation 44, 158–160
demonstrations 44

Index

1974 37, 38
Thailand 153
Department of Education and Culture
   student magazine 116
Department of Information 62, 63–65
   KMD program 47
   ministerial decree 1969 67
   permits to print, issuing authority
      35, 48
   warnings 94, 101
Department of Trade and Cooperatives
   76
deregulation 53, 143, 144, 151
detention of journalists 26, 30
DeTIK 41, 48, 51, 69, 96, 97
Development Unity Party (PPP) 84
Dili Massacre, 147, 98, 102, 145, 146
Director–General of Press and
   Graphics 38, 62, 63, 64, 112,
   132
'dumping' of papers practice 95
Dutch colonialism 26
Dutch East Indies 26
Dutch Governor–General, power to
ban publications 26
Dutch language, banned 27
Dutch–language newspapers 26
Dutch–language press, decline 28
Dutch publications 25
Dutch transfer of Sovereignty 27, 28

E

East Java 118, 121, 122
East Timor 121, 155
East Timor massacre 52
   economic fluctuations 140–143
Editor 41, 48 90
El Bahar (The Sea) 35, 36
English–language
   magazines 130
   newspapers 91, 128–131
   press 28, 29
'entertainment' papers 36
entrepreneurs 43, 53, 73, 82, 92,
   97–104, 132, 140, 142

F

FDWY (Forum Diskusi Wartawan
   Yogyakarta) 72, 73
Fifteenth of January Disaster 37
financial
   deregulation 159
   donations 28
financiers of early Indonesian/Malay
   newspapers 26
First Family, beyond explicit criticism 46
foreign interests, prohibition 150
foreign investment 43, 75, 151,
   152, 153
   acts and regulations 151–152
   government policies affecting
      media 42
foreign publications, Parliamentary
   Decision 132
free and responsible press 61, 62
free speech 44
freedom of the press 34, 35, 36, 44,
   50, 139, 156, 159
   breach 148

G

Gatra 88
General Elections 28, 38, 44
Golkar (government political organisation) 40, 63, 83, 92
   Chairperson 42, 50, 63, 68
   leaders, shares in Pelita 45
   papers 36, 45, 91, 129, 141, 147
   Pelita 125
   treasurer 89
government
   action against press 26, 30, 37
   officials, owners of press publica-
      tions 103
   power over press 29, 34–51, 83,
      148, 155–158
government agencies and industry
   bodies 61–77
government gazette 25
government policies
   criticism, papers banned 45
   public criticism 37
government press conferences, journalists excluded 47
government regulation *see* regulation

government–sponsored publications 45
Gulf War 121, 140, 141

H
Haatzaai Artikelen (Sowing of Hatred Articles) 26
Hadi, Parni 68, 69
Harian Indonesia 132, 133
Harian KAMI 35, 36, 37, 38, 46, 115
Harian Rakyat (People's Daily) 29, 30
Hasan, Mohammad 88
Hatta, Mohammad 27
Heryanto, Ariel 35

I
illegal publications 113
independence 29, 34, 114, 131
   movement 26
   proclamation 27
Indonesia (Republic) 27
Indonesia Merdeka (Free Indonesia) 114
Indonesia Pos 37
Indonesia Raya (Gloriuos Indonesia) 36, 38
Indonesian Advertising Companies Association (PPPI) 65, 75–77
Indonesian Communist Party *see* Partai Kommunist Indonesia (PKI) 'Indonesian identity' 25
Indonesian Journalists' Association (PWI, Persatuan Wartawan Indonesia) 26, 34, 50, 65, 67–73
Indonesian–language newspapers, early 25–26, 27
Indonesian–language periodicals early restrictions 26
Indonesian Nationalist Party *see* Partai Nasional Indonesia (PNI)
Indonesian Raya (Glorious Indonesia) 36, 37, 38, 70
Indonesian Socialist Party see Partai Socialis Partai (PSI)
Indonesian Student Journalists' League 114
Indonesian Student Press League 114, 115
The Indonesian Times 37

international competition 150
investment in media 66, 81–82, 91, 92, 97, 98, 99, 103, 143, 151
Irian campaign 28
Irian Jaya 28
Iskan, Dahan 90, 148, 149, 153
Islamic media 124–128

J
jailing
   Arswendo 41
   journalists 30
Jakarta Post 130, 131
Japanese
   censorship 26
   Occupation of Dutch East Indies 26–27, 123
   sponsor of Indonesian–language daily 27
   training programs for journalists 27
Jarot, Eros 155
Javanese–language publications 25, 123, 124
Jawa Pos (Java Post) 88–91, 121, 122, 124, 141
Jenkins, David 154
journalists
   arrests 34, 35
   detention of 26, 30
   'envelopes' payments 70, 71
   Indonesian Chinese Community 26
   jailing 30
   killing 35
   Japanese training programs 26
   PWI membership 70
   professional body need 72
   responsibility 61
   role during 1931–26 26
   sackings 35, 44
   self–censorship 46
   shadow language grammar 46
   training 149, 150
   working with banned papers, re–employment letter 38
journals 1970s 35
Jurnal Ekuin (Economy, Finance and Industry Journal) 39

— 180 —

Index

K
KMD (Koran Masuk Desa, newspapers to villages program) 47, 48, 64
Katoppo, Aristides 46, 47, 150
Kompas (Compass) 36, 38, 46, 54, 83, 84, 84, 141
Kompas–Gramedia Group 40, 52, 83–86

L
labour union protection 71
legal security 151
legislation
see also Press Act; regulations
Basic Press Law 1966 150, 151
colonial 26
legislative controls 61, 62
early 35–37
regulation and permits 47–51
Lubis, Mochtar 27, 28, 37, 38
Lubis, Sofyan 47, 68

M
magazines 30, 85, 88, 89
oldest commercial publication 123
sole remaining newsweekly 100
Mahasiwa Indonesia (Indonesian Student) 35
market stratagems 145–149
Makarim, Nono Anwar 46
Malay newspapers 26
Malari demonstrations 37, 115, 153, 154
Malik, Adam 27
Manila, Marcos regime 154
martial law 30, 38
Martial Law Administration 131
mass media 35, 139
massacres during New Order 35
Masyumi 30
Medan Priyayi (Aristocrats' Domain) 25
Mederka (Freedom) 36, 37, 38, 50, 144
Media Indonesia 54, 66, 94–97, 102, 125
Media Indonesia/Surya Persindo Group 91–97
Members of Parliament
Chairperson of newspaper phoenix 40

military *see* armed forces
Minister for Information
authority in press dealing 62
Decision (1965) 29
Harmoko 41, 42, 43, 49, 50, 63, 68, 93, 147, 151, 160
Murtopo 34, 50
Regulations (1984) 49, 50
student papers, permits cancellation 116
Minister for Reasearch and Technology, Habibie 41, 42, 68, 126
Ministry of Education 39
'MISS SARAH' 45, 46
Mohamad, Gunawan 49, 70, 72
Monitor 40, 41, 51, 52, 85, 126, 141, 159
monopoly of press empires 83, 104, 143
movement (pergerakan) 26, 132
Muslims
newspapers 36, 124, 125
offended by *Monitor* report 40–41, 126
population 124, 140
staff 145

N
national development 62, 63, 64, 139
national papers 27, 28, 144
collaborative agreements with smaller papers 87, 88
future decline 148
radical 36
nationalist press 25, 26, 27
not subject to censorship, legislation 35, 49
political reporting 44
responsible press freedom 62
task and duty 34
nationalists 25
Navy and Marines officers, protecting *El Bahar* 35, 36
Newspaper Publishers Association (SPS, Serikat Penerbit Suratkabar) 52, 65, 73–75, 120
newspapers
Chinese Malay 26
classification 36, 143–144

— 181 —

collaborative agreements 53, 54, 87, 88, 120, 148
colour photos 92
Dutch East Indies 25
first modern 25
for the villages (KMD) 47, 48, 64
government–affiliated 61, 83, 102
Indonesian language, early 25–26
Indonesian/Malay, early 25–26
prices 95, 141
sales 141
supporting emergence of New Order 35, 36, 37
world's oldest weekly 25
Nieuwsgier 28
non–commercial publications 111–118

O
Opini (Opinion) 88
Oyong, P.K. 84

P
PDI *see* Partai Demokrasi Indonesia
PKI *see* Partai Kommunist Indonesia
PNI *see* Partai Nasional Indonesia
PPP *see* Partai Persatuan
PSI *see* Partai Socialis Indonesia
PWI *see* Indonesian Journalists' Association
Paloh, Surya 40, 50, 51, 69, 92–97, 102–103, 142
Pancasila Press 34, 40, 61, 62, 63, 76, 139
Pancasila Socialist Press 62
Partai Demokrasi Indonesia (PDI, Christian Indonesian Democracy Party) 84
Partai Kommunist Indonesia (PKI, Indonesian Communist Party) 29, 34, 69, 114
Partai Nasional Indonesia (PNI, Indonesian Nationalist Party) 30, 36
Partai Persatuan Pembangunan (PPP, Development Unity Party) 83
Partai Socialis Indonesia (PSI, Indonesian Socialist Party 29,30, 35

Pedoman (Guide) 29, 30, 36, 37, 38
Pelita 37, 45
'pergerakan' (the movement) 25
periodicals
  circulation 53
  political party affiliation 29
'perjuangan' style of journalism 29, 81
permit to print *see* printing permits
permit to publish *see* publishing permits
permits 47–51
registration 111, 112
'pers perjuangan' (press of political struggle) 27, 37, 103, 144 149, 150
Pertima 38
political parties
  links with newspapers 29, 30, 36, 83, 102
  media promotion 27
  papers 29, 30, 36
political reporting 145
politically critical publications 101
population 28, 29, 30, 124, 140
  Chinese 131
  Christian communities 83
  rural 48
Pos Kota (City Post) 36, 50, 84, 144
Post 129
pre–publication censorship 26
press
  role and function 61, 139
  supression 30, 34
  see also bans on publications systems 61
Press Act 1931 (Persbreidel Ordonnatie) 26
Press Act 1966 35, 62
Press Act 1982 34, 49, 62, 76, 81, 104, 156
Press Council (Dewan Pers) 48, 52, 61, 62, 64–66, 75, 150
press empires 54, 73, 81–104, 120, 121, 144, 147, 148
press 'family' 65, 76, 90
regional 119
Press Graphics Association (SGP) 65, 75

press industry bodies 61–77
press offences
 and penalties 50, 81, 104
 seminar 73
press licences, legislation 103
press organisations, representation on Press Council 75
Press Publication Enterprise Permit (SUIPP, Surat Izin Usaha Penerbitan Pers) 48, 49, 53, 54, 63, 64, 65, 88, 111, 112
 application, Surya Paloh 93
 government restrictions 85, 118
 legislation 49–50
 limits on numbers 52, 53, 77
 ministerial power 49–50, 52
 Monitor case 52
 moratorium on new 53
 numbers 142, 143
 press licensing law 139
 protection of press workers 71
 Republica 126
 revocation challenge 160
publications 113
 revocation order 93
 Senang Case 52
 withdrawal regulations 49, 50, 51, 52
 withdrawals 52, 85,
printing permit (SIC) 35, 63, 131
 withdrawals 37, 38
Prioritas (Priority) 40, 50, 92, 93
Proclamation of Independence 27
Protestant communities 82
Protestant journal 35
public criticism of government policies 37
publishing permit (SIT, Surat Izin Terbit) 35, 48, 131
 see also Press Publication Enterprise Permit (SUIPP)
 withdrawn 37, 39, 41
publishing restrictions 45–47

R
radical Nationalist papers 36
radical press, New Order 36
regional government 148
 collaboration with Newspaper

Publishers Association 120–121
regional language press 123–124
regional papers 47, 48, 54, 85, 94, 141, 141
 closures 95
 future rise 148, 149, 153
 national chain 95
 regional press 111
 in Indonesian language 118–123
 regional publications 94
 registration permits (STT, Surat Tanda Terdaftar) 111, 112
regulation
 Australian 140
 government 47–51, 61, 159
 No. 20 151, 152
 under challenge 140
 self– 51–54
 threat 72
regulations
 1984 Peraturan Menpen 49, 50
 colonial 26
 registration permits 112
Rendra, W.S. 44
Republic of Indonesia 27
Republika 68, 126–128, 145
Rivai, Abdul 25
Rukmana, Hardiyanti 99, 101, 113

S
SIC *see* printing permits
SIT *see* publishing permits
SIUPP (Indonesian Solidarity for Press Freedom) 44, 72
SIUPP *see* Press Publication Enterprise Permit
SPS *see* Newspaper Publishers Association
STT *see* registration permits
sackings 71, 125
Samola, Eric 53, 89
Santa Cruz massacre 155
secular papers 128, 143–145
self–censorship 46
self–regulation 51–54, 154, 155–156
Senang (Happy) 52
shares
 Pelita 45

press companies 49, 90, 91, 93
Republica 128
Siahaan, Semsar 44
Simponi (Symphony) 97
Sinar 100, 101
Sinar Galih Declaration 72–73
Sinar Harapan (Ray of Hope) 35, 38, 40, 44, 46, 86–88
Sinar Kasih Group 86–88
social revolution 29
special publications (non-commercial) 111–118
sponsorship of publications 45
Star Weekly 84
State Intelligence Coordinating Body (BAKIN) 64, 97, 133
State of War and Seige 30
State–press relations 46, 62
  1970s 37, 38
  1990s 96, 97, 103
  corporatist approach 64–65
  power shift 139, 140
statistics
  national press market 118
  press publishers 118
student
  arrests 39
  militant movement 35
  Normalisation of Campus Life policy (NKK) 39, 116, 117
  papers 35, 36
  press 38, 39, 114–118
  protests 38, 39
  underground publications 117
Suara Karya (Work Voice) 36, 45
Suara Pembaruan 39, 54, 86, 87
subsidies
  government newsprint 30
  KMD village editions 47
  university newspapers 116
Sudanese-language weeklies 123, 124
Sudwikatmono 99, 100
Suharto, President 41, 42, 50, 62, 96, 113, 139, 140
  anticipated departure 43
  associates 99
  compared with Pharaoh 94
  curbing the press 103

Editor, story on son 41–42
  family interests in press and television 99–104
  First Family, beyond explicit criticism 46, 102, 156
  Marcos-like President article 154
  post, era 104
  relative, owner of Sinar 44
  son 82, 83, 92, 99
Sukarno, President 25, 27, 29, 30, 62
  family criticised 39
Sulah Berita 37
Suluh Indonesia (Indonesian Torch) 30, 36
Sunda Berta (West Java News) 25
Supreme Court
  Judicial Review of mininsterial provisions for banning newspapers 103
  ruling on SIUPP withdrawal 51
  Surya Paloh's challenge 50–51, 69, 103
Surabaya Daily News 91
Surya Persindo Group 91–97
  relationship with Bimantara Group 101–103

T
taboos (topics) and warnings 44–47
Tambu, Charles 28
technology 81, 117, 118, 120, 141, 148, 149, 153
television 151
  advertising 76, 77, 119, 141
  licences 99
Tempo 41, 44, 54, 88–91
Tempo–Grafiti Group 53, 88–91
Thai Rath 83
Thailand, student demonstrations 153
This Earth of Mankind 25
The Times of Indonesia 28
Tirtoadisuryo 25
Topic (Topic) 44–45
trade unions 71, 72, 73
Trihatmojo, Bambang 82, 83, 92, 99
Tur, Pramudya Ananta, This Earth of Mankind 25, 117

U
universities
  campus press 114–118
  educational policies, re-evaluation 39
  NKK policy 39, 116, 117
  student councils, disbanded 39, 116
Utama, Yakob 52, 53, 83, 84, 86, 117

V
villages, newspapers for, KMD program 47, 48, 64
Vista TV 93

Y
Yogyakarta Journalists' Discussion Forum (FDWY) 72, 73
Youth Conference and Pledge (1928) 26

W
wages
  press workers 28, 70, 71
West Papua (now Irian Jaya) 28
Wijaya, Sugeng 67
workers' organisations, unofficial 72, 73